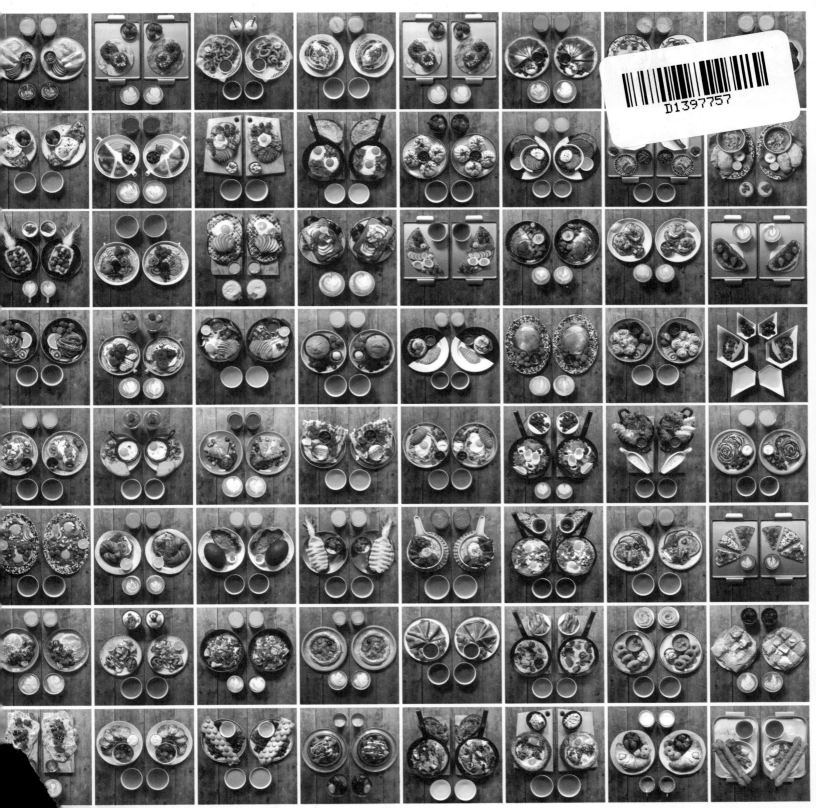

D1397757

SYMMETRYBREAKFAST

Mark, without you there would be no symmetry, no one to make breakfast for, and no reason to get out of bed.

You are my best friend, my love. Will you marry me?

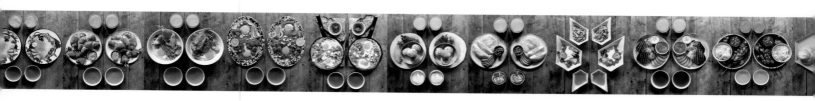

641.52 Z43s ✓

FEV '17

SYMMETRYBREAKFAST

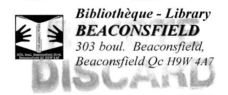

Bibliothèque - Library
BEACONSFIELD
303 boul. Beaconsfield,
Beaconsfield Qc H9W 4A7

DISCARD

100 RECIPES FOR THE LOVING COOK

Michael Zee

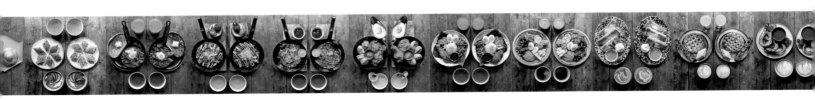

pH powerHouse Books Brooklyn, NY

INTRODUCTION
SOMEWHERE IN THE WORLD IT'S BREAKFAST TIME

Love makes you do stupid things. We've all done or said something in the name of love that later makes us cringe. Then again, often something is born out of love that is really wonderful. I'd like to think that this book is one of those things.

When I started arranging breakfasts on the table symmetrically and taking photos, I hadn't the slightest clue what it would lead to or what I would learn. Three years later, I'm still so humbled that it's brought the opportunity to write this book. Honestly, it was never about the food, or done to create a following – for the first 600 images I had a full–time job teaching at the V&A.

It isn't even about commitment; it's about spending quality time together.

I've learned a few things while writing this book.

Firstly, I have discovered that, all around the world, most people are actually really nice. Beyond political boundaries, historical ties or physical traits, many strangers – lots of whom are now great friends – have been thrilled to show us how to cook the food they love and are honored that I want to know more. I love people, I love meeting new people, and that love has made me want to know more about the food people eat and how they share it with each other.

Secondly, I've learned that food is a deeply political beast. Just try ordering a Full English in Glasgow, a cappuccino after noon in Italy, or questioning the origins of shakshuka with an Israeli. Food is important

to us because it defines who we are as individuals, our personal preferences, but it also represents our collective identity. Writing a cookbook, then, becomes a challenge not only to put together the best recipes, but to avoid treading on anyone's toes. I hope I've succeeded.

Some recipes have been easy to pin down, others defy political and geographical boundaries. So, thirdly, I've learned that there is no definition of what breakfast is or should be. And I quote Massimo Montanari – one of the world's leading experts in food studies – here: "You say 'breakfast,' and that seems obvious to you." Yet I still get the same comment almost every day: "That's not breakfast."

I get a lot of comments every time I post, as is the way with social media, but that one is the one that annoys me the most. It's not because those who say it are wrong – it's certainly not their idea of breakfast – it's that they fail to see beyond their own lives. My personal traditions reinforce what I believe is normal, but for me there's pleasure in looking beyond normal. Most traditions are not universally shared and not everyone is open to other people's traditions. This book attempts to share.

What social media seems to do so well, books have done for centuries, albeit a tad more slowly. Superficially it can seem that digital and analog are at odds, but they complement each other better than you think. From the beginning it felt right that I should shoot this book myself, entirely on my iPhone. It's the common thread that connects my Instagram account to the physical object you're holding right now.

Many of us have smartphones in our pockets but do we really understand their potential to change the way we eat and think about food?

Our food customs come from our respective cultures, so it makes sense that a quintessential breakfast from India is going to be spicy and in China they'll drink tea. These norms have been constructed over a very long time. Globalization is changing what "traditions" are and what they mean. I can see on my phone, in real time, what someone in Hong Kong is eating for breakfast. To my parents it's rather novel. To my ancestors it would be witchcraft.

I think that being a northern, working–class, gay, bit Scottish, bit Chinese man might just be enough to give me the credibility to ask, What is tradition? Or, more importantly, why should I allow it to dictate how I live my life? But you don't have to be a mongrel like me to ask that question. I grew up eating foods from different cultures at the same time and on the same plate – not to be controversial, but because that's just how we rolled in the Zee family. In an increasingly cosmopolitan society, I imagine it's how many others live too.

Fourthly, I've learned not to make any demands of anyone. If you don't like breakfast, I can't force you to like it, nor will I preach the virtues of nutrition or health. If you twitch at the thought of eating the same thing as your partner, you don't have to! Don't like tea? Well, too bad for you, but that's fine too! I want what I cook to inspire you, not to make you feel bad. I started making breakfast for Mark because our time spent together each day was limited to mornings. There are practical considerations that might prevent you from doing the same – 5 a.m. is kind of early to get up – but I hope you can agree that time is a luxury we can't afford to waste. Breakfast time can be about spending precious moments with the people we love. For me, it's about making that time count.

Many of the recipes in this book could be described as authentic. Cultural appropriation can be a prickly pear, but perfect is the enemy of good, as my mother used to say. I've learned that you can't please everyone all the time and nor should you try. I've watched people at McDonald's in Beijing eat French fries with chopsticks and had better madeleines at St. JOHN in London's Smithfield than anywhere in France. And so recipes range from long–forgotten medieval dishes to the more modern and Instagram–friendly.

Food is a way into culture, not into nations; you shouldn't glorify authenticity, but it's damned hard not to. How can one recipe from Myanmar or a stateless nation ever reflect the complexities, the people, and the history? It can't. But I've given it a go anyway.

Finally, to end on a high, we're back to love. My love for Mark hasn't lessened or waxed and waned since we met. Neither has our love of food or travelling, or our love of each other's company. And although I'm still waiting for him to get up and make breakfast, until he does, I'll carry on. As I say, it's all about love.

MICHAEL ZEE, JULY 2016

Coffee is delicious. Don't get me wrong. It can be sublime . . . but very rarely would I drink coffee with breakfast. When you are eating, tea just works better.

Coffee completely fills the palate. It's not a good sharer. It competes quite aggressively with anything you're eating. Like a sumo wrestler, it barges anything subtle or dainty out of the arena. It needs a big partner – like a Portuguese custard tart or a doughnut, something dominated by texture and sweetness – that you can sink your teeth into. Coffee needs a rich, sugary density to balance the dark bitterness.

If you add milk you do tone down the sumo into a mere heavyweight boxer – but he's still pretty intense and wants to knock any competition out of the ring. Whereas tea – well, tea is far more accommodating. Tea is more of a gentleman. He's a lover, not a fighter – deep and romantic. He gets along with anyone and plays extremely nicely. And there is so much more to him – from white through to green, oolong, black and pu'er.

Michael's breakfasts are, of course, as diverse as they are delicious. So much work and effort has gone into each creation, you don't want to overpower the brilliance. He doesn't need a huge, half–naked man with glistening buttocks – an Arnie Schwarzenegger, say – to dominate his breakfast genius. Tea is more of a Michael Fassbender shimmying elegantly across your tastebuds.

There is, of course, more to tea at breakfast time than English Breakfast. When it is beautifully put together, using great teas, it can be a tea of real beauty. But it is only a part of the tea spectrum. You'll notice that Michael very rarely has a milky cup. He's a flavor adventurer. There is no porridge (well, no traditional porridge), no avocado on toast, and no cereal here. He is looking beyond what we are all familiar with. It is the combinations of flavor and the truly exciting choices that we are all drawn to and for which we adore him.

A favorite tea – like Emperor's Breakfast, which is a dreamily delicate and caramelly black tea from China – will work with many dishes. Sometimes a deeper, more malty partner is required and he brings out the Malawi teas. There's Speedy Breakfast for when a strong backbone is required, or Shire Highlands when he's looking for rich, hidden depths.

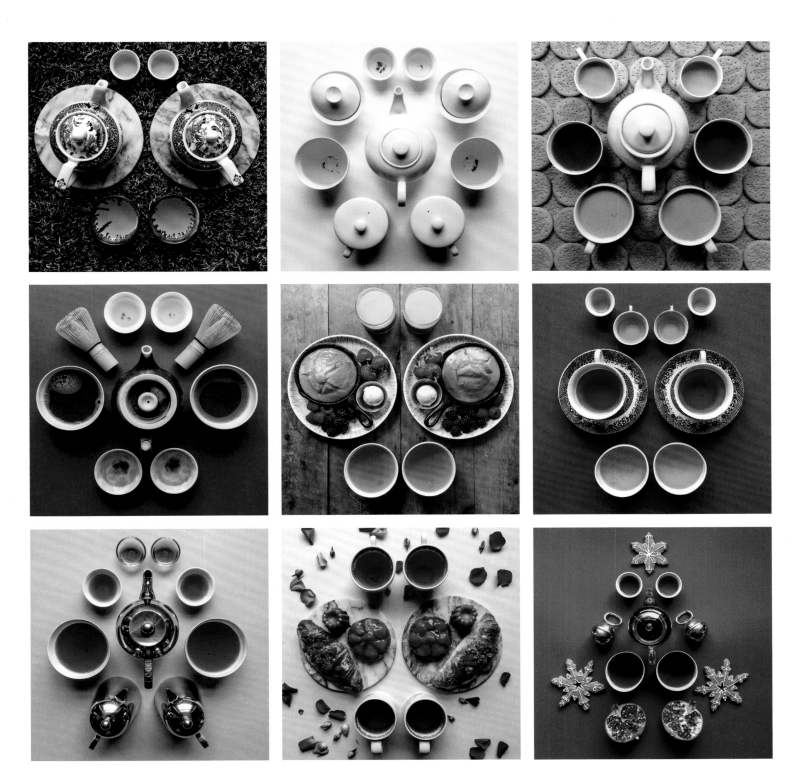

Green teas work well with oily fish and oolongs like the Iron Goddess of Mercy pair especially brilliantly with cheese. My friend René Redzepi of Noma enjoys pu'er with his porridge. I adore white silver tip with ripe pears. I'd never drink Lapsang suchong with kippers, but I would drink it with marmalade on toast. I could go on and on. I hope you will. Experiment with great tea. Certain leaves will really bring out the flavors of specific dishes. It isn't just a matter of a liquid to drink along with your breakfast – it can be a melding of flavors that work in perfect harmony.

Always choose leaf over bags and look for suppliers who source direct from the farms. When you bypass the brokers, the farmer gets a better deal and the tea companies who deal direct are really serious about their tea. They are looking for relationships with craftsmen and truly delicious taste rather than bulk to fill a bag. Be adventurous. Be like Michael.

This is the story of a simple app, set up to post photographs and glimpse into people's lives, a site that has the power to transform lives. This is the story of the social side of social media, of finding friends and sharing food, of holding up a phone torch to illuminate a plate of cheesecake for its moment of fame, and collapsing in laughter at the table: of suddenly realizing – this is absurd, yet it is utterly normal.

I first read about Michael online, of course, in a passing reference to his Instagram account. I followed it, intrigued and impressed by the simple beauty of the idea, the almost mesmeric geometry of those symmetrical plates, and the story of the love behind the images which were so beautifully arranged, so full of joy. Somehow I heard he had fallen off his bike and had broken his collarbone – I sent him and Mark a package full of chocolates and sweets. I hoped it wouldn't seem weird. It didn't: we became instant friends.

We met up properly at the first SymmetryBreakfast pop–up, at London's Town Hall hotel – and we haven't looked back. At the time, the account was still taking off: we had no idea then of the heights it has reached since.

For Instagram has taken me to places I never dreamed were possible: to Italian palazzos and Michelin–star kitchens, to baking classes on rural farms, to Alpine cheese dairies, to Hungarian strudel shops. There is the constant excitement of meals out, new restaurants and pop–ups and supper clubs, and breakfasts, always breakfasts. No slice of cake goes unphotographed, salads are arranged artfully in a bowl sent specially by a potter, posed on the kitchen table in a snatched lunchbreak from work, before being shoved back in a Tupperware box to eat later, at a desk. After more than a quarter of a century writing the nightly TV news, I suddenly have a whole new sideline as a food writer, one which has brought endless joy and countless friends.

It honestly never stops. These are the snapshots from a world now framed by snapshots: carrying lunch around a restaurant, chasing the best light; meals tweaked into perfection with filters, storied with a forest of hashtags; lighting up phone screens with heart–shaped "likes," one hundred, two hundred, three hundred, more.

But the best bit is not really those tiny adrenaline shots of approval: it is rather about friendship. Not just glimpsing other lives but starting conversations that begin in the ether and then continue in reality. I would never have met Michael and Mark without it, would never have met any of the people I now see, never have fallen into this amazing whirlwind which is now my life.

And for Michael – it's meant a whole new career, and a book which will undoubtedly be the first of many. Instead of cycling off each morning to his old job, teaching at a museum, he has been writing recipes, seeking out dishes and ideas from other cultures, ever curious, always learning more. His eye for detail, his aesthetic, his love of design and his sheer imagination are all astonishing.

It is art without a shred of artifice. This project was born out of love – without Mark, after all, there would be no symmetry.

It has taken dedication, and hard work. Cooking all those breakfasts and photographing them every day, without fail, even the day he broke his collarbone, even the hungover days when he'd rather not get out of bed at all – none of it is easy. But for someone without the privilege of a rich family or a background which automatically opens doors, it has opened doors. "Could any of us have ever imagined," he said to me the other day, "how all this could have happened, just thanks to an app on a phone?" We could not.

And so – the simplicity of a site which turns life into a series of gently tinted, highly colorized snaps. Instagram is like a home kitchen whose windows are flung open to the world. Just hear the quiet hum of the smartphone, fizzing with hundreds of thousands of ticks of approval for a breakfast made for two. It might be absurd, yet it has become the new normal; hushed only by the mute button. Be still, my bleeping hearts.

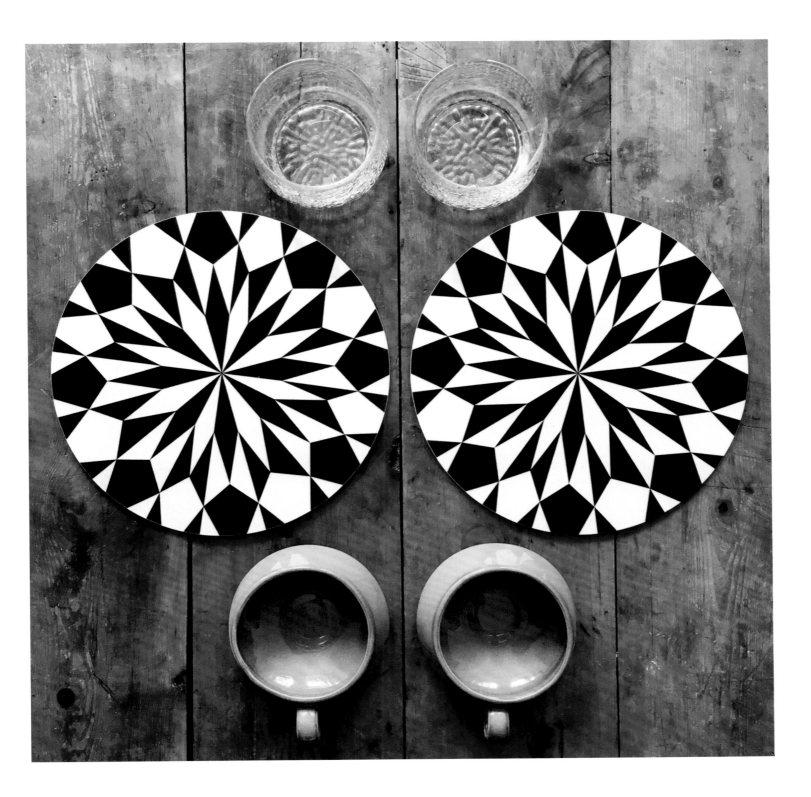

1 RISE AND SHINE
UNITED KINGDOM, PORTUGAL, MOROCCO, NIGERIA, WEST AFRICA

The full English, one of the most famous breakfasts in the world, is absent here, usurped by the Ulster fry, a lesser known but technically superior dish #doublecarbs. Flying the flag for England is frumenty, an ancient recipe that ties in to the rising trend in ancient grains – the recipe comes straight from the court of King Richard II in 1390.

Hopping over to Nigeria, we discover that they understand the joys of carbohydrates too: a bowl of ogi, a fermented cornstarch, and akara, deep-fried bean cakes – a breakfast to savor and dip.

But if you're searching for something sweet, Portugal's pastel de nata or Morocco's m'smmen involve skilfully folded pastry layers, which are hours in the preparation, seconds in the eating. No one can resist their complete deliciousness.

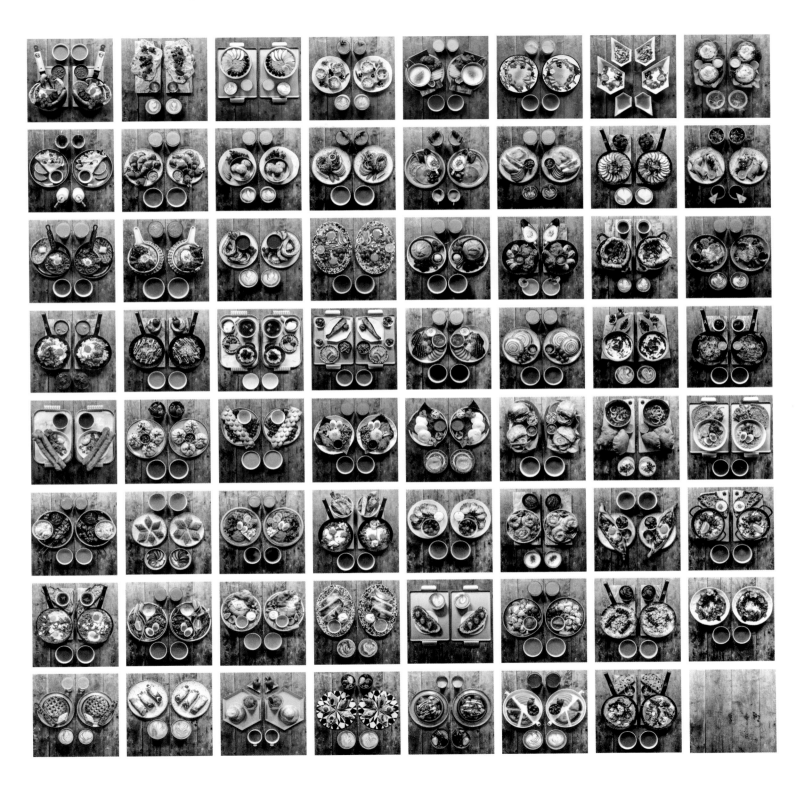

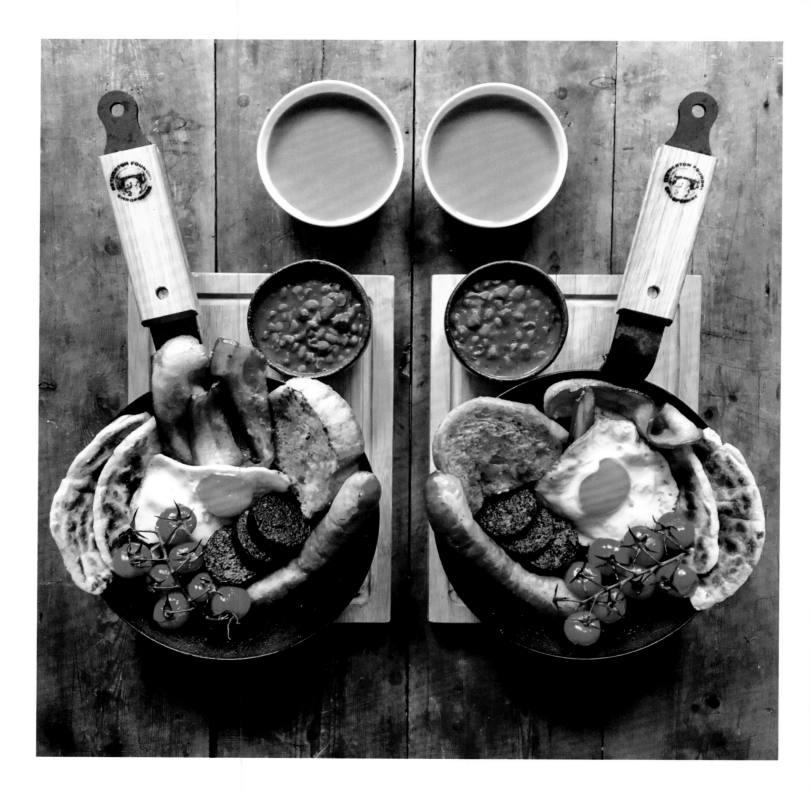

Apologies to England, Wales, and Scotland, but in my opinion Northern Ireland wins the crown for the best fry-up.

The Ulster fry takes the fry-up to the next level, with a portion of soda bread and a potato farl alongside the traditional bacon, sausage, black pudding, egg, and tomato (beans are dangerous territory).

The potato farl is where bread meets potato, and is the perfect way to use up leftover mash. Its name comes from the early Scots word *fardell*, meaning a quarter, something that will become apparent in the shaping of the dough.

It's important to cook everything in the same pan, either at the same time if it's big enough, or in succession. Not just because it will make washing up easier, but because the fried soda bread will absorb all the flavor of the meat and absolutely nothing will be wasted.

THE ULSTER FRY

For the Potato Farls

3 medium potatoes, peeled, boiled, and mashed
2 tbsp plain flour, plus extra for dusting
1 tsp baking powder
1 tbsp butter, melted

For the Soda Bread

Makes one loaf
2¾ cups plain flour
1¼ cups buttermilk
1 tsp salt
1 tsp baking soda

For the potato farls, combine the ingredients in a bowl and mix until a dough forms. Roll out the dough into a circle about 8 in in diameter and ½ in thick. Cut into quarters.

In a dry pan on a medium heat, cook the farls for 3–4 minutes on each side until golden brown. Set aside but keep warm.

Preheat your oven to 425°F.

Sift the flour, salt, and baking soda together, add the buttermilk and, using your hands, work into a ball. You may need to add more flour. As soon as it's a cohesive mass stop handling it.

Lightly dust a baking sheet and transfer the dough to it. Using a wooden spoon or chopstick, press a cross into the dough, going about 2 in deep. This will help with even cooking.

Bake for 20 minutes at 425°F, then reduce the temperature to 400°F for another 20–25 minutes. The bread is ready if it sounds hollow when tapped on the bottom.

Leave to cool on a wire rack, then slice and fry in the same pan as the rest of the fry-up ingredients.

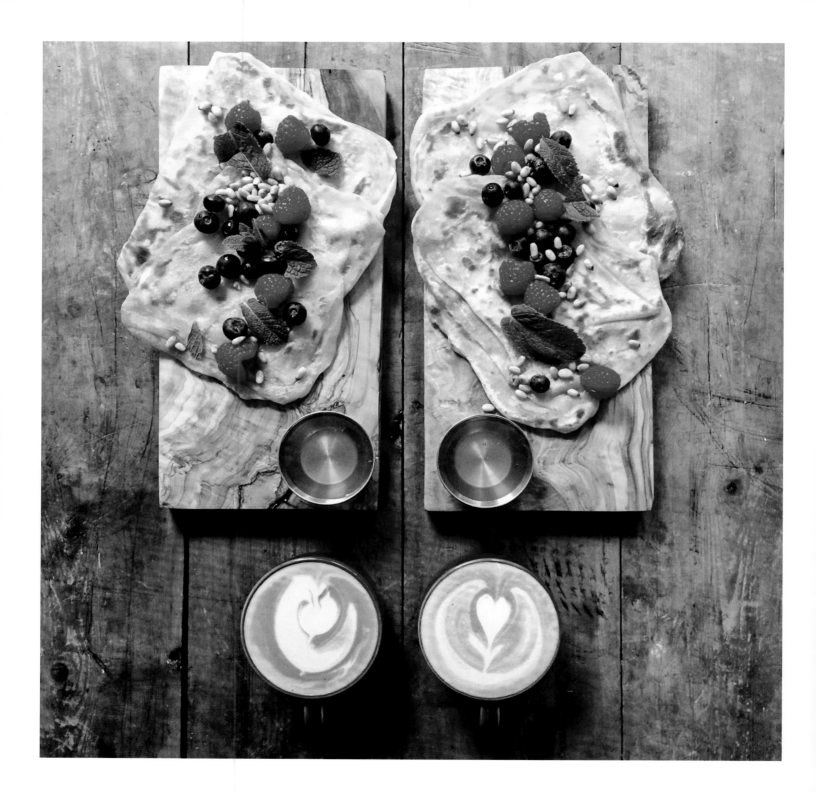

M'smmen are a lovely flaky pancake from Morocco. I first came across these when a friend, Dana (@arganicldn), gave me a bottle of her argan oil as a present and I started to research what to do with it. Culinary argan oil, made from toasted argan kernels, is nicknamed "liquid gold" and quite rightly so. The process is done by hand, mainly by Moroccan Berber women, and the final product is a nutty oil, perfect for dipping bread or drizzling over a salad.

This recipe is very forgiving; there is no need to be a perfectionist. As you stretch the dough, you will inevitably get holes, but as you fold they will become hidden within the layers.

The result is flaky on the outside, chewy on the inside. Serving it with honey and lashings of argan oil is particularly lovely, accompanied by fresh mint tea or a milky coffee.

M'SMMEN CRISPY MOROCCAN PANCAKES

For the Dough
3 cups plain flour
¾ cup fine semolina
1 tsp caster sugar
1 tsp salt
1 tsp fast–action yeast
1 ¼ cups tepid water

For Folding
Sunflower oil
1 stick soft butter
¾ cup semolina

For the Toppings
Honey
Argan oil (go easy on this)
Pine nuts, lightly toasted
Mixed berries

Put all the dry ingredients for the dough into a bowl or mixer and add the water until the mix forms a slightly sticky dough. Be careful that you don't add too much water at the start. If you're using a mixer, knead the dough for about 5 minutes using a dough hook. If you're working by hand, knead the dough on a floured surface for about 10 minutes. It should be smooth and elastic.

Split the dough into 10 balls and, using the sunflower oil, lightly coat each one so that it doesn't dry out. Clear a large work surface to prepare your pancakes and generously oil so that the dough doesn't stick.

Take a ball of dough and, with oiled hands, press it flat. Working from the middle outwards, keep going until the pancake is so thin you can almost see through it; don't worry if you make some holes. Scantly spread some butter over and sprinkle some semolina on – this will help the flaky layers form when cooking.

Like folding a letter, fold the left two thirds in and then bring the right side over. You should have a narrow strip now. Bring the top down two thirds of the way and fold the bottom up to match. Now you have a square. Repeat until all the balls are folded.

Preheat a dry pan over a medium–high heat. Starting with the first square, flatten it out until it's about twice its original size. Fry each pancake for about 5 minutes on each side until golden brown, flipping several times throughout.

Drizzle with honey, argan oil, pine nuts, and berries.

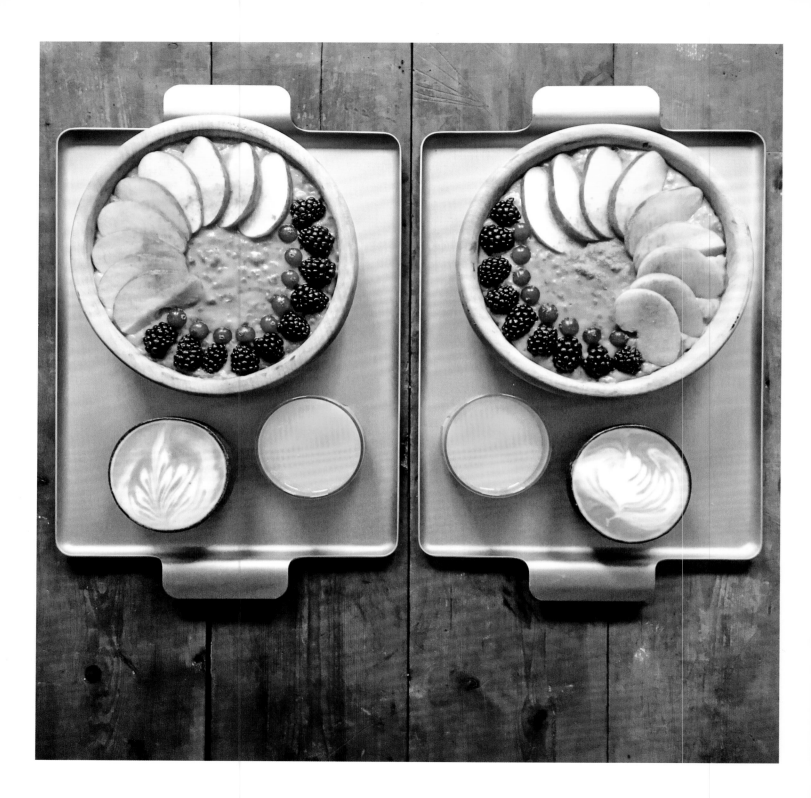

With the current unstoppable appetite for ancient grains, I thought it might be fun to have a recipe for England's oldest national dish, frumenty. It's like a Bircher muesli (that wonderful combination of oatmeal, apples, and thick yellow cream) that is then cooked, but because it is made with beer (I know, for breakfast) it's already a thousand times better than porridge.

Frumenty appears in Richard II's manuscript for cooking, *The Forme of Cury*. Published in 1390, it is the oldest cookery guide in the world. The "Methods of Cooking," as it is called in modern English, is a scroll of 205 recipes written on calfskin and housed at the British Library.

The recipe bears a striking resemblance to Persian haleem, with cooked wheat grains being combined with spices like cinnamon and saffron, egg yolks, and cooked venison or game birds.

FRUMENTY MEDIEVAL PORRIDGE WITH BEER

1 cup ancient grain of your choice: I used siyez, also known as einkorn, from the Belazu Ingredient Company, but farro, spelt, or Khorasan will work equally well; or you can use regular oats instead

2 cups ale or beer, or something darker like a porter or stout

½ cup water

1 egg

⅓ cup currants

½ tsp cinnamon

½ tsp dried ginger

½ tsp nutmeg

3-4 tbsp cream

1 tbsp sugar (optional)

Soak your choice of grain in the beer or ale overnight. If the grain is cracked (which means it's been crushed into smaller pieces) it might absorb the liquid much more quickly, but this shouldn't be a problem.

Put the boozy grain mix into a pan with the water and bring to a boil. Boil for 15 minutes, by which time the grain will be starting to break down and the mix will be thickening. Reduce the heat to low and add the currants and spices.

Take off the heat and leave to cool for 5 minutes. Add the egg and cream and stir well. Sprinkle with sugar, if using, and add any additional toppings of your choice – chopped nuts, extra cinnamon, sliced apple, fresh berries, or a knob of butter really bring this alive.

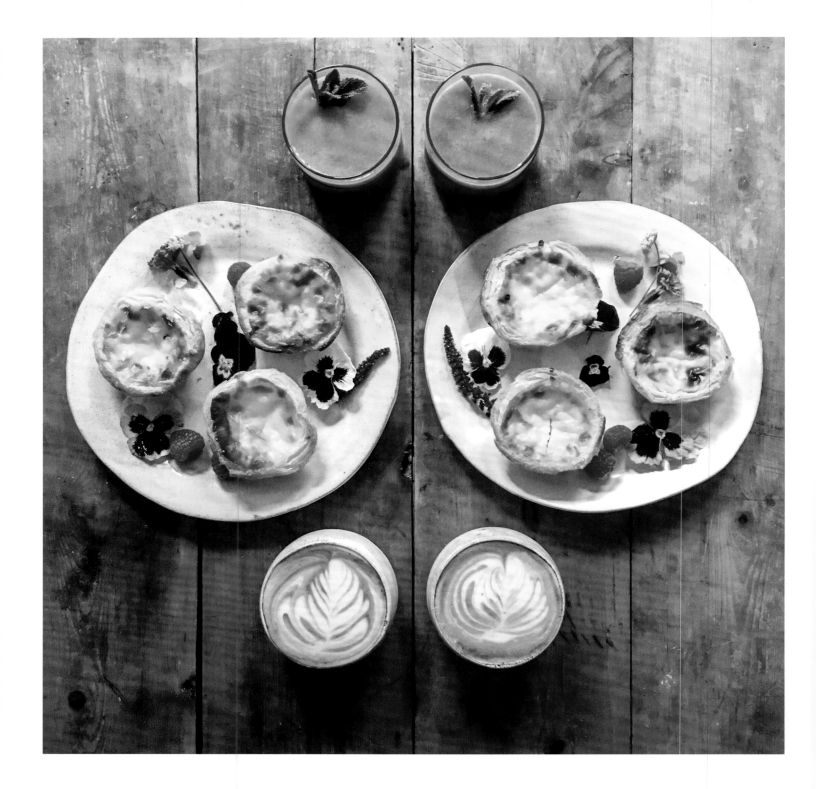

These custard tarts are so achingly delicious, crisp, and flaky, I can only have them a few times a year because of the risk that over-exposure might lead to apathy.

One of my favorite cafés, which makes them fresh every day, is Taberna do Mercado in Spitalfields, East London. It is sufficient distance from home that, should I want one, I have to make a concerted effort to get one. Any closer would be dangerous.

The secret is in the way the pastry is molded in the tin – not like a mince pie, but a wedge of rolled flaky pastry that is teased up the sides. The underside should resemble the rings of a felled tree.

My version cheats on the pastry but doesn't scrimp on the custard. I prefer a nata with a hint of lemon, rather than vanilla.

PASTEL DE NATA EGG CUSTARD TARTS

Makes 12 tarts

1 pack ready-rolled puff pastry (13.8 oz is standard in most supermarkets)
1 whole egg
2 egg yolks
⅔ cup superfine sugar
2 tbsp cornflour
1 ⅔ cups whole milk
Zest of ½ lemon

Take the pastry out of the fridge and packaging at least 30 minutes before unrolling.

In a cold pan, place the egg and egg yolks, sugar, and cornflour, and mix until combined. Pour in the milk and gently whisk until you have a smooth liquid. Place the pan on a medium–low heat whilst continuing to whisk. The secret to smooth custard is to take your time; if the heat is too high you risk making scrambled eggs.

Once it starts to thicken you can turn the heat up very slightly and continue to stir for another 5 minutes. Remove from the heat and add the lemon zest. The custard should have a thick yet pourable consistency.

Pour the custard into a glass bowl and cover with cling film to prevent a skin from forming.

Preheat your oven to 425°F.

Unroll the pastry and remove the plastic. Cut it in half lengthways and place the sheets on top of each other. With the long side facing you, roll the pastry tightly into a long sausage and cut it into 12 discs.

Place each disc in a lightly greased muffin tin. Dip your thumbs into some water and press into the middle of each round. You want to flatten the bottom and push the pastry up the edges. It is OK if the edges come up a little above the tin.

Divide the cooled custard between the 12 pastry cases and bake for 20–25 minutes. You want the tops of the tarts to be burnished with black spots and the insides still to be soft, with a little wobble.

Leave the nata to cool and enjoy them like the Portuguese do, with a small coffee – *um pingo* (espresso with a touch of milk) – and eat with a teaspoon. That way it seems to last longer.

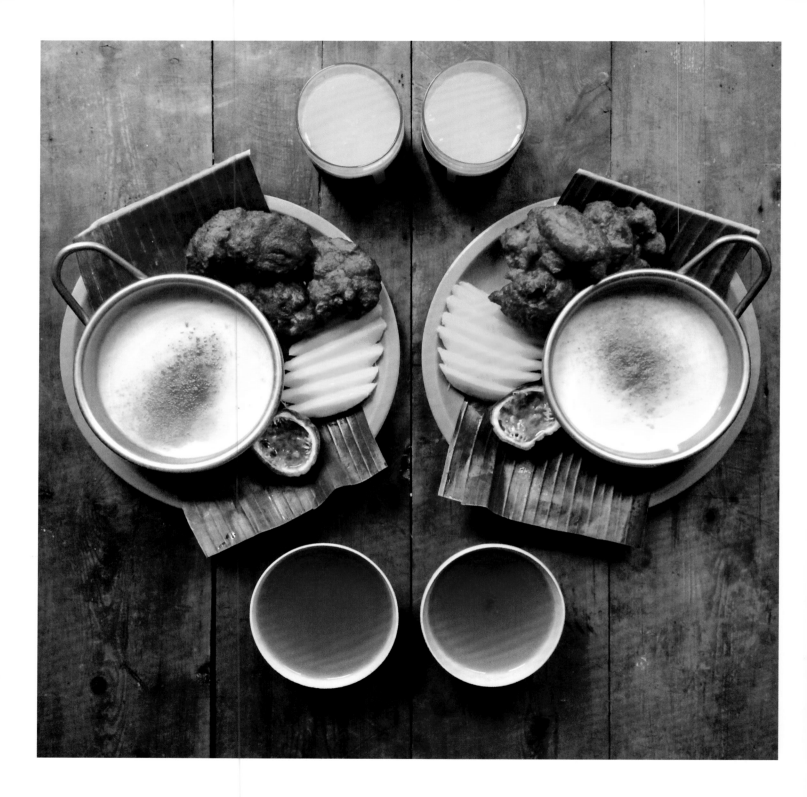

On a quiet Friday morning, around 5 a.m., I met the lovely @dooneyskitchen at Billingsgate Market. She is one of those extraordinary people on a mission to show the world what traditional and contemporary Nigerian cuisine really is.

OGI WITH AKARA
NIGERIAN CORNSTARCH PORRIDGE WITH BEAN FRITTERS

Before her intervention, I had no idea what to expect from Nigerian food. It's extremely hearty and full of goodness. She had very kindly made me some homemade ogi, also known as pap or koko. This is a type of porridge, made from fermented and soured cornstarch. To say that it is an acquired taste is an understatement, so be sure to start with plenty of sugar and milk, but I promise it grows on you. To make ogi from scratch is a long and laborious process, but you can find it ready made in both yellow and white varieties in specialist Nigerian shops and online.

Akara is a fritter made from black–eyed peas and, although it involves some soaking time, it's easy to make and is absolutely delicious. I have also discovered a handy method for de–hulling the beans in no time.

(continued on following page)

For the Akara
3 heaped tbsp ogi
½ cup water at room temperature, plus 1 ½ quarts boiling water
1 cup evaporated milk
Sugar to taste

For the Ogi
1 ½ cups dried black–eyed peas
1 stock cube, your choice of flavor
1 scotch bonnet pepper
3 scallions (just the white part)
Salt and pepper to taste
Oil for frying

Cover the black–eyed peas in water and soak for 10 minutes. Pour them, with the water, into a food processor or blender and pulse the beans around; this will loosen most of the skins. Pour the beans into a large bowl and chafe any remaining skins off by rubbing handfuls together. Discard the skins along with the water.

Place the now-shelled beans into fresh water and leave them to soak for at least 5 hours or overnight.

Once the beans have soaked, put them back in the blender with the rest of the akara ingredients (except the oil, of course) and add ¼ cup of water. Purée the mix into a thick batter.

Heat the oil in a pan over a medium–high heat. It's important that your oil is not too hot or the outside of the akara will burn before the inside is cooked.

Drop dessertspoons of the akara batter into the oil and turn them over after about 3 minutes.

Split one open to check if it's cooked all the way through and adjust your fritter size or cooking time accordingly. The aim is for a golden brown color, and each fritter should be roughly the size of a plum.

Drain on kitchen paper.

To prepare the ogi, first crumble it into a large bowl. Add a small amount of tepid water until you have a smooth paste, then add the rest of the cold water so you have a thick paste roughly the consistency of cream.

With a spoon in one hand and the kettle in the other – a real test of your coordination – pour in the boiling water in a circular motion and stir. Keep stirring and pouring until the mix starts to thicken, then, once this begins, stop stirring but keep pouring! It will thicken on standing.

Pour over the evaporated milk and add sugar to taste. Serve with a side of 3–4 akara.

I first made this with a glut of plums that just didn't want to ripen in the bowl and found that the bergamot in the Earl Grey adds a lovely uplifting zing to what would essentially be jam for lazy folk.

Once you've selected your fruit, weigh it and then calculate the amount of sugar you need. I usually go for a ratio of 1 part sugar to 8 parts fruit if it's very unripe, but use less if your plums are ripe.

EARL GREY AND PLUM COMPOTE

Makes a large jar of compote

1.5 lbs plums, pitted
½ cup sugar
2 tsp Earl Grey – loose-leaf is best
1 cup boiling water
Zest of an orange

Roughly chop the plums. I like to use a range of sizes, as some will soften into a purée whilst larger pieces will give you something to bite. Put the plums and the sugar into a large, heavy pan.

Make a cup of tea using boiling water and let the leaves sit for a minute or two longer than you would if you were going to drink it – best make a cup for yourself at the same time (no milk for me, please). Strain out the leaves and add the liquid to the plums and sugar. Grate in the orange zest.

Bring to a gentle simmer and cover. After about 30 minutes the plums should begin to break down into a mush. Turn your heat down to its lowest at this point and leave the pan to simmer uncovered for another 15 minutes.

I leave the mix to cool before decanting into a jar or airtight container, but bear in mind that this is not a jam and will probably only keep in the fridge for a week at the most.

This is absolutely delicious with all sorts of pancakes, crêpes and, my personal favorite, Dutch poffertjes (see page 191).

Even though flavored here with Earl Grey, this also works wonderfully with a smoky Keemun or oolong tea.

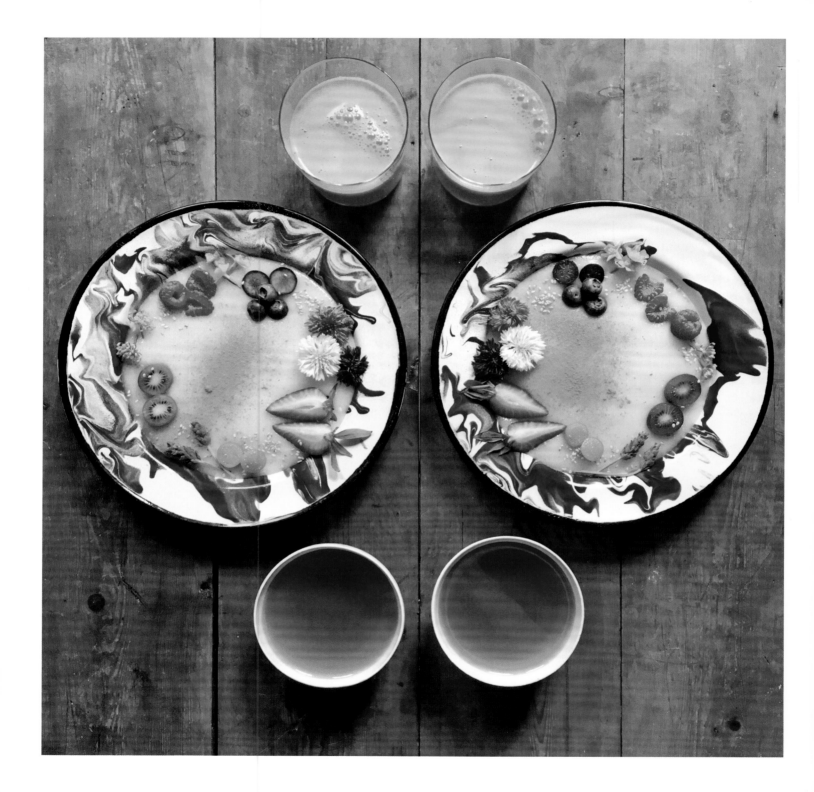

This is porridge plus. Cassava has double the calories and carbs of other tubers, so if you're about to run a marathon give it a go. If you're a slob, then perhaps just have it once in a while.

Make sure to peel and cook the root thoroughly as it can be slightly toxic, but don't let a little bit of poison put you off. A few hundred million people across South America, Africa, and Asia eat cassava every day, so don't be a wuss.

This recipe is also much easier to make by volume than by weight as it depends on what size cassava you buy. The key measurement is 1 part root to 4 parts water.

CASSAVA PORRIDGE

1 cup peeled and
   diced cassava
4 cups water
2 bay leaves
½ tsp salt
1 tsp vanilla extract
¼ cup condensed milk
Cinnamon and nutmeg
   to serve

Pop the peeled and diced cassava into a blender with 2 cups of the water and blend until smooth.

Put the other 2 cups of water, the bay leaves, and salt into a pan and bring to a boil. Remove the leaves, then add the puréed cassava mix.

On a medium heat, keep stirring until the mixture thickens. It should look semi–translucent and smooth.

Finally, add the vanilla extract and condensed milk to taste. Serve with freshly ground cinnamon and nutmeg.

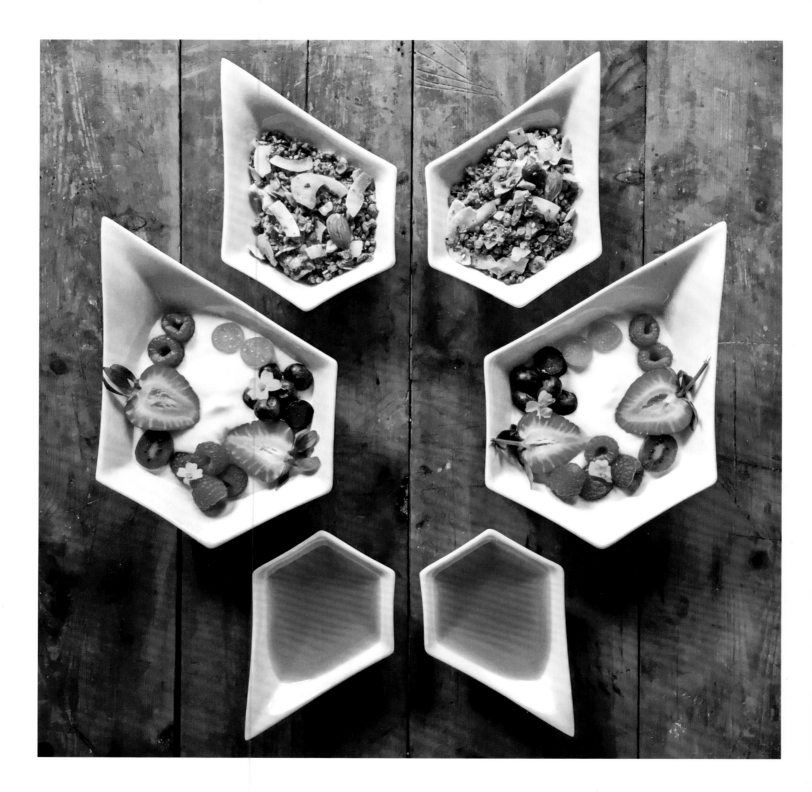

My friend Scarlett @thepantherswhiskers is an awesome cook and chef. She also makes possibly the best granola in the world. As someone who eats cereal for breakfast maybe just once a year (why would you when there are so many wonderful alternatives?), I think that's incredibly high praise.

This recipe could last you a week or a day, depending on how quickly you go back for seconds, and it has the added benefits of being vegan, gluten-free, and is a great make-ahead recipe. Make a big batch over the weekend and enjoy it all through the week.

NUTTY SLACK THE GREATEST CEREAL IN THE WORLD

2 cups oats, regular or gluten-free

⅔ cup unroasted buckwheat groats or sprouted buckwheat groats

5 tbsp coconut oil

6 tbsp maple syrup

3 heaped tbsp unsweetened desiccated coconut or coconut flakes

½ cup roughly chopped pistachios and hazelnuts

½ cup finely chopped dates, crystallized ginger, and dried apricots

2 heaped tsp ground ginger

2 tsp cardamom

1 tsp cinnamon

1 tsp vanilla powder (optional, as it's a pricey ingredient)

Preheat your oven to 350°F. Prepare a baking tray with some greaseproof paper. Combine the oats and the buckwheat in a large mixing bowl.

Gently melt the coconut oil in a pan and add the maple syrup. Add the liquid to the oats and mix thoroughly so that everything is coated. Spread the mix out on the baking tray and pop it in the oven. After 10–15 minutes, give the mix a good stir so that everything cooks evenly.

After a further 5 minutes, add the coconut and the chopped nuts and stir again. Check every 5 minutes until the mixture is dark golden brown. The toasting should take between 20 and 30 minutes but may take longer – it's a fine line between being perfectly done and overdone, but when it's nice and dark brown it will have the great flavor you're looking for.

Tip the hot mixture into a large mixing bowl. Add the dried fruit and the spices. Give everything one final stir. Leave the granola to cool completely, then store in an airtight container or in a pretty jar.

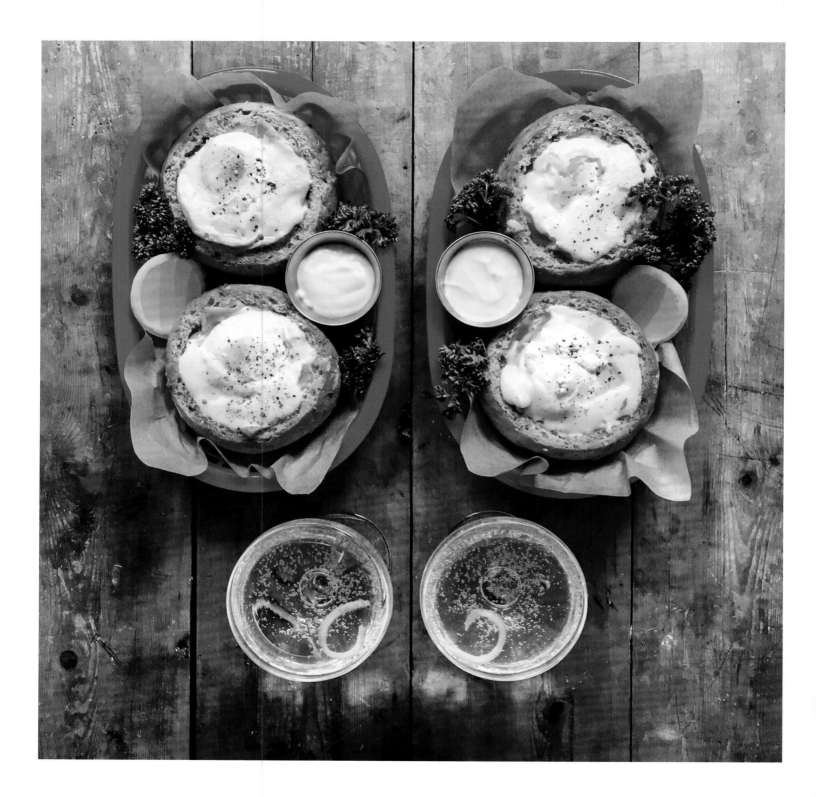

Mark and I absolutely adore bread. The wonderful thing is that really good bread available today is timeless, the recipe unchanged over the last two millennia.

Many cultures and countries have hollowed out their loaves. The Poles fill them with sour rye soup called zurek, the French enjoy a *pain surprise* for a picnic, while in South Africa you might come across bunnychow, a bread roll filled with mutton curry.

BREAKFAST IN BREAD
BENNY BUNS AND SHAKSHUKA BUNS, AKA THE LOVE SHACK

This recipe is a great time–saver. Not only is it quick to make and assemble, but you will reap benefits later: minimal or no washing up gives you more free time to enjoy afterwards. It's perfect for camping (if you're into that) or if you need to feed a lot of people and really fill them up.

My two favorite bready breakfasts are benny buns and the love shack, or shakshuka buns, and the recipes for both are as simple as hollowing out a bread roll of your choice and filling it up.

Shakshuka (see page 179), literally meaning "all mixed up," needs a sourdough roll or loaf as the crust will keep it together much longer than a brioche bun. Not only will it hold up, but when all the sauce is gone you'll be left with a rich treat to rip apart and devour! Otherwise you run the risk of it all disintegrating in your hands. Not a good way to start the day.

(continued on following page)

For the Benny Buns

Brioche buns
Slices of ham or shredded
  ham hock
Hollandaise sauce (see
  page 57)
Eggs
Black pepper

For the Benny buns, preheat your oven to 400°F.

Depending on the size of your buns, you can decide if you want to have one each or two each. Slice a lid off each bun, about 1 cm down from the top, and keep it to one side.

Carefully pinch out the center of the bun and make sure you don't accidentally rip a hole in the side! You want to end up with a bread bowl.

Line the inside with a slice or two of ham and a good smearing of hollandaise sauce, then crack in your egg. Give a good twist of seasoning and replace the lid.

Wrap the bun in foil like a little present and place on a baking tray. Bake for 15–20 minutes until the egg is just set.

Remove from the oven and rip open the foil slightly to allow the steam to escape. Serve with some fresh parsley leaves and a wedge of lemon.

For the Shakshuka Buns

Crusty rolls or a loaf
Olive oil
Thick Greek yogurt, or
    labneh, a very thick
    yogurt from the Levant
Shakshuka (see page 179)
Eggs
Salt and black pepper

For the love shack buns, preheat your oven to 400°F.

Slice a lid off each roll or loaf about 1cm from the top and gently pinch out the inside.

Brush some olive oil on the inside and bake in the oven for 5 minutes. This will help prevent hot shakshuka bursting out everywhere when you're eating it.

Remove from the oven and allow to cool for a minute. Spread the yogurt or labneh around the inside of the buns and spoon in pre–made shakshuka. It's fine if it's cold, just not fridge cold.

Crack in an egg or two, season well, and replace the lid. Bake in the oven for 15 minutes.

Remove and allow to cool slightly before serving with plenty of freshly chopped parsley and black tea.

2 BREAKFAST AND BREAKSLOW
BRAZIL, VENEZUELA, DOMINICAN REPUBLIC

Ordering a coffee around the world can be a complicated business. Ask for a *carioca* in Portugal, and you will be served a weak espresso, whereas in Brazil you'll be describing someone from Rio de Janeiro, not caffeine at all! On the other hand, cakes and pastries like pastel de nata (see page 23) and cachitos are available fresh every day from bakeries in São Paulo, Caracas, and Lisbon.

Like a hot coffee, these baked goods are best when fresh – out of the oven and into the mouth as quickly as possible, without even a thought to the pain that might be inflicted. When food is that delicious, time is of the essence.

If you prefer your breakfast to be a more leisurely affair, and a bit less of a health hazard, the Dominican Republic has the answer: a refreshing oat drink to sip in the shade during summer. Just don't forget the cocktail umbrella.

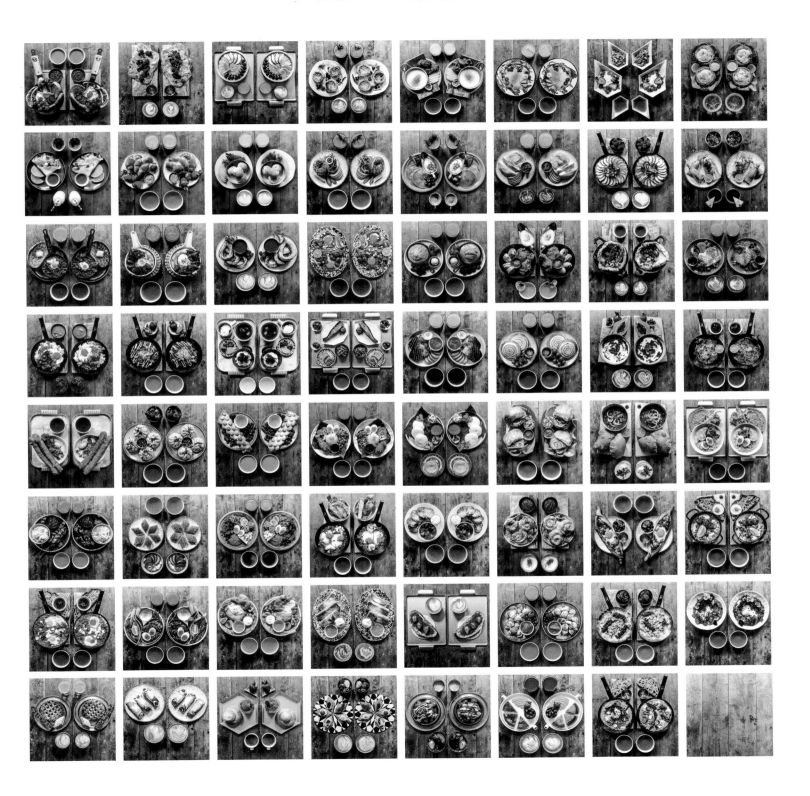

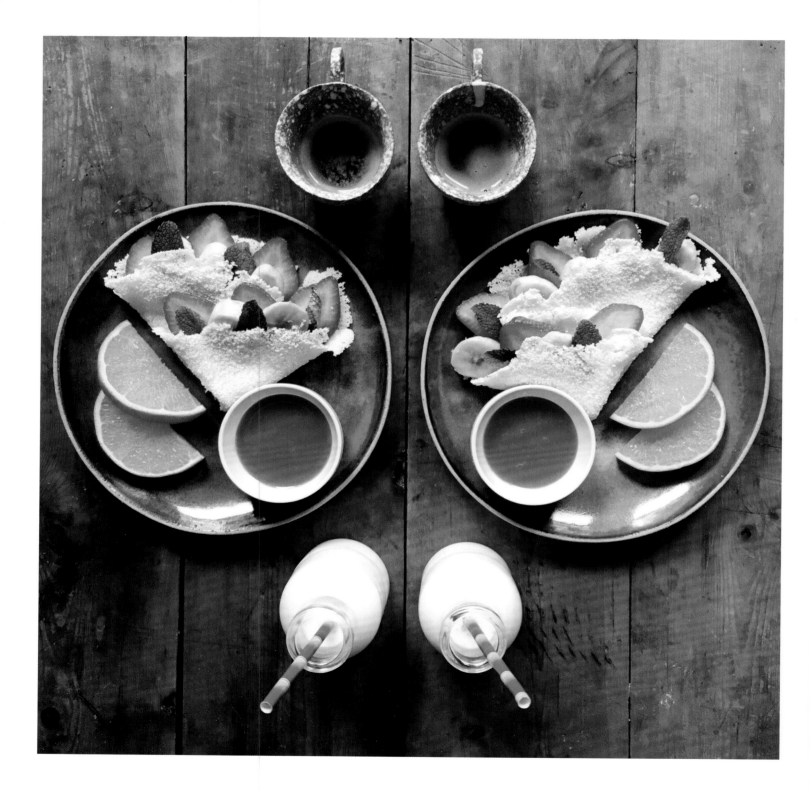

These beautiful pancakes from Brazil are like delicate white lace and, better yet, they're completely gluten-free. They have a chewiness that reminds me of glutinous rice cakes, though that might not be to everyone's taste.

Tapioca flour is used in so many cuisines across South America and is available in many health food shops, South American and Asian supermarkets, as well as online. I use it all the time, but if you've never used it before I would advise watching a YouTube video first. The trick is to add the tiniest amount of water – a few teaspoons are all you'll need. The end result is a fairly bland pancake that can carry sweet or savory fillings of your choice.

PANQUESCAS DE TAPIOCA TAPIOCA PANCAKES

Makes 2 large pancakes

8 heaped tbsp tapioca
    flour – I prefer the sour
    variety
2 tsp water

Put your tapioca flour and water into a bowl. Using your fingers, combine the two until the mixture clumps together. If you add too much water it will transform into a flowing liquid; add some more flour to balance it out.

To remove the clumps, pass the mixture through a sieve into a clean bowl. It should have a texture similar to the one you started with.

Heat a non-stick pan over a medium heat and sprinkle half the mix evenly over the entire surface. After a minute it should form a solid pancake. Flip and cook for another minute. The pancake will have the faintest touch of color but will still be rather white. Wipe the pan clean with some kitchen towel and repeat with the rest of the mixture.

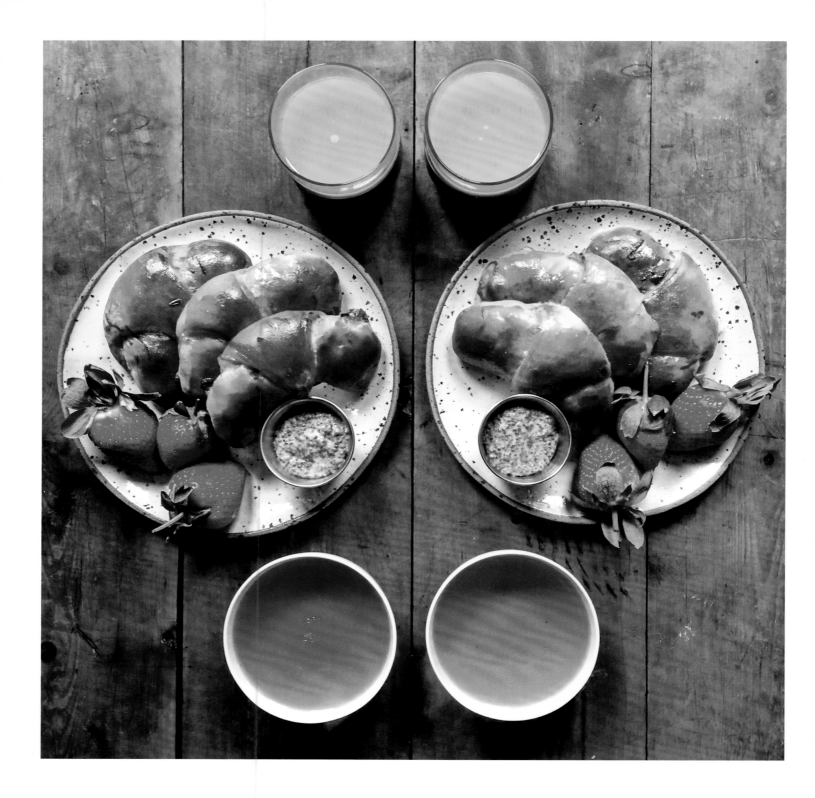

These little crescent–shaped rolls are an incredibly popular breakfast in Venezuela and Central America. A hybrid of a croissant and a bread roll, they are also much easier to make than their French counterparts.

Brought to Venezuela by the Portuguese after the Second World War, they are the most delicious breakfast on the go for Laura Delgado Ranalli @lauritadr21, who sent me this recipe. "These are typically eaten with a nice chocolate milk (we have one called Toddy, which is delicious) or an orange juice," she says. "People usually get them at bakeries and on the go."

You can freeze the buns after baking so you have a constant supply.

CACHITOS VENEZUELAN HAM–FILLED CROISSANTS

Makes 32 buns

1 tsp dried yeast
½ cup sugar
¾ cup milk
½ cup butter, melted, or flavorless vegetable oil
3 eggs
4 cups plain flour, plus extra for dusting
1 tsp salt
2 ½ cups ham, finely chopped
1 ½ cups Cheddar, grated

Dissolve the yeast in ½ cup warm water with 1 tbsp of the sugar and set aside for 10–15 minutes.

In a measuring jug or bowl, combine the remaining sugar with the milk, melted butter or oil, and 2 of the eggs. Add the yeast mixture and stir well.

In a stand mixer or large bowl, mix together the flour and salt. Add the yeast mix and bring everything together into a dough. Knead for 10–15 minutes until the dough is smooth and elastic.

Turn out the dough and shape into a ball. Lightly oil the inside of a large bowl, place the dough inside and cover with a tea towel. Leave in a warm place for 2 hours to double in size.

Lightly flour a work surface and tip the dough out. Punch back the dough – you can literally punch it – to remove the air, then knead it gently for 30 seconds. Shape it into a ball and cut it into 4 equal pieces. Leave them covered with a tea towel for 10 minutes to relax.

Prepare 2 baking sheets with some parchment paper.

Taking one piece of the shaped dough at a time, roll it out on to a floured surface until it forms a circle 10–12 in across.

Cut the dough into 8 slices like a pizza; each slice is one cachito. Take one slice and flatten it further to make it a little bigger, around 2–3 mm thick.

(continued on following page)

With the point of the triangle facing away from you, cover the surface with the chopped ham and grated cheese, leaving a ½ in border all around. Fold the bottom left and right corners together into the middle and then roll away from you. Bend the cachito into the classic crescent shape.

Repeat with the rest of the dough slices, lining the cachitos up on the baking sheet and leaving 2 in around each one so that they have room to expand during cooking. Once you have made them all, cover them with a tea towel and leave them to prove for another hour. They should double in size.

Preheat your oven to 350°F.

Lightly beat the third egg with 2 tsp cold water and brush it all over the cachitos.

Bake for 15 minutes or until golden brown. Remove from the oven and leave to cool slightly before serving with cold chocolate milk or freshly squeezed orange juice.

Who said that the only use for oats in the morning was porridge? If you ever have a gloriously hot summer where you live, you might wake up wanting this refreshing drink from the Dominican Republic.

I've adapted the original recipe by removing the sugar and adding pineapple juice purely because I adore a piña colada, not because I hate the white stuff.

JUGO DE AVENA OAT JUICE

1 cup rolled oats
1 cup water
1 cup pineapple juice
2 cups/13.6 oz can coconut milk
Juice of 3 limes
Handful of ice cubes

Place the oats in a blender with the water and pineapple juice and leave to soak for whatever time you have – an hour is good enough but overnight is also fine.

Add the coconut milk, lime juice, and ice to the blender and blitz until smooth. You can add some extra water if you prefer it a bit thinner. It should be the consistency of a milkshake.

Serve with a maraschino cherry, cocktail umbrella, and a straw.

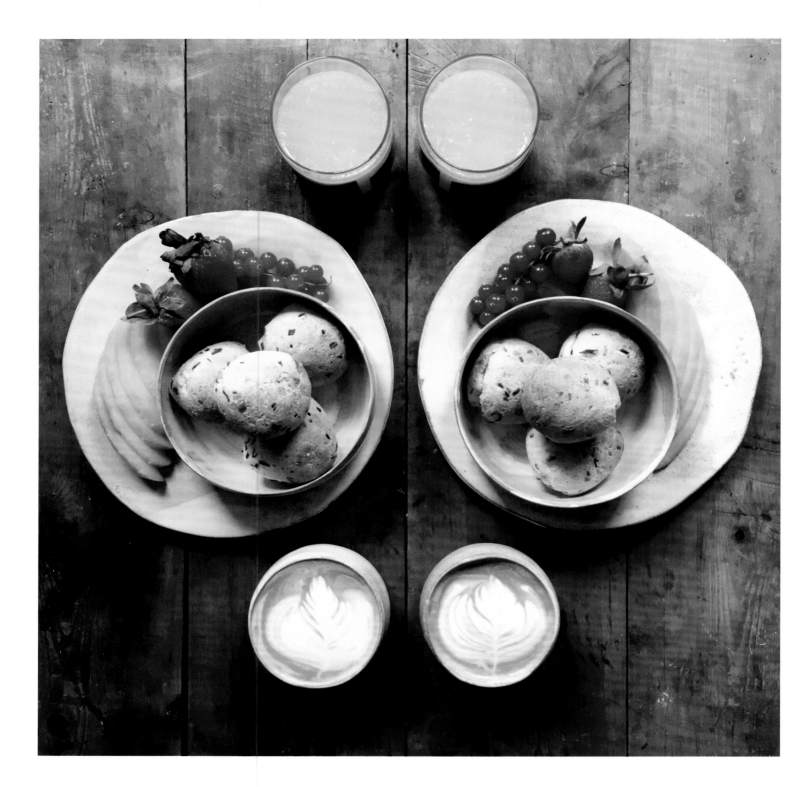

Using the same tapioca flour as for the Brazilian panquescas (see page 39), these are delightful, springy, cheesy balls of joy – one of my favorite breakfasts. The tapioca flour is available in many health food shops, South American and Asian supermarkets, as well as online.

Similar to a choux pastry or gougères, these are gluten–free breakfast bites, ready in just a few minutes and delicious with a short espresso.

Traditionally made with cheese from the Minas region of Brazil, queijo de minas, you can if you like substitute Mexican queso fresco instead. Failing that, I often use a mixture of Parmesan and Cheddar or a mature Gruyère to save me schlepping across town.

PAO DE QUIEJO BRAZILIAN CHEESE BREADS

Makes 10-12 rolls

1 cup milk
1 stick melted butter
1 tsp salt
2 cups tapioca flour
2 eggs
1 ½ cups finely grated
    cheese of your choice
1 tsp chives, chopped
    (optional)

Preheat your oven to 400°F.

In a saucepan, mix the milk, butter, and salt and bring to a boil. Remove from heat and stir in the tapioca flour. Leave to cool for 10 minutes.

Stir in the eggs, grated cheese, and chives (if using), and mix well.

Using either an ice–cream scoop or an oiled spoon, scoop out golf–ball–size portions on to a baking tray lined with parchment.

Bake for 20 minutes but check at 15 minutes. They should be puffy and golden. Serve immediately.

3 IN SEARCH OF A CURE
COLOMBIA, PERU, NORTHEAST USA

This chapter is one of my favorites. Bagels, arepas, and tamales – what other choice of vehicle do flavorsome fillings need? Better yet, you can eat all these things with your hands; no more pesky forks or spoons slowing you down.

One of the few examples of intentional miscategorization in this book is the inclusion of hollandaise sauce in this section. It has been around for centuries and is more likely French or Dutch in origin, but it was catapulted to fame as part of a recipe for eggs Benedict. The dish has uncertain origins, but I prefer the story that a Wall Street banker, Lemuel Benedict, created eggs Benny in 1894 whilst looking to cure his hangover. The kitchens at the Waldorf Hotel were more than happy to oblige his request. I assume it worked, as we still often turn to eggs Benedict when we're not feeling our very best in the morning.

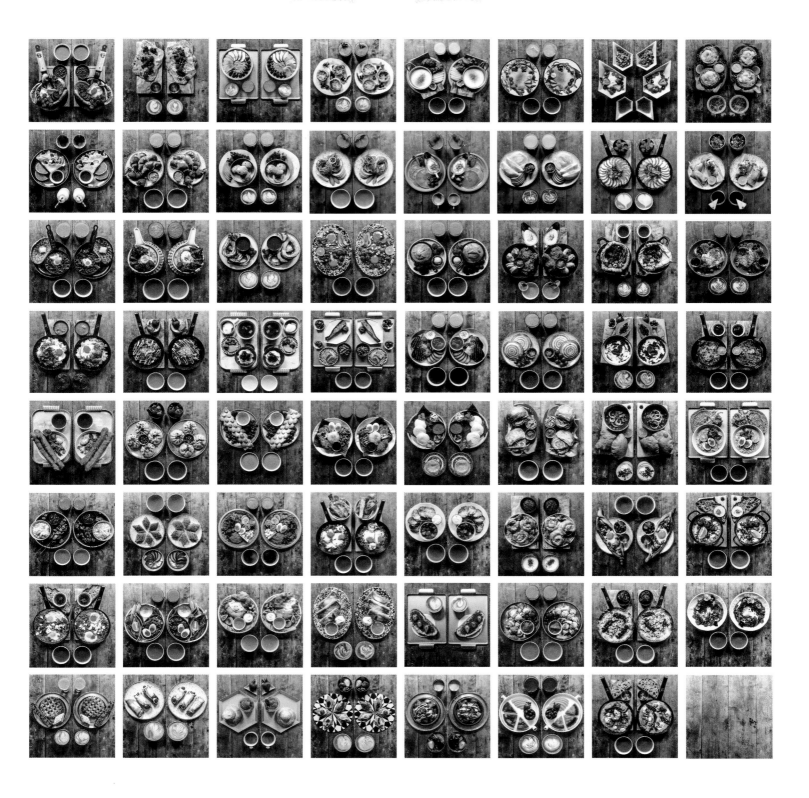

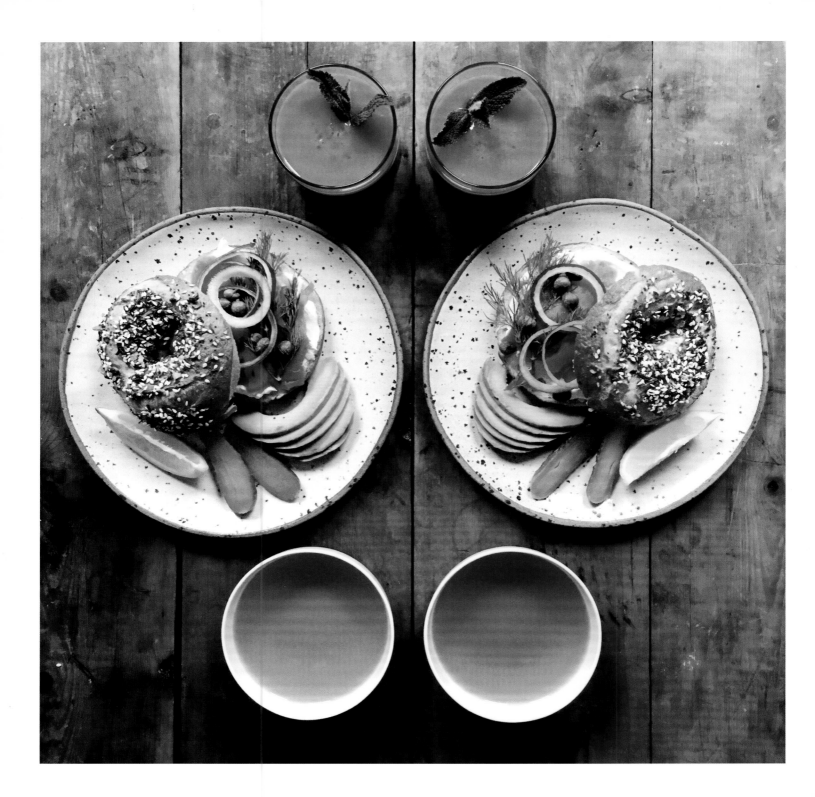

I only know of one bakery in London that makes everything bagels, which is sad really because they are the king of bagels.

They're named "everything" because they combine all the other flavors of New York into one joyous carb-fest. Sesame, caraway, poppy, onion, and garlic might seem full-on flavor, but they really work together.

EVERYTHING BAGELS

The spice blend is also delicious on baked potatoes, chicken, and in salads, so keep any you have left over in a jar for later.

The fillings are endless but nothing beats smoked salmon and cream cheese with some thinly sliced raw onion, capers, and dill.

(continued on following page)

For the Everything Spice Mix

4 tbsp poppy seeds
4 tbsp caraway seeds
4 tbsp sesame seeds
4 tbsp dried onions
4 tbsp dried garlic
2 tbsp sea salt

Mix together all the ingredients for the everything spice mix in a large jar and give it a shake. If you are using dried garlic or onion flakes and they are very large, give them a rough chop first.

Makes 8 bagels

For the Bagels

3 cups strong white bread
   flour
1 cup strong wholemeal
   bread flour
1 ⅓ cup warm water
2 tsp dried yeast
1 tbsp brown sugar
2 tsp salt

For the Water Bath

3 tbsp honey or 1 tsp
   baking soda
8 quarts water, or however
   much your pan can take

Combine the yeast and warm water in a bowl and set aside for 5 minutes.

Place the flours, salt, and sugar in the bowl of a stand mixer and combine thoroughly using a dough hook attachment. On a gentle speed, add the yeast water and knead for 8 minutes. You may need to stop and scrape down the sides occasionally. The dough should be soft but not sticky at this stage. If you are doing this by hand, combine everything and knead for 15 minutes.

Tip the dough out on to a clean surface and shape into a ball. Lightly oil a large bowl and coat the dough lightly too. Leave covered in a warm place for 90 minutes; it should almost double in size.

Punch back the dough (literally) – a satisfying task – to remove the build–up of air, then knead it for a minute. Using a knife or pastry cutter, divide the dough into 8 equal pieces and roll each one into a ball.

With a finger dipped in flour, poke a hole in the middle of each ball and stretch it out. The hole should be around an inch across.

Make a water bath by filling a large pan with water and bringing it to a boil. Add the honey or baking soda and stir until dissolved. Preheat your oven to 425°F and prepare two trays with baking parchment, and a wire cooling rack.

In batches of two or three, boil the bagels for 1 minute, then flip them over and boil for a further minute with the other side up; this will give the bagels their characteristic chewy crust. Remove and leave to cool for another minute on the rack. Proceed with the next batch.

Whilst the bagels are still slightly wet, sprinkle lots of the everything spice mix over them.

With four bagels to each baking tray, bake for 25 minutes. Transfer back to the wire rack to cool completely.

These freeze well. I suggest slicing them before freezing as it will make thawing them less painful.

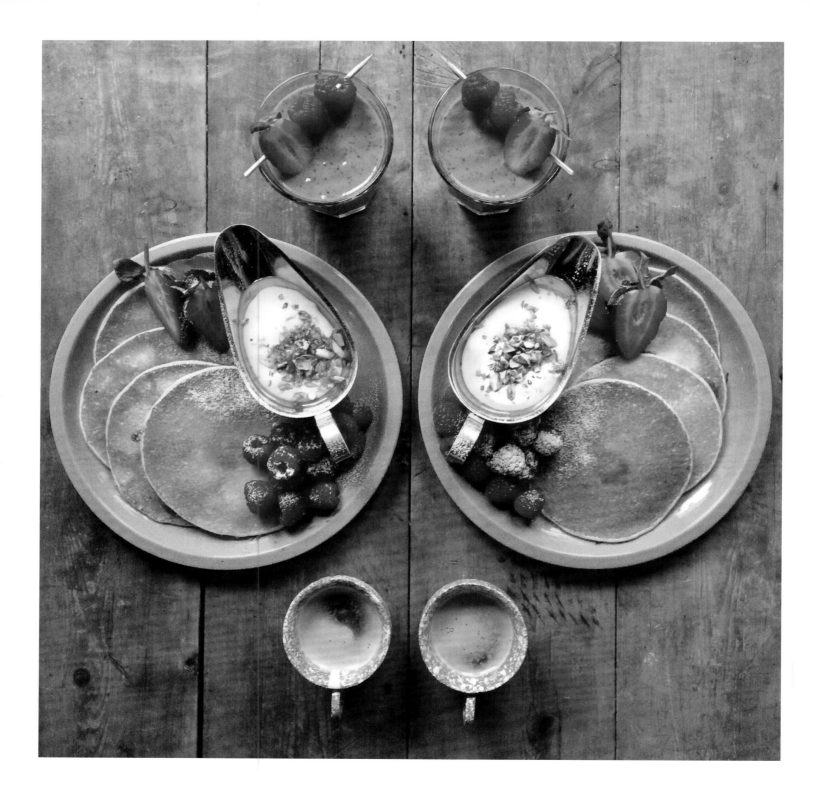

This is a slight tweak of a recipe from one of my favorite cookbooks, *The First American Cookbook,* by Amelia Simmons, which goes way back to 1796. For the first time, an American had written a cookbook using American products. Quintessential dishes like cornbread, Johnny cakes, and these slapjacks were born. Out of it, a distinct American cultural identity emerged.

It is important to stir the batter between ladling each pancake, as the cornmeal (known as "Indian meal" back in the day – hence the recipe's name) will start to sink.

The soft and sweet cornmeal crumb makes these perfect with pretty much any topping you want, but you can't really beat maple syrup.

INDIAN SLAPJACKS

Makes 10-12 pancakes

1 cup cornmeal
2 cups milk
2 eggs
½ cup plain flour
½ stick butter, melted
Pinch of salt

Combine all the ingredients in a bowl and mix well.

Heat a frying pan on a medium–high heat. I personally use a ¼ measuring cup to ladle out each pancake and that will give a pretty short stack all of uniform size, which is pleasing to look at. Alternatively, use an espresso cup. The batter should be quite thin, almost watery looking.

Cook for about 1 minute and flip. Slap that jack! Keep warm under an upturned bowl as you continue to make the rest.

Serve with maple syrup, yogurt, and seasonal fruits.

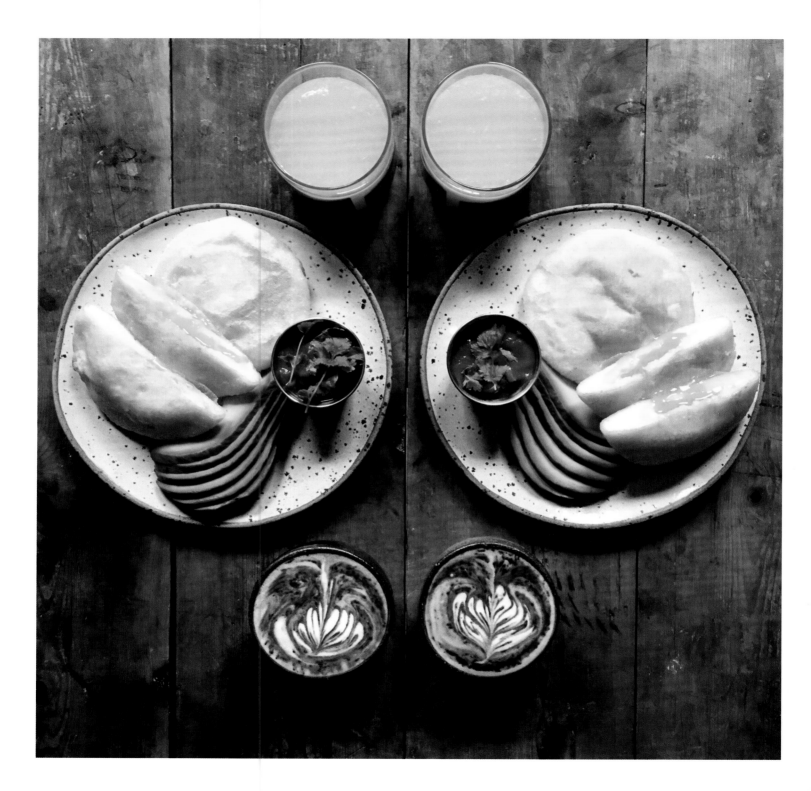

In the past few years Hackney, in east London, has really become my and Mark's home – not just somewhere we live. There are some incredible people there. This recipe was given to me by our friends Esther and Ricardo from @theroastingshed, who make some of my favorite coffee.

Whilst living in Ricardo's native Colombia, they often had these for breakfast, served in greaseproof paper with hogao sauce and chunks of avocado with salt and lime. Freshly squeezed orange juice and black Colombian coffee are essential to wash it all down.

AREPA DE HUEVO EGG–FILLED CORNMEAL CAKES

Makes 6 large arepas

For the Hogao Sauce
2 tbsp virgin olive oil
1 cup scallions, finely chopped
2 cloves garlic, minced
1–2 tsp chili paste (optional)
1 can (14.28 oz) high-quality chopped tomatoes
½ tsp ground cumin
⅓ cup cilantro, chopped
Salt and pepper

First make the hogao sauce. Gently warm the oil in the pan. Add the scallions, garlic, and chili paste (if using) and cook for 3–4 minutes. You want the onions to soften but not brown.

Add the tomatoes and cumin and continue to cook for a further 10–15 minutes, until the mixture starts to thicken.

Add the coriander and season to taste. Allow to cool to room temperature while you make the arepas.

In a bowl, combine the cornmeal, salt and sugar. Slowly add the water and the 1 tbsp

(continued on following page)

For the Arepas

2 cups white PAN Harina Blanca, a pre-cooked white cornmeal

1½ tsp salt

½ tsp sugar

2 ½ cups warm water

1 tbsp rapeseed or peanut oil, plus extra for frying

6 eggs, not too large

oil until a dough forms. With your hands, knead it until it is smooth and divide it evenly into 6 balls.

In a deep pan, heat the oil over a high heat. You want the oil to be 2 in deep.

In Colombia, it is also popular to grill or bake arepas and treat them much like a pita bread. They have some pretty brilliant names too. Unfilled they are known as *la Viuda*, or the Widow, but popular fillings include shredded beef, chicken, beans, and even shark!

Flatten the balls into UFO discs, about 4¾ in in diameter and ½ in thick, and, in batches, gently lower them into the hot oil. After 2–3 minutes, flip them over and then they should really start to puff up. Use a slotted spoon to press them back down into the oil so that they're fully submerged. After another minute, they should be a light golden–brown color.

Remove them from the oil and drain on kitchen paper. Allow them to cool for 5 minutes.

In a small jug with a lip, crack an egg and season with salt and pepper. Take one of the arepas and slice open a small hole in the side. Gently pour the seasoned egg inside and squish the opening closed. Repeat with the remaining arepas and eggs.

Turn the heat up slightly under the oil and fry the arepas a second time for 2 minutes.

Remove and drain again on kitchen paper. Serve with fresh hogao sauce.

Some people might turn their nose up at finding a recipe for hollandaise here. Of course any cook worth his or her mustard will already know how to make it and will have perfected a technique. But a hollandaise recipe is one that I am still asked for at least once a week.

It was actually after having an impressively bad plate of eggs Benedict and home fries in a New York diner that I was spurred into learning to make my own. Never again would poor little Mark have to suffer.

My version uses a blender, which means that it is incredibly unlikely to split into a complete mess. Save the egg whites too and make a meringue or, better yet, an Earl Grey Whiskey Sour (see page 233).

HOLLANDAISE

Juice of ½ lemon
3 tbsp white wine or cider
  vinegar
3 egg yolks
2 sticks or 1 cup butter

In a small pan, heat together the lemon juice and vinegar until it starts to steam. Then take it off the heat.

Separate the eggs and put the yolks into a blender. If you have a removable pouring spout, then slowly add the lemon juice and vinegar on a low speed. If you don't, allow the mix to cool slightly, then bung it all in at once and blitz on high for 30 seconds. It will turn a paler shade of yellow and become frothy.

Melt the butter over a low heat. Incorporate the butter into the egg, either in a steady stream or by the spoonful, with the blender on a low speed.

If you want the mixture a little thicker, pour it into the buttery pan and gently warm through. As it cools it will thicken. It will happily sit on the lowest heat for 10–15 minutes whilst you get on with the rest of the Benedict. If you want to thin the sauce, then use hot water, a few tablespoons at most.

This hollandaise will keep in a jar in the fridge for a week.

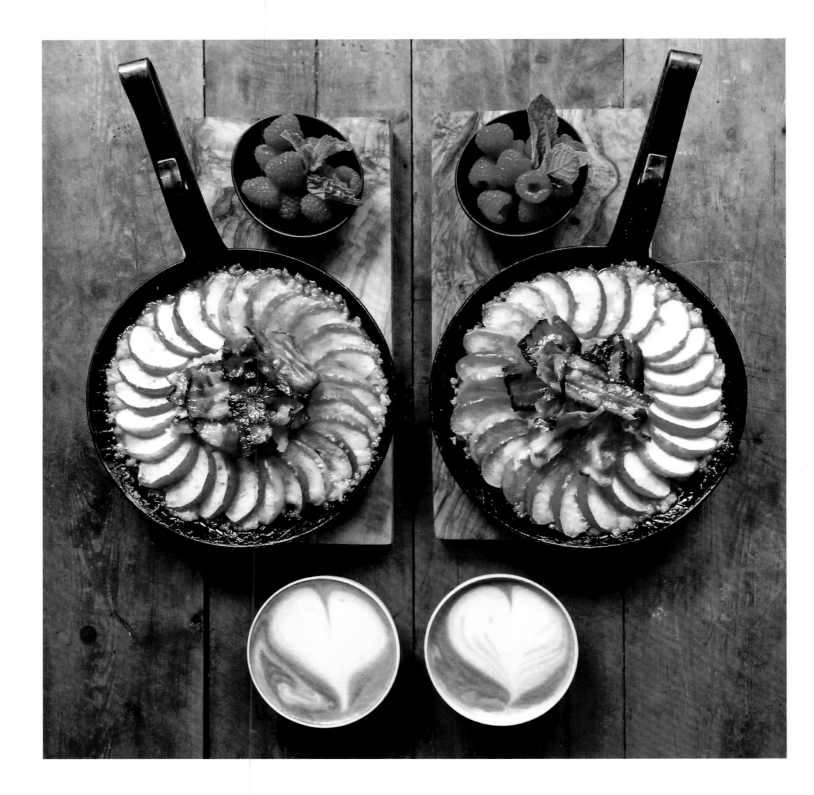

Some people think I'm mad for making a different – and sometimes quite elaborate – breakfast every single day. I think people are crazy for eating porridge every single day. Swings and roundabouts. That said, I couldn't leave porridge out of this book; it is after all a breakfast staple. But then again, I'm not going to teach you how to suck eggs. If you're keen to shake up your breakfast habits then each recipe needs to be worth your time. So this is porridge with a twist.

I started toasting my oats in a dry frying pan, a trick I learned from the brilliant @elicitycloake. A few minutes on the heat will pay dividends later. In this recipe, the hidden layer of nuts and dried cranberries at the bottom gives welcome crunch and sourness to an otherwise ordinary bowl of porridge. Topped with sliced apple, a scant sprinkling of sugar, and a hefty dose of cinnamon, this is porridge with literal and sensorial depth.

The ginger beer bacon is totally optional, but if you want a vegetarian option I would seriously invest in some J&D's bacon salt, which you can buy online. You can thank me later.

BAKED OATS WITH GINGER BEER BACON

1 cup oats
1 cup water
1 cup milk of your choice
½ tsp salt
¼ cup nuts of your choice
¼ cup dried cranberries
2 small apples, finely sliced
1 tbsp dark brown sugar
2 tsp cinnamon
2 tbsp syrup – I used ginger but maple is also good

Preheat your oven to 350°F.

Add the oats to a frying pan over a medium heat. Move them around the pan for a good 5 minutes to stop them from burning. They should get a bit darker in color. This stage can also be done in advance; you just have to let them cool completely before storing.

Add the water, milk, and salt, stirring continuously for 3 minutes until the mixture starts to thicken. At this point take it off the heat, as you want it fairly runny.

Scatter the nuts and cranberries at the bottom of a small ovenproof dish or skillet and pour the oats over. Top with apple, sugar, cinnamon, and syrup, then bake for 15 minutes.

For the Ginger Beer Bacon

This is very, very simple. Before bed, stick the bacon of your choice in a bowl with some ginger beer and pop it in the fridge. A 12 oz can will easily do a whole pack of bacon. Avoid using diet ginger beer, but do use the extra–fiery stuff; it's available from most corner stores. Next morning, fry the bacon as normal, until caramelized, and enjoy.

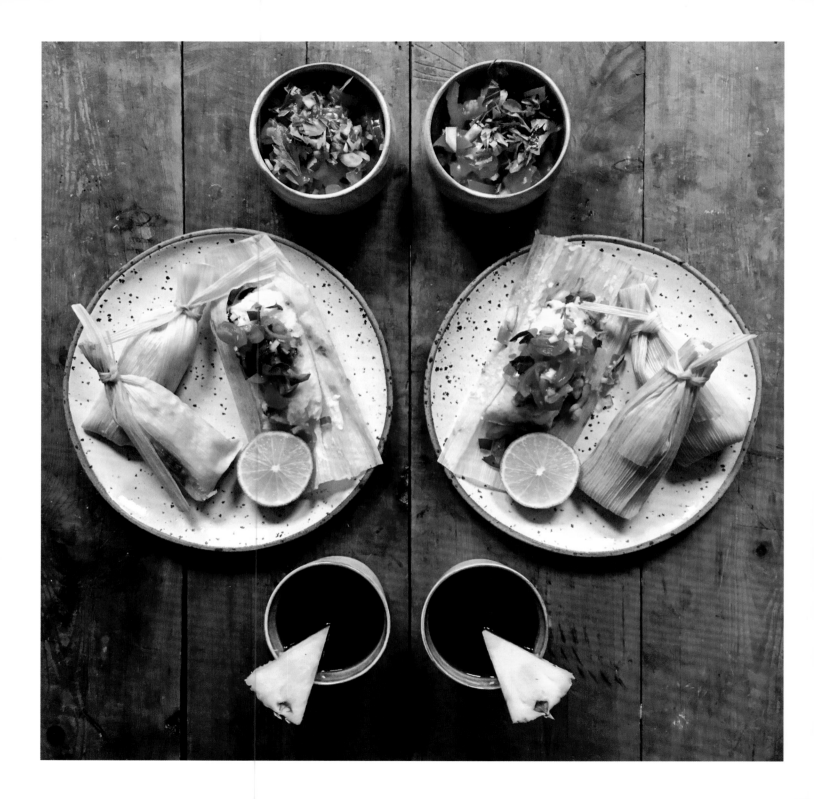

This recipe came from two of my sweetest followers @dantooley and his girlfriend @gracefully_ frank. This is what they wrote:

"What started as a bit of fun has grown into something so much more. We research for hours finding the most authentic recipes the internet can supply. We have discovered shops we would have never entered, learnt new techniques, used ingredients we can not pronounce and find ourselves getting out of bed at 6:30 a.m. on a weekend! It has grown into something more than just the breakfast."

Similar to the Mexican tamale, this is a simple corn batter steamed in a soft corn husk. Humitas can be left plain and served with refried beans, cooked meat or fish, or even made sweet.

HUMITAS WITH SALSA PERUVIAN TAMALES WITH SALSA

Makes 10 to 15 humitas

For the Corn Dough
6 corn husks (banana or
   plantain leaves are a
   great substitute)
2 ears corn
½ stick butter
1 tsp chili flakes (or more if
   you like it hot)
3 cloves crushed garlic
Pinch of salt
Pinch of granulated sugar
2 egg yolks

Soak the corn husks in freshly boiled water and set aside to soften. This prevents them from breaking when you come to assemble the dish later.

Cut the corn kernels off the cobs and place them in a food processor with 3–4 tbsp water. Blitz into a creamy purée.

Heat the butter in a pan on a medium heat and add the chili flakes and garlic. Be careful not to burn the garlic. Pour in the puréed corn, add the salt and sugar, and cook for 10 minutes, stirring constantly. Remove from heat and leave to cool.

Finely chop all the ingredients for the filling and add this to the cooled corn mix. Add the egg yolks to the batter and stir well to combine.

(continued on following page)

For the Humita Filling

¼ cup cashew nuts

¼ cup raisins

½ cup sweet potato, peeled, diced and cooked

50g black olives

Pinch of salt

2 large hard-boiled eggs

1 tsp ground cumin

1 tsp oregano

1 tsp paprika

Hot sauce or Tabasco to taste

For the Peruvian Salsa

1 medium red onion

2 tomatoes, skinned and de-seeded

1 green chili, de-seeded

Juice of 1 lime

1 tbsp olive oil

Handful of cilantro, chopped

Salt and pepper

Folding a tamale can sound complicated, but there are many guides online if you're not sure! This is how I do it. Flatten out a soft corn husk with the narrow end facing you. Place 2 tablespoons of the corn mix in the middle and spread it towards the left side and to the top edge, but not towards the right–hand side. If you want to add anything else, chicken or pork, for example, add it now.

Bring the left side of the tamale over to the right edge of the corn mix but not to the edge of the husk. Fold the bottom upwards and then continue to roll it towards the right. You should end up with what looks like a burrito with an open top.

Repeat with the rest of the corn and husks.

In a steamer, stand the tamales up against each other and steam for 45 minutes.

Whilst the tamales are steaming, prepare the salsa. Peel and thinly slice the onion and soak it in some ice–cold water for 10 minutes – this will soften the harsh flavor. Drain well and combine with the rest of the salsa ingredients.

Serve with a refreshing glass of chicha morada (page 63).

If you're looking for a fabulous non–alcoholic drink to serve at a party or brunch, then you need to turn your attention to what the Peruvians do.

Aromatic, sweet, and a deep purple in color, I think Julius Caesar or Henry VIII would have loved a sip of chicha morada if they'd had the chance.

CHICHA MORADA PURPLE CORN DRINK FROM PERU

Makes enough for 20 servings

1 gallon water
1 pineapple
3 dried purple corn cobs
2 apples, quartered, or 1 quince, roughly chopped
4 sticks cinnamon or cassia bark
6 cloves
3 star anise
1 cup sugar or agave syrup
Juice of 2 limes

Put the water in a large pan and bring to a boil.

Wash your pineapple thoroughly. Top and tail it, and discard the leaves. Cut all the way around with a sharp knife and add the skin to the water. Quarter the pineapple, cut out the core and add the core to the pan.

Dice the flesh of the pineapple, place this on a baking sheet lined with some parchment and freeze. These chunks will act as ice cubes when serving, without watering down your drink.

Add the corn, quartered apples, cinnamon, cloves and star anise to the pan and bring to a boil. Turn the heat down, cover, and simmer gently for 30 minutes.

Using a slotted spoon, fish out all the flavorings and discard; make sure you count the cloves out. Whilst still hot, add the sugar or syrup and the lime juice. Allow to cool completely before refrigerating.

Serve in a tall glass with frozen pineapple cubes.

4 KEEP IT SIMPLE
MEXICO, SOUTHERN USA, CANADA

The simple things are often the most difficult to get right. Fried chicken demands care, perfectly cooked grits don't just happen, and black coffee is all too easy to overcomplicate. Attention to detail or lack thereof is of the utmost importance here. You want to appear like an experienced cook, combining flavors like a maestro and knowing when it's done without breaking a sweat.

Spice and seasoning is bold yet complex. Under-season your baked beans and they'll be bland; hours of waiting will be wasted. Over-spice your huevos and you will feel the burn and probably not much else for the rest of the morning.

Coffee and tea, miles away from infusion timers and tattooed baristas, are served straight up and unadulterated.

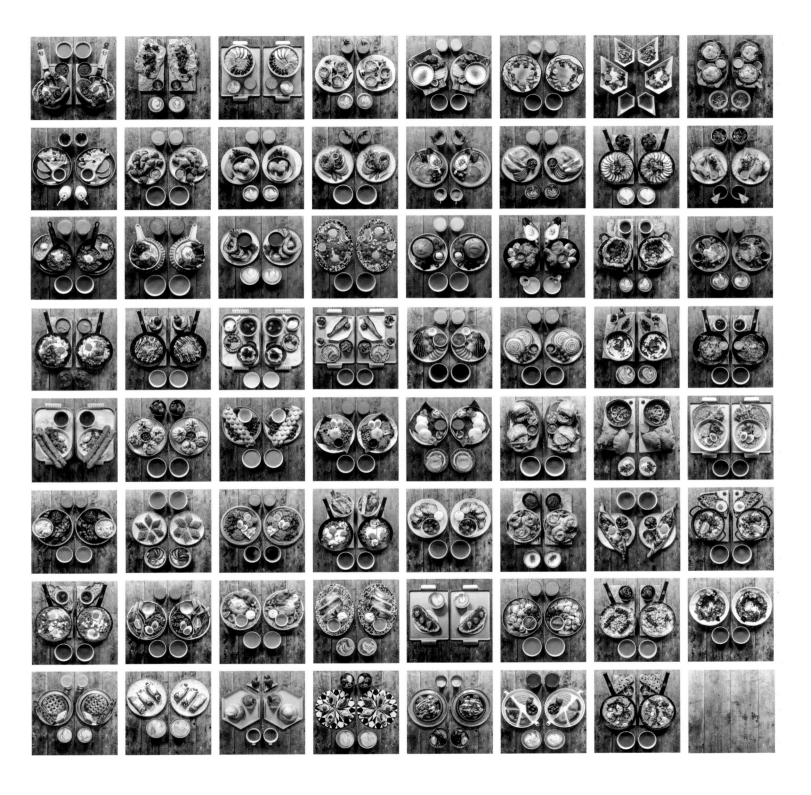

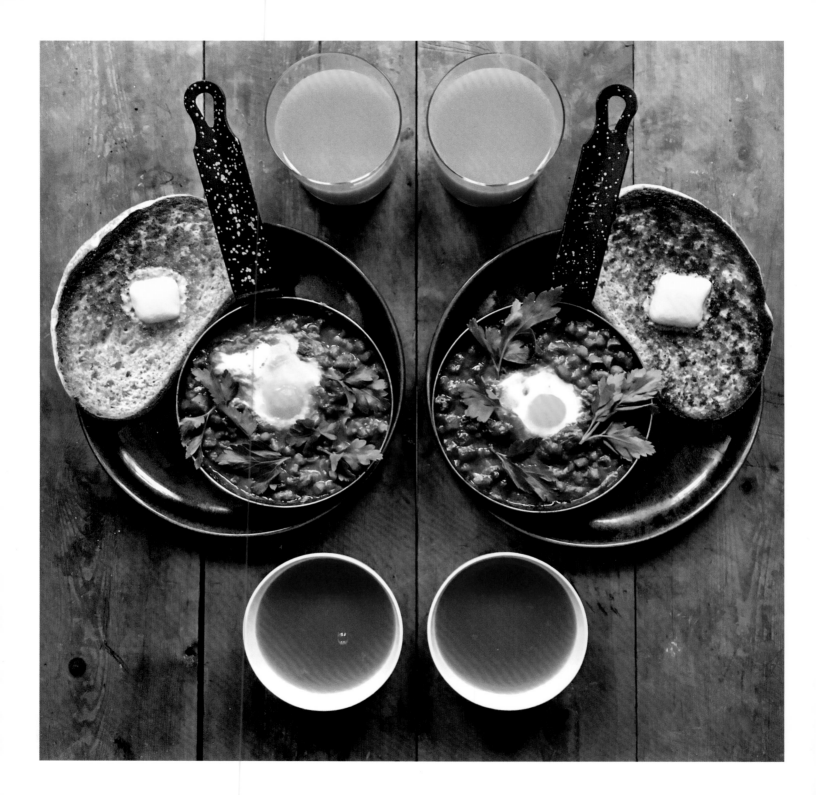

I am firmly in the camp of those who believe that baked beans are an integral part of a full English breakfast. They are the gravy that binds it all together. That said, who wants to go through all the effort of making a vague and often inferior approximation of what you can get in a tin?

These beans, however, are jam-packed full of flavor: delicate, sweet, spiced, and salty, and completely different from their canned cousins.

I use boczek for this recipe (basically, it's Polish bacon), as they have a Polish section in my local supermarket. It's a wonderfully smoky, fatty pork that's not too salty and half the price of pancetta.

I'd also advise starting this on a Saturday morning, putting the beans on to soak, ready for a delicious Sunday brunch. This recipe is also brilliant if you have a pressure or slow cooker.

FATTY BOY BEANS

Serves 4

1 lb or 2 cups dried navy beans
2 cups chopped boczek (smoked streaky bacon is a fine substitute)
4 tbsp date molasses
1 tbsp English mustard
10 pickled onions, halved
1 tsp liquid smoke
1 tbsp sweet paprika
1 tsp black pepper
1 tsp salt
1 tbsp white miso paste (optional but really good)

Put the beans in a large ovenproof pan and cover with cold water. Leave to soak for at least 8 hours or overnight.

Refresh the water and boil the beans on a high heat for 15 minutes. You may need to top up the water a little to make sure they are completely covered. Turn the heat down to a gentle simmer and leave for a further 30 minutes.

Preheat your oven to 275°F.

Chop the boczek or bacon into small cubes and add to the pan along with all the ingredients except for the salt and white miso paste. Stir until everything is dissolved.

Cover with a lid and cook in the oven for 4 hours, stirring occasionally throughout that time. Once cooked, mix in the salt and miso paste, and bake for another hour uncovered.

These are even better the day after, I promise you.

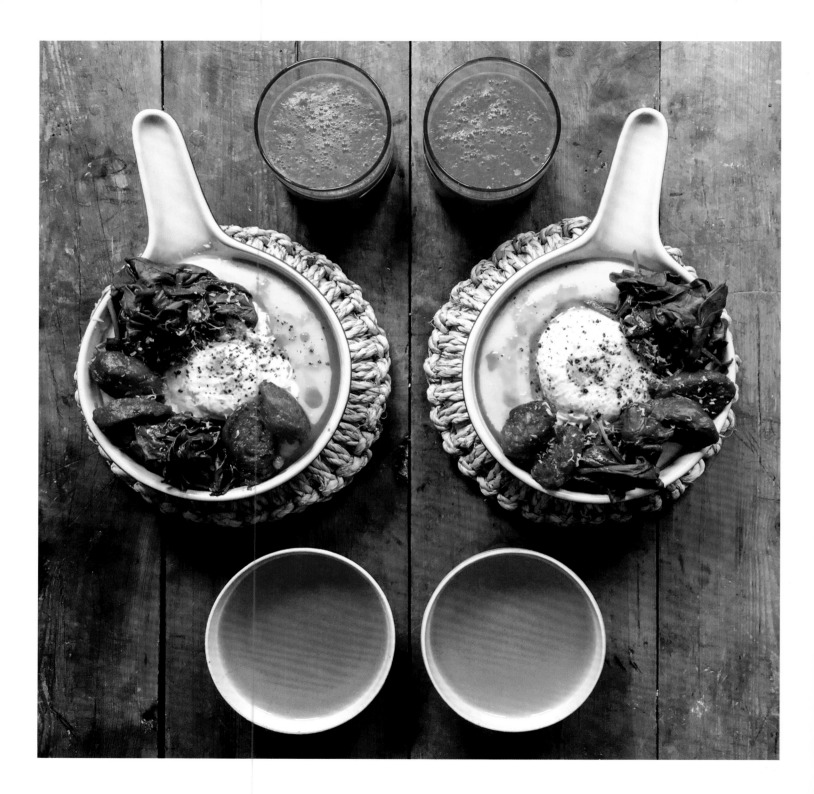

"Are we to believe that boiling water, soaks into a grit, faster in your kitchen, than in any place on the face of the Earth?! Well perhaps the laws of physics cease to exist on your stove! Were these 'magic grits?!'"

—**Joe Pesci** as Vinny in the 1992 classic *My Cousin Vinny*

Grits always remind me of the incredible film *My Cousin Vinny.* I watched it repeatedly when I was growing up, the story of a teenager accused of murder who is saved by his blundering cousin Vinny, who realizes a key witness is lying because he tells the jury his grits were ready in 5 minutes rather than 20. No self-respecting Southerner uses instant grits.

This was in fact my first encounter with American breakfasts – when Vinny looks at the menu in the diner and there are just three options: Breakfast $1.99, Lunch $2.49, and Dinner $3.49. If only more restaurants took this approach!

Personally, I love grits. The coarsely ground corn porridge is perfect with just a knob of butter, but is also the ideal canvas for topping with egg, cheese, shrimp, bacon, or chorizo.

MAGIC GRITS

½ cup milk
1 ¾ cups water
1 tsp salt
½ tsp black pepper
½ cup grits (Palmetto Farms is my favorite)
½ cup grated sharp or mature Cheddar
2 tbsp butter

Add the milk, water, salt, and pepper to a heavy saucepan and bring to a boil.

Turn the heat down to low and add the grits, stirring continuously for 5 minutes. The aim here is low and slow. If the grits start to bubble, then your heat is too high. Cover with a lid and continue to cook on low for 20 minutes, stirring every 5 minutes. Taste to check if they are tender and cooked.

Take off the heat and add the cheese and butter, stirring until melted.

Serve the grits as they are with an extra knob of butter, or with crispy bacon and fresh grilled jumbo shrimp, egg, or perhaps with chorizo or spicy merguez sausage. The beauty of grits is that they're a vehicle. Go to town with the flavors: perhaps make them with half milk and half stock, or add some chili paste and a teaspoon of honey.

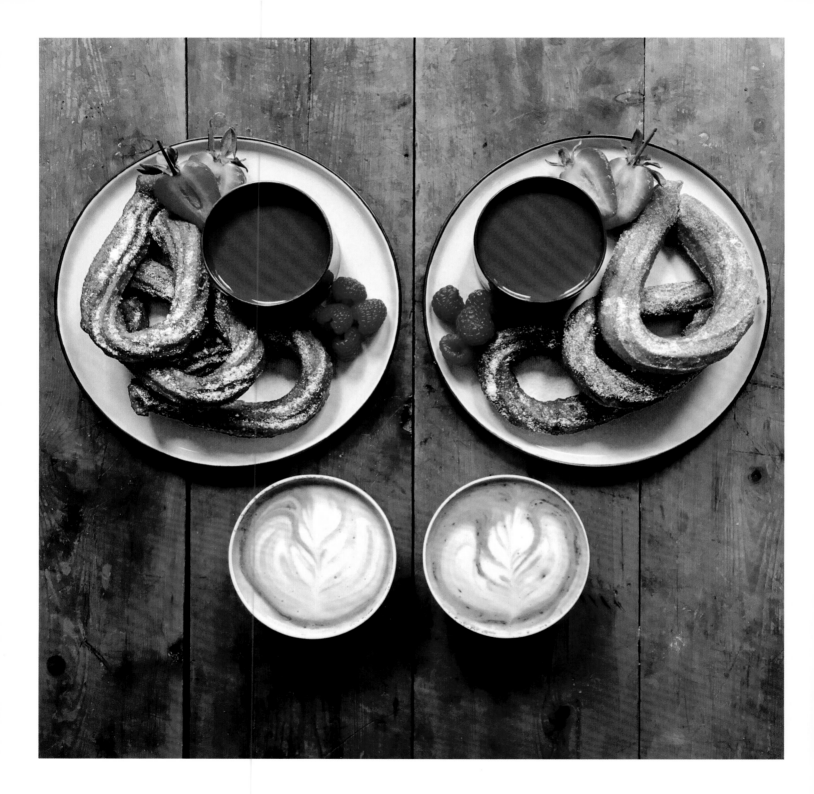

Last year Mark and I went to San Sebastián in Spain. One morning, whilst walking around the Old Town, it became pretty evident that breakfast is not really a thing there – but then again neither is waking up at 8 a.m. The streets were practically deserted.

Thankfully, San Sebastián is not very big and we quickly discovered one restaurant that was open, called Santa Lucia. The place is a like a Soviet–era canteen, complete with strip–lighting. The furniture is bolted to the floor. Depressing stuff. But those churros, made fresh to order, with a cup of chocolate sauce so dark it looked like Armus from *Star Trek: TNG* (you may need to Google this – it's good), were so delicious I was able to forgive them.

Now because I am a big fan of twisting tradition, I added that other Spanish classic, jamon to the churros batter for savory umami.

Cajeta is the Mexican cousin of dulce de leche; however, it is made using goat's milk, prepared in a copper pan, and develops its flavor through a Maillard reaction – the same chemical reaction that gives bread its crust and coffee its roast – rather than through caramelization. In Central and South America, panela is unrefined cane sugar that comes pressed in small blocks, but I would suggest a light muscovado sugar as a substitute. The baking soda is there to prevent the milk solids from coagulating before they've had a chance to develop the deepest possible flavor.

This is perfect for dipping churros as well as a topping for ice cream or just to eat by the spoonful. I make a big batch because it's quite time–intensive, but it will sit in the fridge for 6 months. Trust me, you'll never look back.

CHURROS Y JAMON CON CAJETA
CHURROS WITH HAM AND CARAMEL DIPPING SAUCE

For the Cajeta

Makes 3 jam jars of sauce

2 quarts goats milk
2 cups grated panela, or
    light muscovado sugar
1 tsp vanilla
½ tsp baking soda

To make the cajeta, place the milk, sugar, and vanilla in a large, heavy–bottomed pan (large is important and you'll see why later). A copper pan is traditional in Mexico, but any heavy–based enamel or steel pan will work fine. I'd advise against using cast iron because of the risk of damaging the pan.

Over a low heat, slowly melt the sugar into the milk and add the vanilla extract. Bring to a gentle simmer, stirring constantly with a wooden spoon, so you don't burn your hand.

Dissolve the baking soda in a tablespoon of water and quickly add this to the milk, still stirring. Within seconds the liquid will double in volume, so quickly turn the heat down if you need to.

(continued on following page)

For the Churros

Makes 8 churros

1 cup water
Oil for deep frying
3 tbsp light brown sugar
1 stick butter
1 cup plain flour
½ tsp salt
2 eggs
1 tsp vanilla extract
⅓ cup minced Serrano ham
1 cup superfine sugar
2 tsp cinnamon
8 squares of baking parchment, 4 x 4 in

Now, for the next 4–5 hours, with the heat on low, it is a matter of stirring occasionally and making sure it doesn't burn. Perhaps use this time to finish those odd jobs around the house you've been putting off.

Sterilize three jam jars. The easiest method is to wash them in hot soapy water, rinse but not dry them, and then bake them in the oven at 350°F for 15 minutes.

The cajeta should now be glossy and caramel colored. It will thicken as it cools. Carefully pour into the sterilized jars, screw on the lids, then immediately turn the jars upside down and leave to cool completely. This will create a vacuum seal and it simply means that you'll be able to keep the cajeta for longer. You can store it in a cupboard until opened, then keep it in the fridge and use within 6 months (if you can manage it; it's more likely that you'll scarf the lot).

To make the churros, you'll need to invest in a heavy–duty piping bag with a star nozzle or a specialist churro gun, which you can find online.

Gently heat the oil in a heavy pan. You want the oil to be at least an inch deep.

In a separate pan, add the water, light brown sugar, and butter, and melt. Bring it to a boil and add the flour and salt. Combine the lot with a spoon and some elbow grease until you have a batter that looks like wallpaper paste.

Beat the eggs in a bowl with the vanilla and combine this with the flour mix. You will now have a smooth, glossy batter.

Finely mince the Serrano ham and add this to the batter. Combine the superfine sugar and cinnamon and set aside.

Load up your churro gun or piping bag with the nozzle already inserted. Test the temperature of the oil with a pea–sized ball of the batter. If it browns fully in 90 seconds then it's ready.

To create the classic teardrop shape, pipe the mix on to a sheet of the baking parchment and, using a pair of scissors, snip the batter clean from the nozzle.

Gently lower the churro, paper attached, into the hot oil. After 30 seconds it will come free of the paper; using tongs, carefully discard the paper.

Continue to cook for 1 minute, then flip and cook for another minute. Remove from the oil and drain on kitchen paper. Repeat with the remaining batter. Leave to cool for a minute so that you don't burn yourself, then sprinkle each churro gently with cinnamon-sugar. Serve with cajeta and coffee.

Another of the questions I get asked all the time is, "What happens if Mark wants something different for breakfast?" My reply is always the same: "DIVORCE!"

Don't worry – I am joking. The situation has never arisen, but I do have to say that having a different breakfast prepared lovingly every day is hardly a raw deal.

Huevos divorciados, or divorced eggs, are the perfect solution. Two eggs with spicy red salsa on one side, spicy green salsa on the other. A wall of refried beans separating the two. Distinct but complementary, together but different. It's not really divorce; it's more like a compromise.

Huevos de compromiso just doesn't have the same ring, though.

The one ingredient you might struggle to find is the tomatillo. I buy them online from SousChef or Cool Chile Co. in a whopping 26 oz can. Any leftovers should be drained of the liquid and popped in the freezer.

HUEVOS DIVORCIADOS DIVORCED EGGS

For the Salsa Roja

3 very ripe tomatoes
1 medium onion
2 cloves garlic
1 fresh jalapeño chili
2 dried chipotle chilis (or any other smoky chili)
2 dried Anaheim chilis (or any other mildly spicy variety, e.g. mulato or ancho)
⅓ cup cilantro, chopped
½ tsp salt

For both of the salsas the preparation is the same, just remember to do them separately!

Preheat your oven to 400°F. Roughly chop the tomatoes or tomatillos with the onion, garlic, and fresh jalapeño, and put in an ovenproof dish. Cook for 15–20 minutes until the onion starts to brown.

In a dry pan, toast the dried chilis for 3–4 minutes over a medium heat. Allow to cool completely and remove the stem.

Combine the roasted with the toasted in a food processor, add the cilantro and salt and blitz into a purée. Pour into a bowl. These processes can be done a day in advance.

To prepare the refried beans, drain the tin of beans and add it to a pan with the rest of the ingredients. Add enough water just to cover the beans and cook over a medium heat with the lid on for 20–30 minutes until they are soft.

Fish out the chili and remove the stem, then pop the chili back in. Using a potato masher or a stick blender, purée the beans until you have your desired smoothness or chunkiness.

(continued on following page)

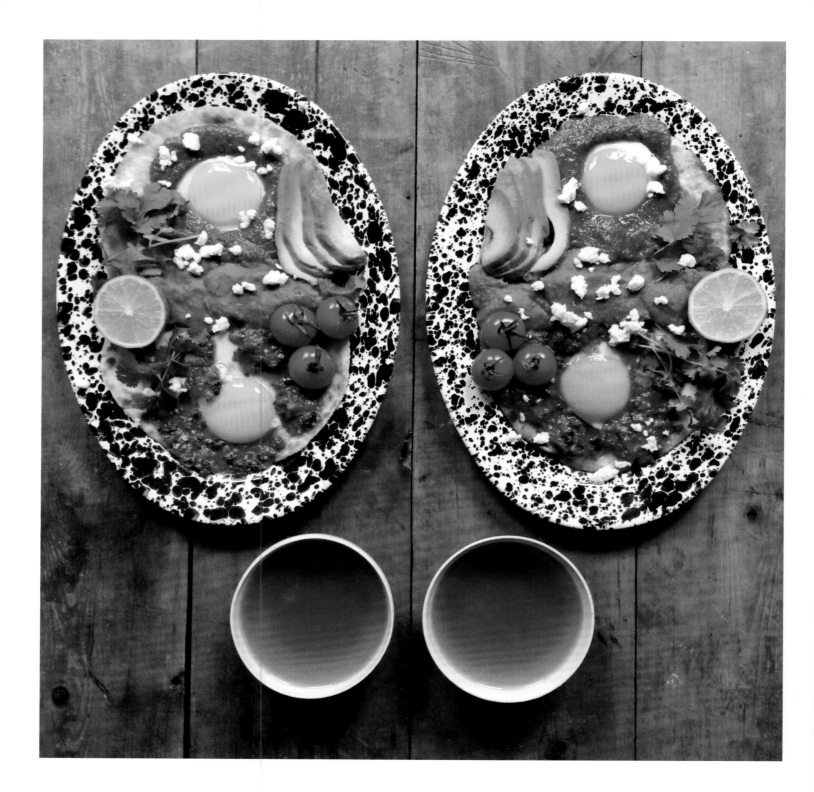

For the Salsa Verde

4 fresh tomatillos, or 1 ½
   cups canned tomatillos
1 medium onion
2 cloves garlic
1 fresh jalapeño chili
⅓ cup cilantro, chopped
½ tsp salt

For the Refried Beans

Ready–prepared refried
beans are available now in
most supermarkets. If you
really want to make them
from scratch you'll need:
2 cups/13.6 oz can pinto
   beans
1 small onion, finely diced
2 cloves garlic, minced
1 dried chipotle chili
½ tsp cayenne pepper
Salt and pepper
Oil for frying

To Serve

4 small corn or flour
   tortillas
4 eggs
2 cups queso fresco (any
   cheese really – feta or
   Cheddar are good)
1 lime
Cilantro

To assemble the dish, add a few tablespoons of oil to a frying pan and heat on high. Fry the tortillas until lightly browned with crisp edges. Remove and drain on some kitchen paper. Add some extra oil to the pan and fry the eggs.

You can serve this one of two ways: on a plate with the tortillas underneath; or in individual serving dishes or pans with the crispy tortillas on the side. Garnish with fresh cheese, lime wedges, and fresh cilantro.

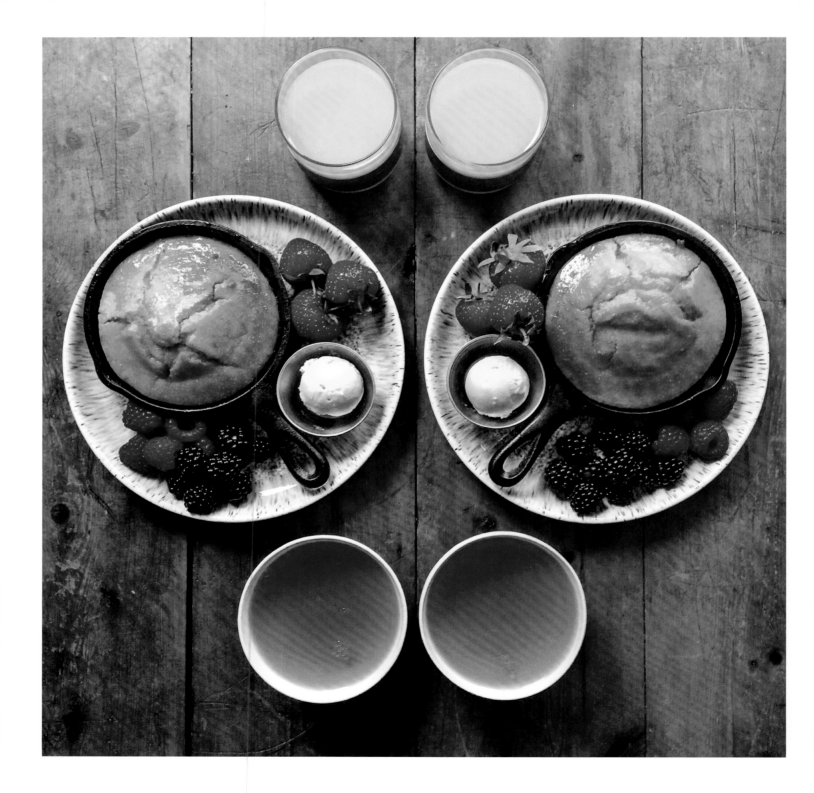

There is no one definitive way to make cornbread, in the same way that there is no one way to make regular bread. However, it makes sense that if you want to make really good cornbread you need to start with really good cornmeal.

Is there a difference between the white and yellow varieties? Does it matter if the germ or the bran is left in? Does stoneground make a tastier crumb? Being the honest man that I am, I'd say it doesn't. I personally like Palmetto Farms' cornmeal.

Cornbread is one of those recipes that, if it is the first time you've made it, I *insist* that you adapt the recipe afterwards and make it your own. Maple syrup, Cheddar cheese, creamed corn, jalapeño, and soft fruits are just some of the ways you can put a twist on it, though obviously not all at the same time. I also make mine in a cast-iron skillet, primarily because it can go from the range to the oven but also because it looks gorgeous on the table.

CORNBREAD

Makes one 10-in skillet or two 5-in skillets

1 ½ cups cornmeal
1 cup buttermilk
⅓ cup milk
½ tsp salt
2 tsp baking powder
2 eggs
2 tbsp beef dripping

Preheat your oven to 425°F.

In a bowl, mix all the ingredients together except for the beef dripping.

Over a high heat, melt 1 tbsp of dripping in each pan if you are using two smaller skillets, or 2 tbsp in a large skillet until hot and smoking.

If you're using smaller skillets, divide the mix between the two. You won't get much rise, so don't be afraid to fill them. Cook on the range for about 2–3 minutes. This will help to give a crisp bottom.

Transfer to the oven for about 20 minutes, checking at 15 minutes with a skewer – it will come out clean when the cornbread is done.

Cold, day-old cornbread is delicious toasted or fried with either sweet or savory toppings and a cup of Cowboy Coffee (see page 83).

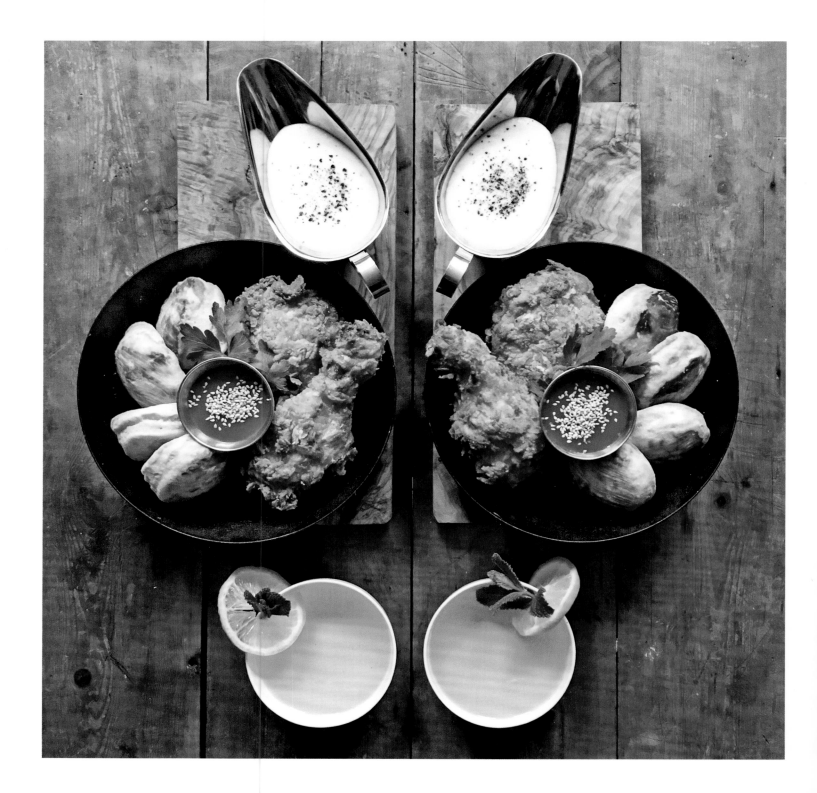

I've asked a lot of people the same question: "What one food could you not face eating first thing in the morning?"

The top three, surprisingly, are chili, chocolate, and chicken (not all together). Chili and chocolate for breakfast are dealt with elsewhere (see pages 141, 157, and 109), but for me the best way to approach chicken first thing in the morning is to deep fry it.

My favorite is Southern style. No gimmicky cornflake or Rice Krispie coating in sight, but I've decided to deviate from tradition and soak my chicken in yogurt rather than buttermilk.

I also use Aromat in this recipe. It's a great all-round seasoning mix, but some flavor purists might call it cheating as it contains MSG. Good thing this isn't the Olympics. Feel free to leave it out, but I am firmly leaving it in.

CHICKEN AND BISCUITS

Serves 2 fatties, 4 thinnies

For the Fried Chicken

8 pieces of chicken with the skin on (I like a mix of thigh and leg)

2 cups plain yogurt

3 cups plain flour

¼ cup rice flour or cornflour

3 tsp salt

1 tsp mixed spice

1 tsp sweet paprika

1 tsp cayenne pepper

1 tsp hot chili powder

1 tsp ground black pepper

1 tsp Aromat

2 quarts oil for frying

In a large bowl, place the chicken and most of the yogurt and mix so that every piece is well covered. Leave covered (purely for hygiene reasons) in the fridge, ideally overnight but for at least 1 hour.

Mix all the dry ingredients in another bowl and add the remaining yogurt. It should be a very dry coating with large, shaggy clumps. Shaggy clumps means crunch.

Heat your oil in a heavy–bottomed pan. You want it nice and hot. Preheat your oven to 400°F.

Take one yogurt–drenched piece of chicken at a time and dump it into the flour mix. I suggest you even press the flour into each piece for maximum effect.

Fry the chicken in batches in the hot oil. Don't overcrowd the pan, so do 2–3 pieces at a time for about 10 minutes, then remove and drain on kitchen paper. Once your last batch is done, transfer the chicken to a roasting tray, put in the oven, and continue cooking for another 10–12 minutes to make sure each piece is fully cooked.

(continued on following page)

American–style biscuits require the most delicate hand. Barely touching the dough gives you a light, moist crumb. Again, you could substitute yogurt for the buttermilk, but these are really worth the effort so go for the buttermilk if you can.

BUTTERMILK BISCUITS

2 cups plain flour
2 tsp baking powder
1 tsp salt
1 tsp sugar
7 tbsp butter (cold)
¾ cup buttermilk, plus 2
    tbsp for brushing

To make the biscuits, put all your dry ingredients in a large bowl and mix well. Cut the butter into cubes and, using your fingers and thumbs, massage the lot together until you have a loose crumb.

Add the buttermilk and, with a gentle hand, mix until you have a dough. Don't knead it at all, and stop once it's combined.

Preheat your oven to 400°F and prepare a tray with some baking parchment.

Dust a clean work surface with flour and tip out the dough. Roll it into a circle about an inch thick. If you are using a cookie cutter, then dip it in some flour first and again after each cut. You could also cut it like a pizza into 8 wedges, giving you zero waste.

Put the biscuits on the prepared tray, brush the top of each one with buttermilk (careful none goes down the sides) and bake for 15 minutes.

Remove from the oven and cool on a wire rack for a minute, then serve with fried chicken and white gravy (see page 81).

There are lots of misconceived ideas around the consumption of lard or dripping. The white stuff, along with eggs and other fats, were shamed into submission by the health brigade of the 1980s. Now, natural fats and even butter are seen as part of a wholesome, nutritious diet.

Animal fat in general is instantly unappealing to many because of its appearance, but real beauty is more than skin deep. I scarcely use beef dripping but, when I do, there is a strong reason for it – it makes me happy.

My personal favorite is from James Whelan Butchers – the excellent online meat shop. In 2015 their beef dripping was awarded Supreme Champion at the Great Taste Awards and listed as one of the Top 50 Foods in the world, for good reason. Once you try this gravy made with their dripping, you will never look back.

WHITE GRAVY

2 cups chicken stock, or 2 cups boiling water and 2 stock cubes
2 tbsp beef dripping
2 tbsp plain flour or cornflour
2 cups milk
Fresh black pepper

Heat your chicken stock in a pan or in a jug, dissolve the stock cubes in freshly boiled water. Set aside.

In another pan, gently melt the beef dripping. Turn the heat up to medium and add the flour. Combine to make a thick paste and continue to stir until it begins to turn a light golden brown.

Add a third of the hot chicken stock and, using a whisk, blend until you have a smooth but very thick sauce. Add the rest of the stock along with the milk and continue to stir for a further 15 minutes. Adjust with extra hot water to reach your desired consistency. Season well with black pepper and serve on the side of fried chicken and biscuits (see page 79). It is also delicious with just the biscuits and fresh parsley.

One of my favorite cookbooks of all time is *White Trash Cooking* by Ernest Matthew Mickler. It makes me howl with laughter. The title might suggest it is somewhere between parody and comedy, but it's actually a serious book filled with wonderful anthropological observations about food and culture in the Deep South. It's just as important as any French Provençal cookbook.

For Clara Jane's Unforgettable Peach Pie Crust, you're advised simply to forget it – no one left alive can make a pie crust like hers, so you might as well go buy one. They certainly don't make cooks like they used to!

There are three different variations for Ice Tea South in *White Trash Cooking,* but my preferred one is the cold–infusion method. If you make a hot infusion and then cool it, the tea will oxidize in minutes. In cold temperatures this does not happen and you can enjoy your tea for 2–3 days.

ICE TEA SOUTH

Serves 4

5 tsp loose black tea of your choice: Earl Grey, Keemun, and English Breakfast are all excellent
8 x 8 in square of unbleached cheesecloth
8 cups cold water
1 lemon
Sprigs of mint

Weigh out your tea and place it into the center of the cheesecloth. Tie it up like a little bag and pop it into a large jar or jug.

Add the water and leave for a minimum of two hours but a maximum of three. Fish out the bag and discard. Stir the tea and serve with slices of lemon and sprigs of mint.

Sweeten, if you desire with some of the simple syrup from pg 218.

"'How would you like that brewed?' is a question I never want to hear again."
—**Keith Pandolfi**, "The Case for Bad Coffee"

Last year, I read a brilliant article by Keith Pandolfi entitled "The Case for Bad Coffee." In it, he wonders what his dead grandfather would say as he spends $18 on a pound of artisanal roasted coffee beans. "You know what, kid? You're an idiot," is whispered from beyond the grave.

As I slowly lowered the flat white that I had prepared for myself with my rather expensive home espresso machine, I had a sudden feeling of Northern shame. What had I become?

The Argos drip coffee machine, which helped me to power through the nights during my Masters, was given away to a neighbor. My precious Sports Direct mug was abandoned in the kitchen at work. The half–finished bottle of Camp can still be found lurking at the back of the cupboard, years past its use–by date.

Something had to change. I wanted coffee without the paraphernalia or the silly gimmicks. So this is coffee for those moments when you have more important things to discuss than the beans.

COWBOY COFFEE

1 cup ground coffee
1 egg
1½ cup cold water
2 quarts boiling water
12 x 12 in square of cheesecloth, or 2 paper coffee filters

In a small bowl, combine the coffee grounds, egg, and ½ cup of cold water into a thick, sludgy paste.

In a pan, bring 2 quarts of water to a boil. Add the coffee slurry to the boiling water and stir. Boil for 3–4 minutes, then remove from the heat.

Add the remaining cold water, stir gently, and leave for another 2–3 minutes.

Slowly strain the coffee through the filter or cheesecloth, either into an insulated jug or directly into your cup.

Perfect for camping or if you're a cowboy or girl.

5 FROM GOOD TO GREAT
WEST COAST USA, HAWAII

"Is something wrong with your steak?"
"No, it's great."
"What are you doing?"
"I'm tasting my food."
"Why aren't you swallowing it?"
"You think I look this good by eating?"
—**Miranda** eating with Lew in LA in the *Sex and the City* episode "Sex and Another City," 2000

Before our summer holiday to San Francisco, Honolulu, and Los Angeles in 2015, I was full of ideas about what it would be like, mainly that it would be health obsessed. The reality was far more complex than what I had expected. California and Hawaii, bathed year round in sunshine, produce food of an incredible quality and draw influence from cultures around the Pacific Rim and beyond.

On top of all that, I still think about the croissants at Tartine – the famous bakery in San Francisco, which really deserves all the hype – and sigh with happiness. The 30–minute wait is worth it.

This chapter is about taking what is familiar and giving it a twist for the better. How can you make French toast better? How can you make a simple pancake better? How can you make a green smoothie not so . . . green? You might also be asking what French toast is doing in the middle of the ocean. All will become clear.

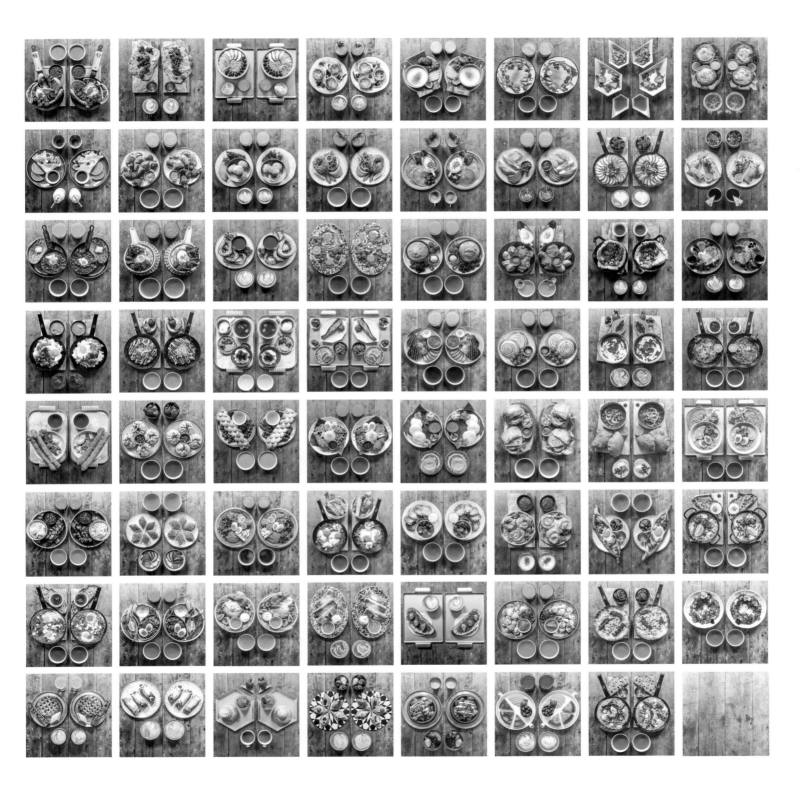

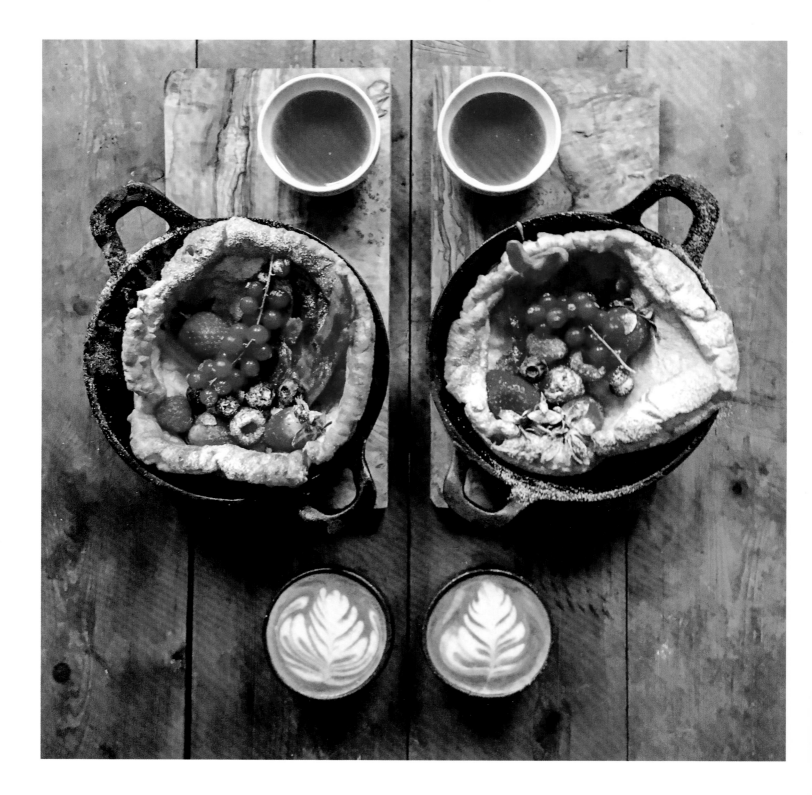

Mark finds the name of this pancake incredibly confusing. Being a Dutch puff himself he wonders why he wasn't informed about his namesake sooner.

Originally made by the German community in America, where Dutch is actually a corruption of the word Deutsche, the Dutch puff (or Dutch baby) found new life as a diner classic in 1940s Seattle.

However, if you, like me, grew up with Yorkshire puddings and roast beef most Sundays, then it can seem a bit odd to have these sweet and for breakfast, but, believe me, it's as versatile as any other pancake. Chuck those traditions out of the window!

I use beef dripping as my fat of choice here too. It will make your babies über–puffy and the smoky meatiness is a great background to all the sugar you are about to consume, but any flavorless oil is a fine substitute.

Serve with your favorite coffee.

DUTCH PUFF

6 rashers streaky bacon
1 cup plain flour (strong bread flour can also be used)
2 tsp superfine sugar
½ tsp salt
⅔ cup milk
3 eggs
1 tsp vanilla extract
2 tbsp beef dripping or oil
Soft fruits: blueberries, strawberries, raspberries, redcurrants
Maple syrup
Powdered sugar

Preheat your oven to 425°F.

Fry the bacon until very crispy and drain on some paper towels. When cooled, crumble into pieces of various sizes. This will make the most excellent topping.

In a bowl, mix the flour, superfine sugar, and salt together with a whisk. Measure out your milk and add the eggs and vanilla extract. Beat until smooth and add this to the flour mix. Whisk until you have a smooth batter, then set aside.

Place two cast–iron skillets on a baking sheet or sturdy tray and add a spoon of the dripping or oil to each. Place them on the middle shelf of your oven with space above for your babies to grow.

Transfer the batter into a measuring jug for easier pouring. After about 15 minutes in the oven the oil should be smoking hot. Quickly and carefully, split the batter between the two pans. Bake for 10–12 minutes. Do not open the oven door until they're done! Your puff should look like a huge cloud of batter with crispy golden edges.

Serve with the soft fruits of your choice, crispy bacon pieces, maple syrup, and a dusting of powdered sugar for beauty. I've also had this with ice cream – much like Spuntino in Soho serves. I recommend it if it's a particularly hot day or you're just a fatty.

Top Tip

My top tip for making sure your batter rises is to bring all your ingredients to room temperature first. Take them out of the fridge at least an hour before you plan to start cooking, if not before you go to bed the night before. Heat is absolutely key: if you put a fridge–cold batter into the oven it will take longer to heat up and rise, and is more likely to fail.

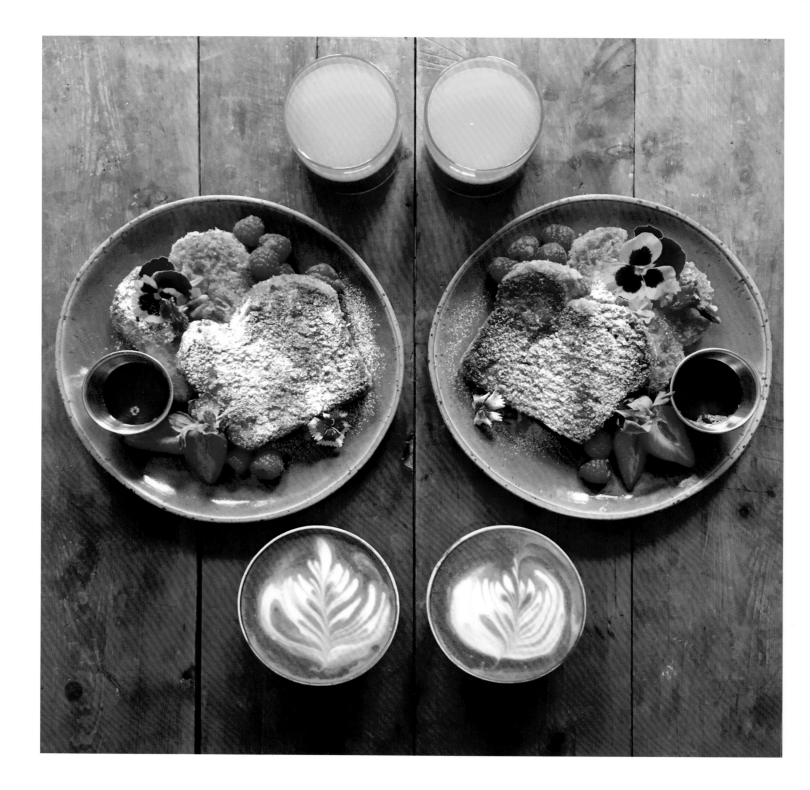

Mark is lucky in the sun. It takes just a few days for him to tan like a bronzed Adonis. I, on the other hand, have a sorry mix of Chinese and Scottish genes and burn, burn, burn.

It was last year, in Hawaii, in the ferociously hot sun, that I could feel the burn through my clothes within mere seconds – from leaving the cab to entering a café. Which is a good excuse for staying indoors and eating.

At chef Lee Anne Wong's restaurant on Oahu, @kokoheadcafe, American, Chinese, and Hawaiian influences are wonderfully fused together. She has the same kind of irreverence for "tradition" that I have. Who says that kimchi can't be deep–fried?

The brunch menu at Koko Head Café includes Dumplings All Day Wong, Miso Smoked Pork Omelette, and Black Sesame Yuzu Muffins – and those are just some of the highlights. I hope that we go back soon.

CORNFLAKE FRENCH TOAST

2 eggs
1⅓ cups whole milk
1 tsp vanilla extract
2 tbsp powdered sugar
5 cups cornflakes
¾ cup ground almonds
4 thick slices brioche
3 tbsp butter

Whisk together the eggs, milk, vanilla, and sugar in a bowl.

In a plastic bag, crush the cornflakes so that you have a range of sizes from whole flakes to dust. Put this in a new bowl with the ground almonds and mix well.

Cut generous slices of brioche, two per person, and dip each into the egg mix until all the liquid has been absorbed.

Carefully, as they'll be pretty squishy, coat the brioche in the cornflake and almonds.

Preheat your oven to 350°F.

Put half of the butter in a frying pan over a medium heat. Add half the brioche and cook for 2–3 minutes per side, then transfer to a baking sheet covered with parchment. Wipe out the pan with some paper towel and repeat with the remaining butter and the second half of the brioche.

Bake the toasted brioche for 10 minutes until crisp. Serve with a dusting of powdered sugar, sliced bananas, maple syrup, and sour berries to balance the sweetness.

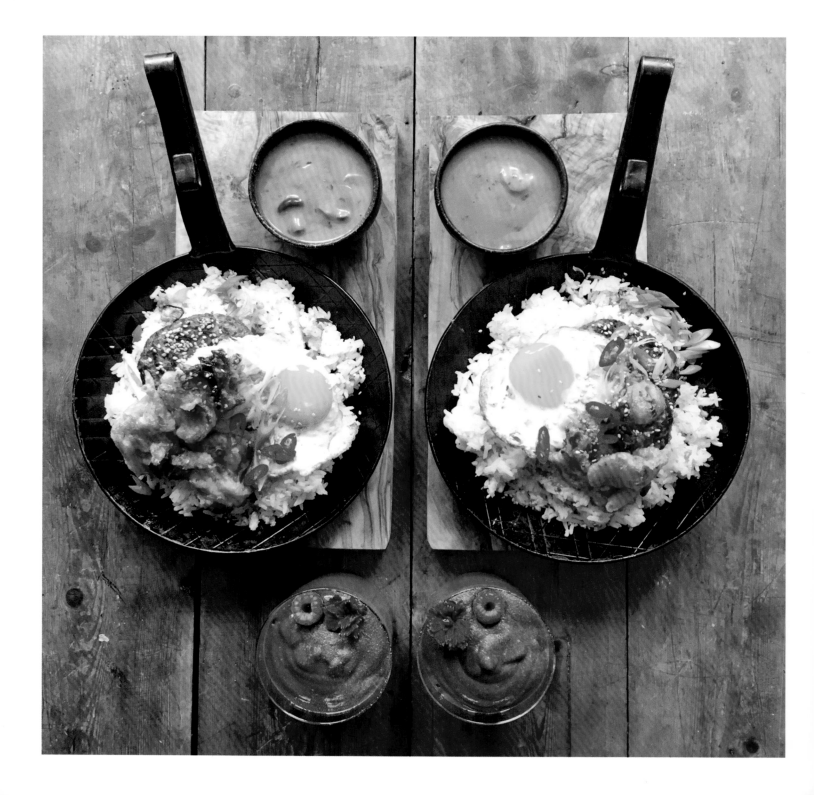

What exactly is a typical Hawaiian breakfast? I was expecting a cornucopia of tropical lush fruit, especially pineapple. Was I wrong!

Hawaii is where East meets West. It is native Polynesian culture sandwiched between Japanese and American. Loco moco might seem a confusing dish on paper – a hamburger patty with boiled rice, a fried egg, and lashings of brown mushroom gravy – but the crazy ideas are always the most exciting.

The @kokoheadcafe version, the Koko Moco, is true to Hawaiian tradition but with a few tweaks, like the addition of tempura kimchi, a small but revolutionary twist. More food should come with it. My version of the loco moco is no exception.

LOCO MOCO

For the Rice
1 cup white long–grain rice
2 cups water

For the Sauce
1 oz dried porcini
    mushrooms
5 oz white mushrooms, or
    10oz if not using wild
5 oz wild mushrooms
    (optional; otherwise
    double quantity of white)
1 onion
¼ cup olive oil
Pinch of salt
2 garlic cloves, minced
½ stick butter
¾ cup single cream
1 slosh of Marsala
    (optional)

Start by putting your sparkling water and mixing bowl for the tempura kimchi in the fridge to chill.

Wash the rice and put it in a pan, add the water and cover with a lid. Cook on a medium–high heat for 15–20 minutes until cooked. Leave the lid on so that it steams.

For the sauce, soak the dried porcini mushrooms in about 1/2 cup freshly boiled water.

Meanwhile, slice the rest of the mushrooms and onion.

In a pan, heat the olive oil over a medium heat, add the onion with a pinch of salt, and cook for 2–3 minutes before adding the garlic. Add the chopped fresh mushrooms. Pour the mushroom liquid from the porcini into the pan and give the now rehydrated mushrooms a rough chop, then add these to the pan. Cook for 5 minutes. Turn the heat down and add the butter and cream. Add the Marsala, if using, and continue cooking for another 5 minutes, checking for seasoning too. Add a splash of water if you prefer it a bit thinner in consistency.

To prepare your burger patty, split the mince into two equal portions and mold each into a round. Whatever you do, don't season the meat until it's about to be cooked, as the salt will make the meat tough. Depending on the fat content of the meat, you may need a teaspoon of oil, or none.

Season the patties with salt and pepper before cooking them in a frying pan on a high heat. Flip when you have a good dark brown color. The whole thing should take 12 minutes max. Leave the patties to rest.

(continued on following page)

For the Patties

½ lb minced beef, or mince
   your own steak
Salt and pepper

For the Tempura Kimchi

Oil for frying
2 egg yolks
3 cups sparkling water
¾ cup plain flour
¼ cup cornflour
4 oz kimchi (see page 106)

For the Egg

1 egg per person
¼ cup oil

For the tempura kimchi, heat the oil in a pan. You want the oil to be 2 in deep.

Add the egg yolks to the chilled mixing bowl. Whisk in the chilled sparkling water and then add the flours until you have a smooth batter.

Dice the kimchi into bite–sized chunks and dip them in the batter. Fry for a few minutes, turning in the oil until just golden, then drain on kitchen paper.

Fry the egg last. If you want a fried egg with a crispy bottom, the trick is to use a bit more oil and make sure it is extremely hot before you put the egg into the pan. It's best to crack the egg into a small cup first. As soon as it hits the mirage–like surface of bubbling oil, turn the heat down and use a spoon to baste, whilst tilting the pan gently.

Finally, assemble your dish: rice first, followed by the patty, egg, mushroom sauce, and lots of tempura kimchi. Enjoy with unsweetened ice tea or, better yet, a cocktail.

"Not in cold blood
Madame. There is
nothing cold about
the Goddess."
—**George Arliss** as
the Rajah in *The Green
Goddess,* 1923

As you can imagine, Hawaii in the summer is ridiculously hot. Bogart's Café is a roadside diner a few minutes' walk from the Diamond Crater. A small, suspicious-looking place, a bit reminiscent of a Hawaiian Little Chef, it turned out to be one of the hottest spots for breakfast.

On offer: Taro Bagels, Mama's Fried Rice, Goldie Lox Benedict, and, the most delicious thing on the menu, the Green Goddess Smoothie, so deliciously thick that it provided a perfect 80s workout for your face muscles.

Fast-forward a few months and, looking back at our holiday photos, we have the urge to try it again. So here it is.

After some research, I decided to give this version a name change. Not only because I think giving food a gender is silly (c'mon, it's the 21st century), but if it did induce some god-like complex, I'd recommend you have your medication checked.

GREEN NON-GENDER-SPECIFIC DEITY SMOOTHIE

Serves 2 to 3

1 mango, pitted, peeled and frozen
2 bananas, peeled and frozen
1 cup coconut water
½ tsp cinnamon
½ lb spinach, fresh
Mint leaves and raspberries for garnish

Here's a tip. Before freezing your mango and banana it is best to cut them into small chunks. It will reduce the chance of them getting stuck in the blender.

In a blender, put the (chopped) frozen mango, banana, coconut water, and cinnamon. Blend on the highest setting until smooth. Add as much spinach as you can fit in the blender – you might need to use a wooden spoon to push the leaves into the mango/banana mix. Repeat if you have any additional spinach you want to use up.

The smoothie should be incredibly thick, almost like ice cream. Garnish with some pretty mint leaves and raspberries, and suck through a straw.

6 SOMETIMES MORE IS MORE
JAPAN, AUSTRALIA, KOREA, THE PHILIPPINES

Leaping across the Pacific, have your timer at the ready because, in true Japanese style, breakfast is as much an art as origami. Many recipes don't require great precision, but onsen tamago is no ordinary egg dish: these eggs need exactly 17 minutes.

Whilst Japan is famous for its umami, it's the Philippines that are secretly obsessed with it. Champorado, the bittersweet chocolate rice, is paired with dried fish called tuyo. I personally don't like chocolate and fish together, but I'll leave it up to you to decide. What I do like in the morning, however, is spice.

The Koreas, both North and South, it has been argued, don't do breakfast. It's not that they don't eat first thing in the morning, but rather there isn't such a great distinction between breakfast and other meals. Many other cultures are the same. Kimchi, the spicy, fermented red cabbage dish, is eaten in all its guises with everything, all the time.

If you're looking for something easier and quicker, like avocado or Vegemite on toast, they're not here – sorry. Australia has been hiding something from us. You could say it's just a toastie, but the humble jaffle is much more fun and might just get you out of the kitchen.

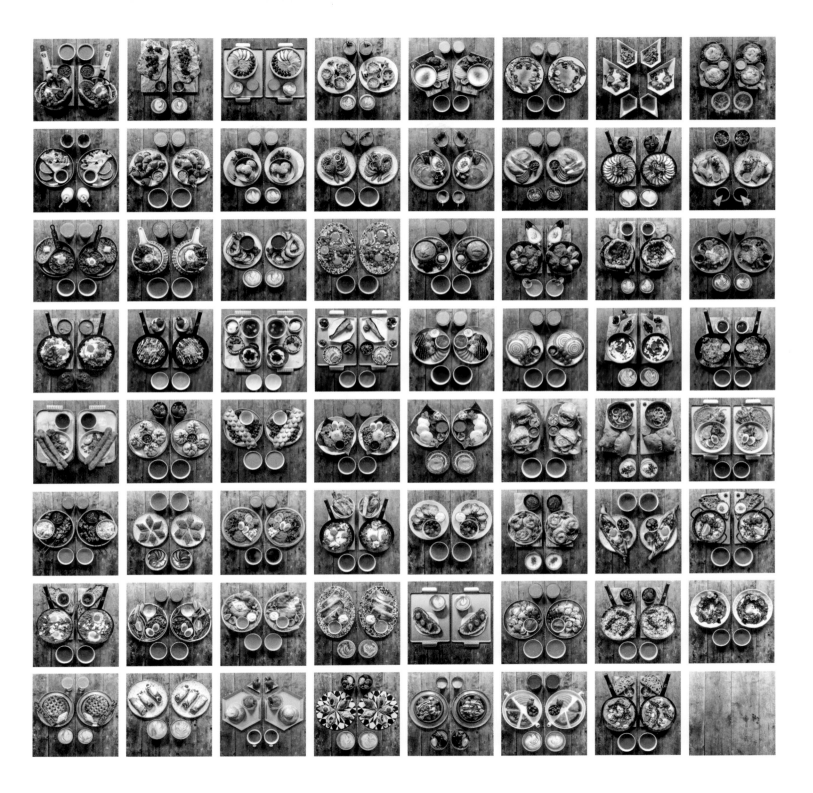

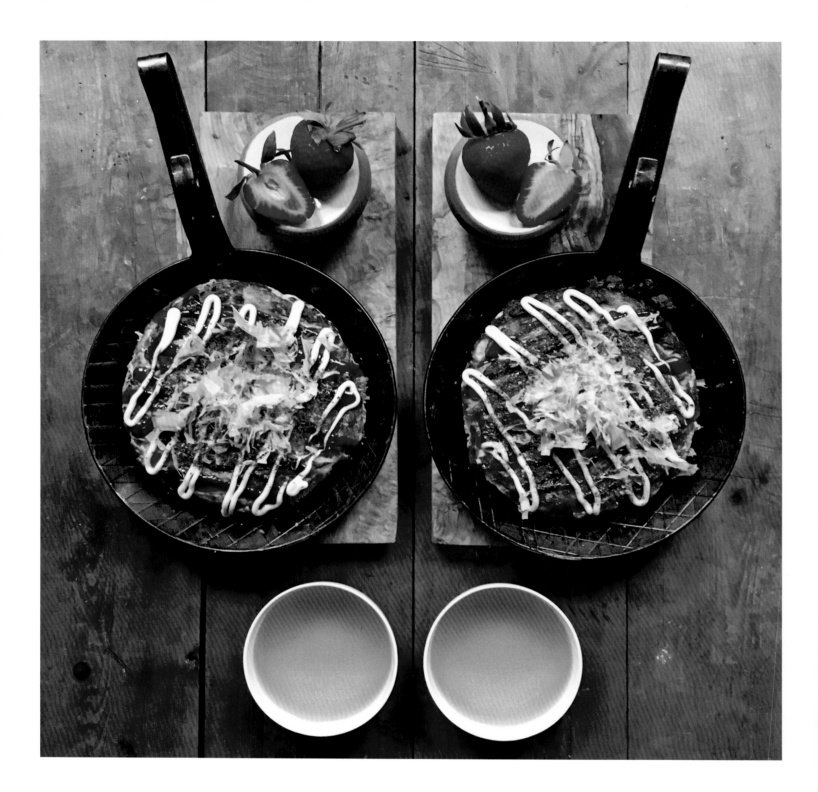

I consider these pancakes to have healthy intentions – that may or may not put you off. We visited an okonomiyaki restaurant in Tokyo, and a large bowl of finely shredded vegetables arrived at the table with the pancake batter and eggs buried underneath. After mixing vigorously for a minute you then have to tip the lot out on to an enormous hot plate. Flipping requires two wide spatulas and is a skill in itself. (I actually hurt my back pretty badly in the process of flipping, as the table is very low and I am very tall, so watch out!)

Although more of a snack than a breakfast, okonomiyaki literally translates as "cooked how you like it" and there is no one recipe for what you can put in this pancake – it's really up to you. The thick batter almost always contains shredded cabbage and beansprouts, but after that it's optional to add bacon, scallion, shredded carrot, pork belly, salted duck egg, cooked noodles, mushrooms, squid, octopus, cheese – the list is endless. Just make sure everything is thinly sliced so that it cooks quickly, and finish with okonomi sauce, Japanese mayo (lots), dried seaweed (aonori) and plenty of katsuobushi flakes. One of my favorites!

Makes 1 giant or 2 individual pancakes

2 eggs
1 cup dashi stock, cold
½ cup katsuobushi (also known as bonito) flakes – tissue–paper–thin, dried and fermented tuna
2½ cups okonomiyaki flour
½ lb cabbage, shredded
1 carrot, grated
2 scallions, sliced
6 thick slices unsmoked bacon
½ cup of your favorite fillings (optional)

Toppings
Okonomi sauce
Japanese mayo – Kewpie brand is my favorite
2 tsp aonori (seaweed)
A few big pinches of katsuobushi flakes

OKONOMIYAKI JAPANESE PANCAKES

Combine the eggs, dashi stock, and katsuobushi in a bowl and whisk. Add the okonomiyaki flour and stir until you have a smooth, thick batter. Add the shredded cabbage, carrot, and scallions and mix thoroughly.

In a cold frying pan with steep sides, lay out the bacon so it covers the entire surface. You might need to trim it to get it to fit. Pour the cabbage mix over and tidy up the edges. It is quite a thick pancake, at least an inch thick.

Cover the pan with a lid, turn the heat up to medium and cook for 10 minutes until golden brown on the bottom and you can see that the bacon is cooked.

Slide the pancake on to a plate, invert the pan and flip the whole thing over. Continue to cook for another 10 minutes.

You can serve direct from the pan at the table or slide the pancake on to a plate. The classic method of topping an okonomiyaki is to have a huge pot of okonomi sauce that is brushed all over the pancake with a freestyle zigzag of mayonnaise. Let your artistic side go wild!

Sprinkle the aonori all over and finish with a big pinch of katsuobushi in the middle, which will gently wave as the heat rises from the pancake.

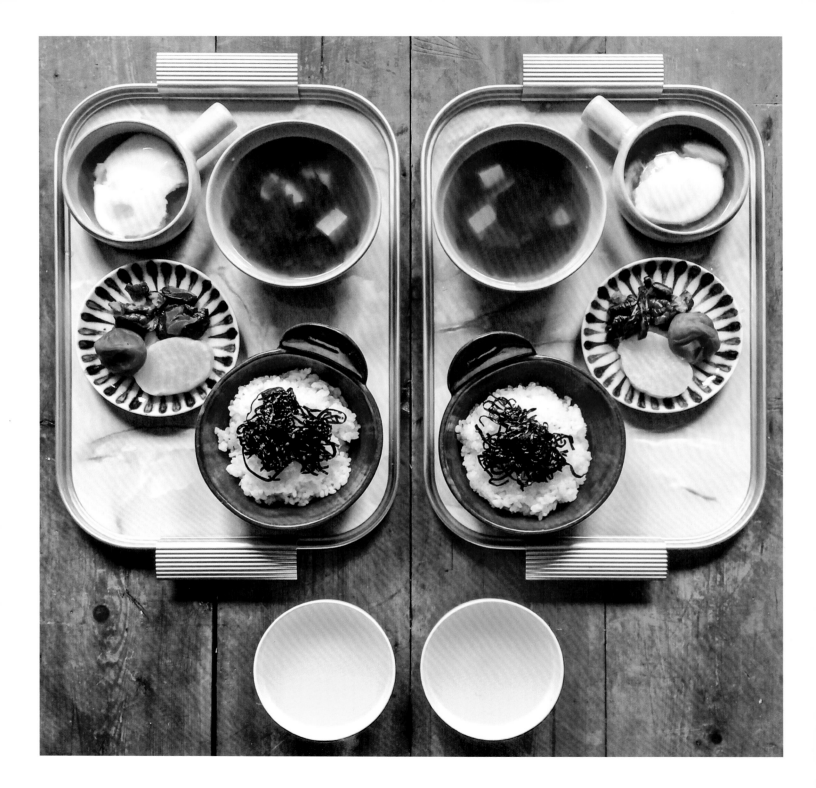

This is a small component of the Japanese breakfast, but as it is quite technical I believe it deserves its own recipe. I genuinely believe that in Japan, especially in culinary terms, perfection is possible. Even in the smallest yakitori bar, I experienced food that was prepared and presented with such skill, care, and attention that I felt it was an immediate bedfellow of SymmetryBreakfast.

Onsen tamago, or hot spring eggs, form part of a traditional Japanese breakfast which is described on page 101, and it offers that possibility of perfection. It was whilst staying in a ryokan in Yudanaka that Mark and I had these semi–soft, custard–like eggs, floating in a moreish dressing. I could have had ten. Perhaps I did.

Easy to make, the ingredients needed for the sauce are used in countless other Japanese dishes, so they're a great thing to have in your cupboard. Dashi is a simple broth made from seaweed and is an essential ingredient in miso soup.

ONSEN TAMAGO HOT SPRING EGGS

4 eggs
3 tbsp mirin
½ cup dashi stock
2 tbsp light soy sauce
⅛ cup katsuobushi (also known as bonito) flakes – tissue–paper–thin, dried and fermented tuna

In a large pan with a lid, boil 1 quart of water. Remove from the heat and add 1 cup cold water.

Carefully place the whole eggs in the water and leave for 17 minutes. Set a timer!

In a small saucepan, bring the mirin, dashi stock, and soy to a boil, then take it off the heat. Add the katsuobushi flakes and leave to soak for 1 minute. Pass the mixture through a sieve and keep it warm.

Remove the eggs from the hot water and place them into cold water for 5 minutes.

Carefully crack an egg into a small bowl. It should be slightly translucent and wobble like jelly. Pour over a few tablespoons of the sauce and serve with hot rice and miso soup.

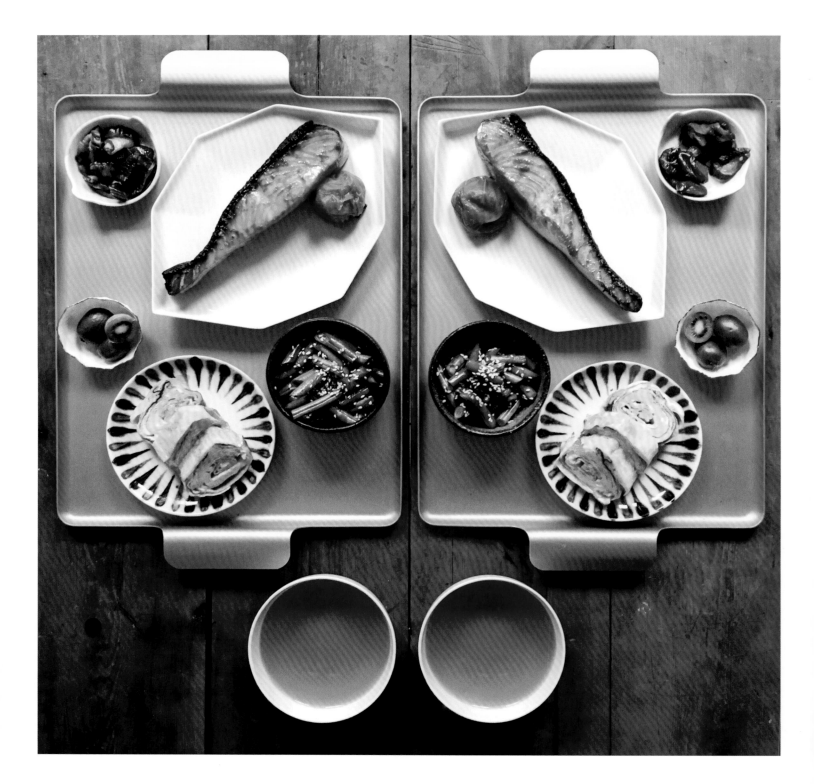

If, like me, you prefer your mornings to start with a salty kick rather than a sweet hit, then you should most certainly try a traditional Japanese breakfast. It's all about healthiness without pretentiousness, filling without stuffing, flavors that have been expertly balanced over centuries.

Formed of several small dishes, this meal has boiled rice at its center. Naturally sweet and sticky, it binds the rest together. Eggs, also an essential component, can be served in a number of ways. My favorite is the onsen tamago (see page 99) with an umami-rich dressing, or, better yet, raw, stirred vigorously into the steaming hot rice.

The rest of the dishes are made up of miso soup, salmon or mackerel marinated in shio koji or amo-koji paste, fresh tofu, green beans with sesame, green tea, and the, infamous natto – soybeans fermented with the *Bacillus subtilis* bacteria, producing what I call pure evil.

A JAPANESE BREAKFAST
GOHAN–SHOKU, OR SALMON WITH GREEN BEANS AND TOFU

For the Koji Salmon
2 fillets salmon
Salt to taste
1 tsp shio–koji (salty) or amo-koji (sweet) paste per fillet; alternatively use miso paste

For the Green Beans (*Goma-ae*)
1 cup fresh green beans
1 tbsp sesame seeds
1 tbsp soy sauce
1 tsp sugar
Pinch of salt

For the Tofu (*Hiyayakko*)
1 block soft tofu (14 oz)
Soy sauce
1 scallion, finely sliced
Piece of fresh ginger, peeled and finely grated
Katsuobushi (also known as bonito) flakes – tissue-paper-thin, dried and fermented tuna

Lightly salt the fish and leave for 20 minutes; this is to extract some of the moisture. Pat dry with a paper towel and smear over the koji or miso paste. Refrigerate overnight.

Grill the fish on a high heat for roughly 10 minutes, turning once if your fillet is thick.

Boil or steam the green beans to your desired tenderness. Once cooked, briefly run them under cold water. In a bowl, mix together the rest of the ingredients to make a dressing. Dress the beans and serve warm.

Split the tofu into two. Leave to rest on a plate for 10 minutes to allow some of the water content to drain out. Serve in small bowls with soy, scallion, ginger, and a large pinch of katsuobushi flakes.

To serve, arrange each of the components on its own small individual plate and drink with Japanese green tea. Genmaicha is my favorite.

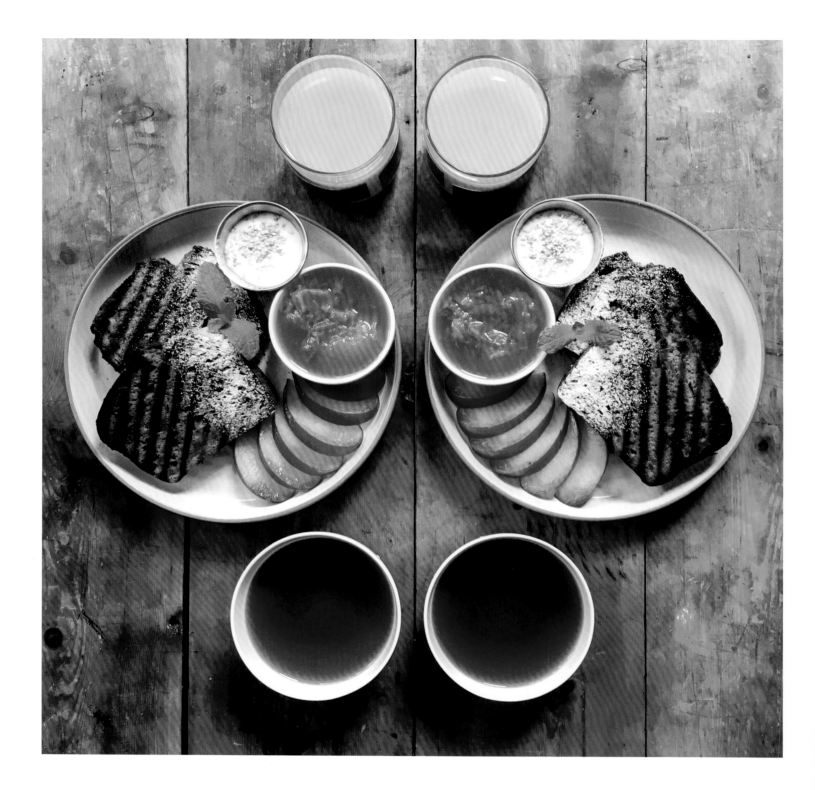

There are few things I am a complete purist about, but banana bread is one of them. I don't want nuts, cocoa nibs, chocolate, or anything interfering with the flavor or texture. What I want is dense, squishy, unadulterated bananariness.*

The one trick I employ to maximize the banana flavor (even if you have a favorite recipe already, you should still do this) is to bake the bananas with their skins on until they go jet black. Even if they are already on the turn, bake them anyway. What you get is maximum starch to sugar conversion. It really is quite transformational.

The second trick for the perfect moist loaf is to whip this up the night before and, after cooling, wrap it in cling film.

*Bananariness – it's a word, trust me.

TOASTED BANANA BREAD

Makes 1 loaf

5 bananas
1½ sticks butter, softened
⅔ cup dark brown sugar
   (muscovado, preferably)
2 eggs
½ cup sour cream
1 tsp vanilla extract
2 shots dark rum
2 cups plain flour
1½ tsp baking powder
½ tsp salt

Preheat your oven to 400°F.

Bake 4 of the bananas on an oven tray for 15–20 minutes until completely black. Remove and leave to cool slightly before peeling and mashing.

Generously butter and flour the inside of a 2 lb loaf tin, or use parchment if you prefer.

In a large bowl, cream together the butter and sugar until it starts to lighten in color. Whisk in the eggs and combine to a smooth batter. Then add the sour cream, vanilla, mashed bananas, and dark rum.

In a second bowl, sieve together the flour, baking powder, and salt. Add this to the wet mixture and combine thoroughly. Pour the batter into the prepared tin, slice the remaining banana in half lengthways and place on top of the batter. This will caramelize during cooking.

Turn the oven down to 350°F and bake for 50 minutes or until a skewer inserted in the center of the loaf comes out clean. Leave to cool in the tin for 15 minutes before turning it out on to a wire rack to cool for a further 30 minutes. Wrap the loaf in clingfilm or in a plastic bag and leave it overnight.

The next day, slice a piece (as thick as you like – I'm not your boss!) and dry–fry it – or use butter if you prefer – in a pan or on a griddle and serve with yogurt, honey, and berries, or simply with some butter and a sprinkle of sea salt.

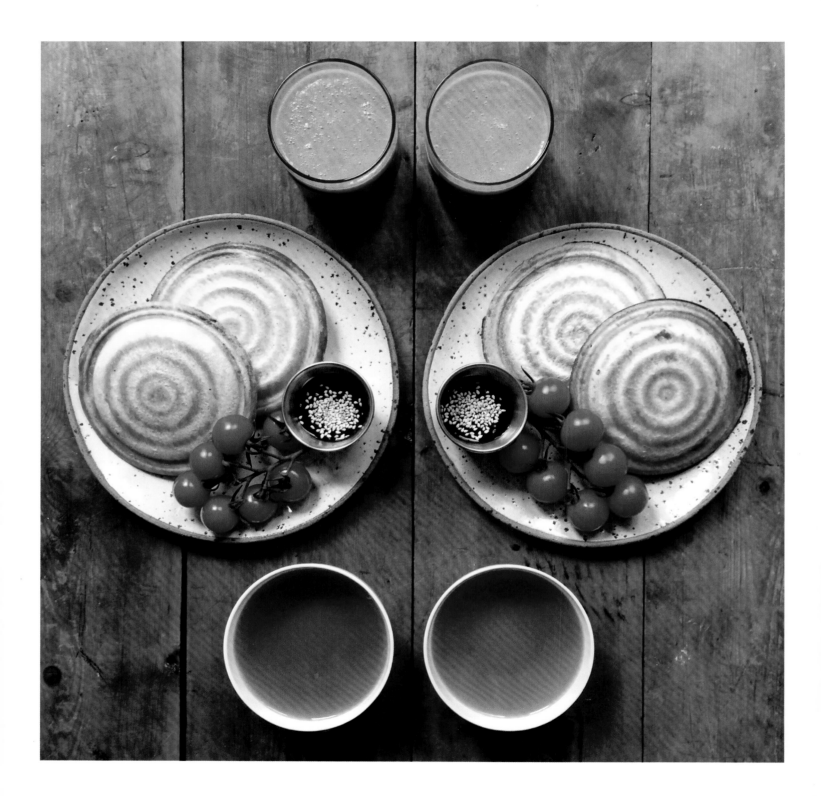

"I'll just have a cup
of coffee."
"Beer it is."
"No, I said coffee."
"Beer?"
"Coff–ee."
"Be . . . eer?"
— **Marge Simpson**
attempting to order a
coffee in Australia,
in the episode
"Bart vs Australia,"
The Simpsons, 1995

It might seem completely unfair and even untrue, I define Australian cuisine by its snack foods. Whether you are enjoying a Chiko roll, a Tim Tam, a lamington, an Iced VoVo or even a slice of fairy bread, you will probably be drinking it with an expertly prepared coffee or an ice–cold beer.

When I was a child, my parents had a Breville sandwich toaster. I remember it because I broke it.

Now, depending on what part of the English– speaking world you are from, you might call a toastie – the ultimate snack – something else. I recently purchased a jaffle iron, a common feature of camping in Australia or at a braai (barbecue) in South Africa. Loaded up with sweet or savory fillings, closed tight and placed straight into the fire or hovered gently over a gas flame.

You too will of course need a jaffle iron, new or vintage. There are some amazing designs available and mine is a replica of a 1949 Toas–Tite.

If you are camping or at least in the garden, I doubt you will weigh or measure anything. Use your own good judgment and you'll be fine.

If you have any leftovers at all, bung them in. So if you've got any chole (see page 145), fatty boy beans (see page 67), kimchi (see page 106) or bits and pieces from any other recipe in this book, feel free to re–appropriate them as you wish.

JAFFLES

Serves however many you want it to!

White plastic bread – leave the sourdough at home
Butter, regular, garlic, or herb
Ham, bacon, leftover meat of any kind, bolognese, curry, etc.
Grated cheese – Cheddar is perfect here, but adding mozzarella raises the game
Eggs – small eggs are best
Baked beans
Hot sauce, Sriracha (hot chili sauce) or Tabasco

Measure your bread against the jaffle iron. If it's just a bit too small, use a rolling pin to flatten it out – but don't worry too much if it's a tight fit. Simply pack it in.

Start by preheating your jaffle iron. Lightly grease or oil the inside first and place it on the edge of the fire or over a low gas flame.

Generously butter your bread. Open the iron and place the first piece inside, butter side down. Start your filling with the meat, then create a ring of grated cheese, break an egg in the middle and add a few teaspoons of beans, then add hot sauce to taste. Place the second slice of bread on top, butter side up, close the iron firmly and lock the handle. Pinch off any excess bread.

Cook over the heat for 1 minute before flipping. Repeat until both sides have had 2 minutes each. The bread will be a lovely light golden brown.

Remove from the heat for a minute before opening. This is to allow the pressure to drop inside, otherwise you could end up with egg yolk shooting out.

Enjoy with strong black tea or Cowboy Coffee (see page 83).

It was watching a documentary about North Korea that inspired me to try making my own kimchi. So deeply entwined in the Korean identity (both North and South), it is recognized by the UN as part of their intangible cultural heritage. Pungent, fresh, sour, and spicy, with just a hint of sweetness that makes it so deeply addictive, kimchi is also wonderfully nutritious and makes its way into breakfast, lunch, and dinner throughout the Korean peninsula.

The benefit of making your own is that you can make it as hot as you can handle, with all the face-numbing qualities. However, it doesn't make much sense to go through all the effort for just one cabbage-worth of kimchi. This recipe makes enough to feed two people for a fortnight if you're eating it on a regular basis. It is common in soups or stews, salads, boiled rice, or, my favorite, in tempura batter.

The recipe requires some specialist ingredients and you may need to invest in a giant plastic bowl or even an onggi – a big, earthenware Korean pot – if you're fancy like that, but some decent-sized airtight containers work too.

KIMCHI

3 Chinese leaf cabbages (also known as Napa cabbage)
12 tbsp salt
1 cup water
2 tbsp cornflour
2 tbsp brown sugar
2 carrots
1 daikon radish
1 Chinese pear
6 scallions

First prepare the cabbages. At the base of each cabbage, cut a cross about an inch deep. Carefully pull the cabbage into two, but not into quarters just yet. You will now have lots of frilly loose leaves. Gently sprinkle salt in between the leaves, getting right down into the core.

Leave the salted cabbage halves in a big bowl (or multiple bowls) for at least 4 hours, but best overnight. Turn the cabbages occasionally so that the salt is evenly distributed. They will become soft and flexible and lose lots of water content.

Next prepare the chili dressing. Put the water, cornflour, and sugar into a pan and bring to a gentle simmer until it thickens. You want the consistency of a thin soup. After roughly 5 minutes remove from the heat and leave to cool. Pour this into a very large bowl.

(continued on following page)

20 cloves garlic

1 white onion

1 thumb–sized piece fresh ginger, peeled

6 oz red Korean chili powder

4 oz fermented shrimp (saeujeot) or fermented anchovies (myeolchijeot)

Finely julienne the carrots, daikon radish, and Chinese pear. Add this to the cornflour mix. Finely chop the scallions and add to the bowl.

Place the garlic, white onion, and ginger in a food processor and mince to a smooth purée. You can do this by hand but, ideally, you want the mince to be extremely smooth. Add this to the large bowl.

Add the chili powder – less or more, depending on your preference. Measure out the fermented shrimp, squeeze the liquid into the bowl, and finely chop the baby shrimp or anchovies, then add them to the mix. Stir well until it is all completely incorporated.

Fill your kitchen sink with cold water and wash each cabbage to remove all the salt. Leave to drain for one hour.

Now, the fun part. I'd definitely advise wearing clean rubber gloves for this, especially if you wear contact lenses like me. You want to take each cabbage half and massage each leaf liberally with handfuls of the chili mix. It is best to do this one at a time. Once every inch of leaf is covered, split each half cabbage into two.

Tightly pack your onggi or plastic tub with the massaged cabbage leaves, folding them in half and pressing down as you go to squeeze out the air. Once full, pop on the lid and leave in a cool place, but not the fridge, for 36–48 hours. An airtight container with a locking lid might need opening every 12 hours to prevent it from exploding!

(You can also eat some of the kimchi unfermented, which is called geotjeori, with boiled rice and toasted sesame seeds, or in a salad.)

The kimchi should be bubbly when pressed with the back of a spoon and should smell mighty fragrant. Stored in the fridge, it should last for several months. To serve, take one leaf, remove the tough end and roughly chop.

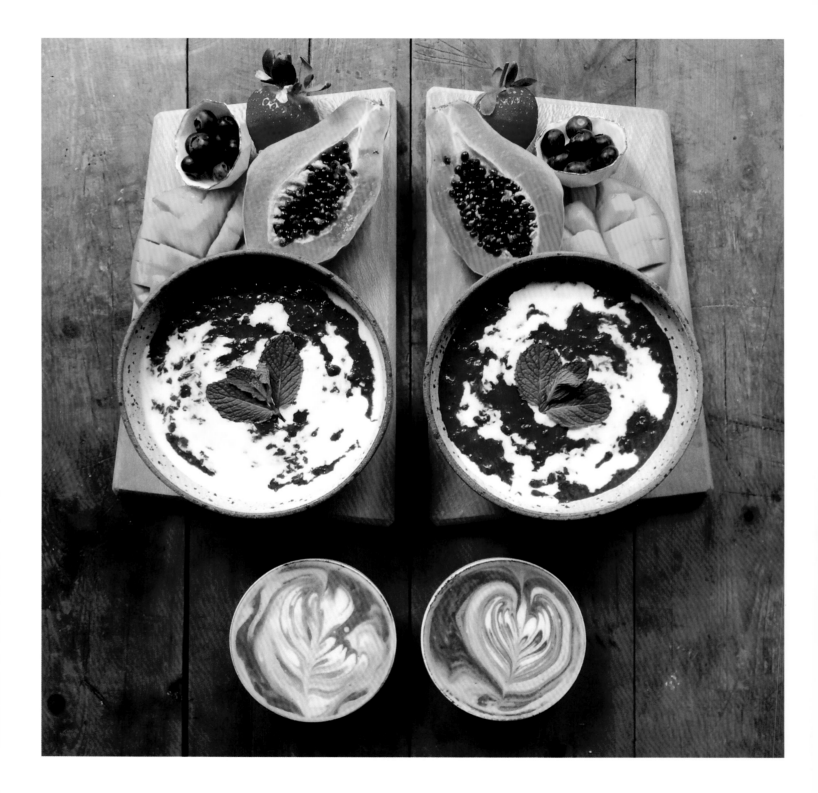

The Philippines is one of those interesting countries that draws its cultural and culinary identity from across continents. A complex mix of Spanish, American, and Austronesian influences, it has some of the most exciting (and shocking) food I know of.

Champorado is the Pinoy answer to Coco Pops, albeit a lot healthier. It's an authentic recipe that requires tablea, intense bittersweet tablets of pure compressed cocoa. The flavor is like no other.

Whilst tablea can be difficult to find, you can make it at home with some patience and a food processor. Dry–fry some cocoa beans until dark and intensely chocolatey, then leave to cool completely. Remove the outer shells and blitz until a dark, sludgy paste forms. Shape into golf balls or small pucks and allow to harden. Failing that, the easiest solution is to use the best–quality dark chocolate you can find – 80 percent cocoa or higher.

CHAMPORADO FILIPINO CHOCOLATE RICE

1 cup glutinous or sticky rice
3½ cups water
4 tablea, or 1 cup pure cocoa or bitter chocolate
¼ cup superfine sugar
⅓ cup milk (regular or evaporated, your choice)

In a pan, bring the rice and water to a boil over a medium heat. Boil for 1 minute, then turn the heat down to low and cover with a lid. Cook for 15 minutes or until the rice is soft.

If you are using tablea, grind it into a powder in a pestle and mortar. If using chocolate, roughly chop into very small pieces.

Remove the rice from the heat. Add the sugar to taste along with the tablea/cocoa/chocolate. Stir thoroughly until combined.

Divide between individual bowls and pour the milk over. Serve with fresh fruit, such as mango or papaya, accompanied by either black tea or, my personal favorite with anything chocolatey, a cup of Jasmine tea.

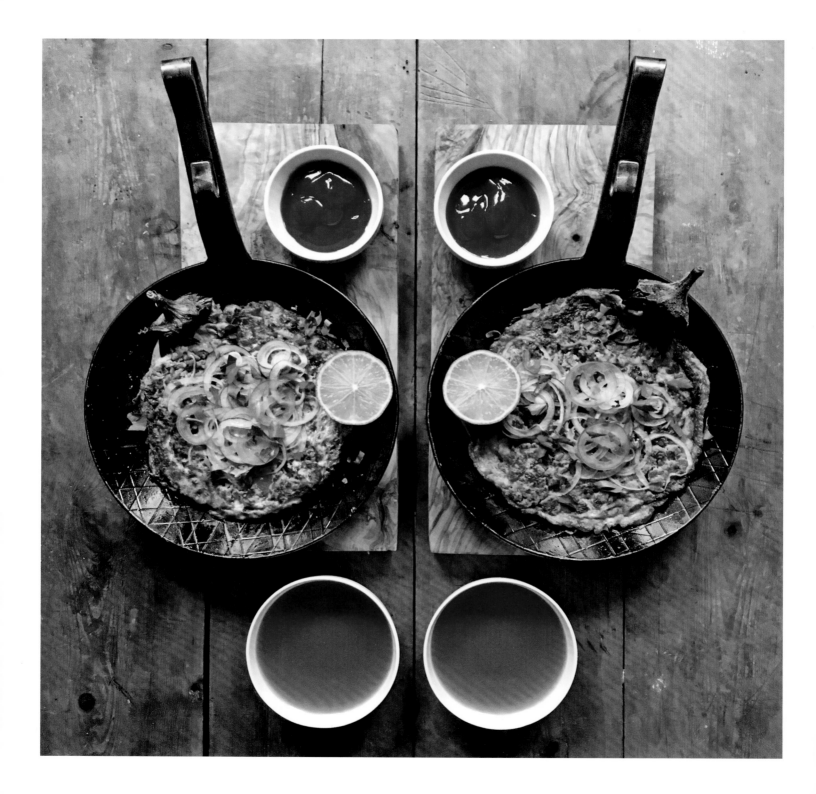

This dish is certainly not going to win any prizes for beauty, but what it lacks in looks, it certainly makes up for in flavor. Very rarely do I think of eggplants – or, in the case of this dish, Chinese eggplant – as breakfast food. The gargantuan black beauties we are more familiar with in Mediterranean cooking don't appear on the breakfast table of Italian, Greek, or Turkish cuisine. But that doesn't mean they shouldn't. The Chinese eggplant is thinner, longer, and a beautiful ultra-violet color.

TORTANG TALONG FILIPINO EGGPLANT OMELETTE

My good friend June @tgi_june has been my Filipino cooking guru for many years. He first recommended balut, a partially developed duck embryo that is boiled and eaten from its shell (which I politely declined), but then he suggested I try tortang talong.

One small prerequisite is the condiment with which to serve it – banana ketchup (see page 113), an innovation born out of a lack of tomato ketchup in the Philippines during the Second World War. It's a sweet and spicy concoction you won't regret trying. How extraordinary that it goes so well with eggplant.

(continued on following page)

4 Chinese eggplants, or 2
  regular black ones
1 medium onion, chopped
2 cloves garlic
Oil for frying
1 tomato, chopped
½ lb minced pork
1 bay leaf
1 tbsp soy sauce
Salt and black pepper
4 eggs
Chives, chopped
2 limes or calamansi,
  common in Asian
  supermarkets
Banana ketchup (see page
  113), to serve

Preheat your oven to 400°F.

Prepare your eggplants by making a shallow cut down one side. This is to make light work of removing the skin later. But beware – you don't want to cut right through.

Put the eggplants on a baking tray and roast for about 10–15 minutes, turning on all sides. The eggplants should become blackened, shrivelled and soft.

While the eggplants are cooking, fry the onion and garlic with 1 tbsp oil on a low heat for about 5 minutes until translucent. Add the tomato and cook until soft. Add the pork, bay leaf, soy sauce, and salt and pepper to taste. Cook over a low heat, stirring frequently, for another 10 minutes and set aside.

Remove the eggplants from the oven and leave to cool. Whisk one egg in a flat, shallow bowl. Being careful not to burn your fingers, peel the skin off one of the eggplants and lay it in the egg with the stem resting on the edge of the bowl.

Heat a few tablespoons of oil in a frying pan.

Using a fork, gently mash the eggplant into the egg mix. Add 3 tablespoons of the pork mix and carefully spoon some of the beaten egg over. Slide the whole eggplant into the oil and pour the remaining egg over.

Cook the eggplant in the frying pan until the egg is set. At this point you can either flip the whole thing over or place it in a broiler to cook on top. Repeat the process with the rest of the eggplants and eggs.

Serve with chopped parsley, wedges of lime, and don't forget the essential banana ketchup.

Now I can't promise that this will replace that well-known brand of tomato ketchup on your bacon sandwich, but it just might!

Faced with a shortage of regular ketchup in the Philippines during the Second World War, a resourceful woman named Maria Orosa created the delicious banana ketchup in its place. Orosa is also credited with inventing Soyalac, a protein-rich soybean preparation, similar in many ways to baby formula, which saved thousands from death caused by malnutrition in Japanese prisoner-of-war camps.

Sweet, spicy, and a touch sour, this is a delicious condiment with tortang talong (see page 111) or just about anything with eggs. A batch will last for about a fortnight in the fridge.

BANANA KETCHUP

Makes 2 jam jars of ketchup

2 tbsp oil
2 medium onions, finely diced
4 garlic cloves, finely sliced
2 jalapeño chilis, de-seeded
1 in fresh ginger, peeled and minced
1 tsp turmeric
4–5 ripe bananas, mashed
¾ cup cider vinegar or white wine vinegar
¼ cup palm sugar or dark brown sugar
2 tbsp tomato paste
1 tsp salt
1 shot dark rum
1 cup water

Put the oil, onion, garlic, chili, and ginger in a large, cold pan and cook gently on a medium heat for 15 minutes. You don't want the onion to brown.

Add all the remaining ingredients and continue to cook on a low heat for 30 more minutes.

Remove from the heat and leave to cool. Whilst still warm, pour the contents into a food processor or blender and purée until very smooth. You may need to add a touch of water to reach the same consistency as ketchup.

Spoon into sterilized jam jars or an empty ketchup bottle and refrigerate. It will keep for 2 weeks.

7 THE GRAIN OF LIFE
CHINA, INDONESIA, HONG KONG

China is a spiritual and cultural home for me. My grandfather was born on the outskirts of Shanghai at the start of the 20th century and settled in Liverpool at the end of the Second World War. Whenever I visit, I understand where my dad gets many of his peculiar mannerisms, especially the way he shovels rice into his mouth.

Rice, the grain of life, sustains and feeds billions across the continent of Asia. The most basic of breakfasts, congee, is a delicious, simple and versatile bowl that can be sweet or savory.

Whilst the Chinese and Indonesians have their fair share of foods for those in a rush, it's the Hong Kongers who take street food so seriously that it now has its own Michelin guide.

You'll need to invest in a special pan to make egg waffles but, if you're anything like me, there will be no chance of it ending up at the back of the cupboard.

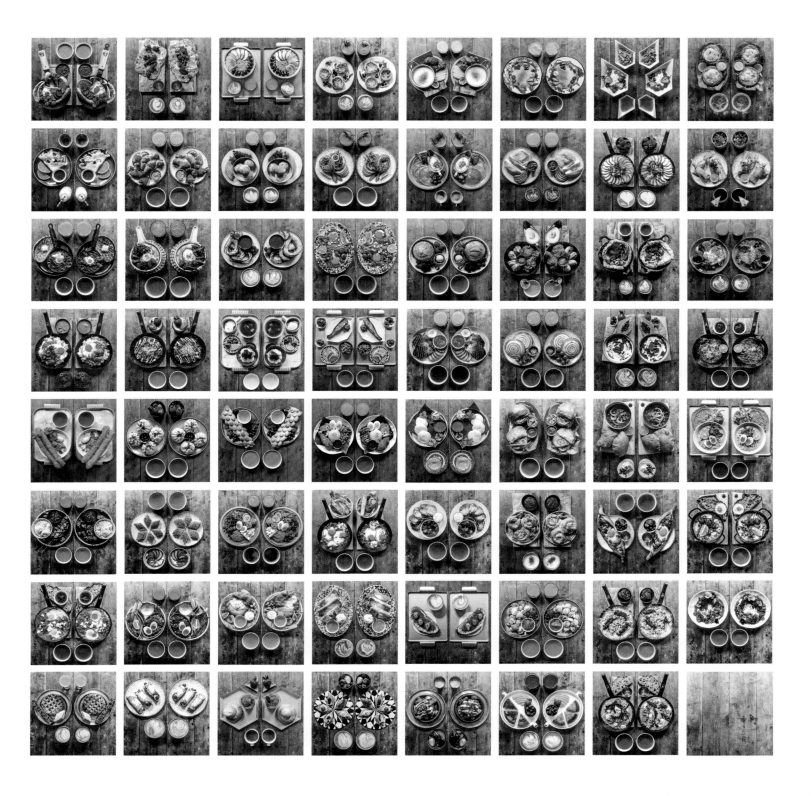

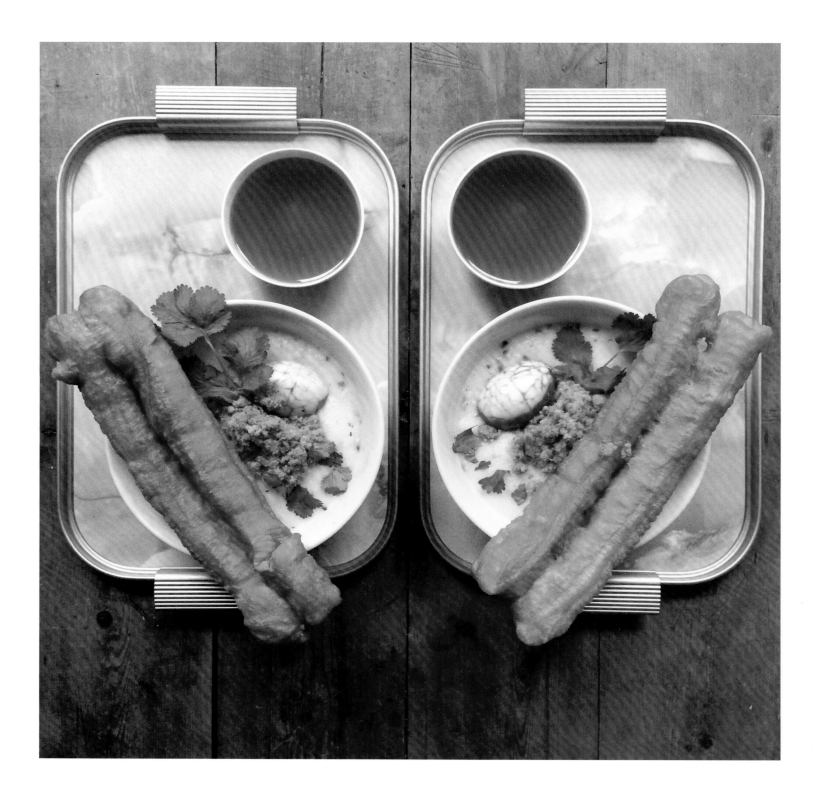

Congee is the porridge of the East. Like the annual competition for the Golden Spurtle, held annually in the Scottish Highlands with the aim of finding the best porridge in the world, there is also great skill in making delicious congee.

I've always eaten chicken–flavored congee with lots of savory toppings: shredded chicken, peanuts, cilantro, pork floss, a soft–boiled egg, and plenty of youtiao (fried Chinese breadsticks) on the side, either whole or sliced and stirred in. The list of what you can do with congee is endless.

CONGEE AND YOUTIAO
RICE PORRIDGE AND FRIED CHINESE BREADSTICKS

Good congee can take a few hours to make and, if you've never tried it before, it makes a wonderful and healthy Sunday breakfast (especially with loads of toppings). But for a weekday alternative, I've included my method for speedy congee.

The most important ingredient is the stock. Use the best you can buy or make your own. Youtiao are available in most Chinese supermarkets in the freezer section, but I insist that you try to make them yourself, at least once. Their distinctive shape sets them apart from other fried breads.

(continued on following page)

For Traditional Congee

Uncooked rice, preferably
long-grain – start with
1 cup
Top-notch chicken
stock, shop-bought or
homemade; or stock
cubes or pods

An Incomplete List of Toppings

Shredded chicken
Pork floss
Chopped peanuts
Cilantro
Preserved radish
Crispy spring onions
Sliced scallion
Finely sliced carrot
Chili oil
Soft-boiled or tea egg

For the Youtia

Makes 6 giant youtiao
1 cup warm milk
1 tsp dried yeast
1 cup strong bread flour,
plus extra for dusting
2 tsp sugar
½ tsp baking powder
1 tsp salt
1 tbsp oil
Oil for deep frying

Firstly, this recipe is all about volume. If you want a medium consistency, then start with 1 cup washed, uncooked rice and 5 cups stock. If you want it thicker, then use 4 cups stock; or if you're cheap and like it thin, then use 6 cups. These quantities will make a medium-thick congee for 2 really hungry people.

Start with a big pot, put in the rice and stock, and bring to a boil. Stir continuously for 5 minutes, then turn down the heat to medium-low and partially cover with a lid. Cook for 45 minutes, stirring every 10 minutes. Once you have reached your preferred consistency, serve in a big bowl with as many of your favorite toppings as you like.

The rice will also thicken on standing, so add some more boiling water if necessary.

To make the youtiao, warm your milk to about 100°F (you can heat half in a microwave and add the cold), add the yeast and set aside for 10 minutes until foamy.

Put the flour, sugar, baking powder, salt, and the 1 tbsp oil in the bowl of a mixer and pour in the yeasty milk. Using a dough hook, mix until you have a sticky dough. Turn it out on to a floured surface and shape it into a ball. Place it in an oiled bowl, cover loosely, and leave in a warm, draft-free place for 45 minutes until it has doubled in size.

Press the dough back with your fingers and split it into two. Shape each half into a rectangle about 16 in long and 4 in wide.

Transfer to a baking tray, cover, and leave for 45 minutes to rise a second time.

In a large pan, heat the oil to 350°F. The oil should be 1½ in deep.

Meanwhile, using a rolling pin, flatten the dough and divide each rectangle lengthways into 6 smaller rectangles.

Take one piece of dough and place it on top of another. Lay a chopstick or skewer lengthways in the middle of the dough and press down to stick the top and bottom pieces together, but don't press so hard that you cut through! Remove the chopstick and gently stretch the youtiao at either end to make it longer; you should be looking at making it about 50 percent longer.

The size of your pan will determine if you need to cut your youtiao to fit; however, there is no rule saying they need to be straight, so you could press the ends together to make a doughnut.

Fry each youtiao until golden brown, turning occasionally, for 3–4 minutes each side, then remove and drain on kitchen paper.

Serve with congee, either on the side to dip in, or sliced into large chunks and stirred through.

As fast as Shanghai's Maglev train, this is congee for those who don't want to spend their time watching rice boil. You do need a blender of some sort and you could cut out even more time by using pre-cooked rice from a vacuum pouch – I won't judge you at all.

CONGEE EXPRESS

1 cup rice
5 cups top-notch chicken stock, shop-bought or homemade; or stock cubes or pods

The night before you'd like to eat this, place the rice and stock in a blender and leave to soak. An hour minimum is enough, but overnight will reduce the cooking time significantly.

In the morning, pulse the mix five times to break down the grains into a range of sizes – you don't want it completely smooth, though.

Pour the congee into a pan and bring to the boil. Turn the heat down and simmer for 15 minutes, stirring occasionally.

Serve with the toppings of your choice.

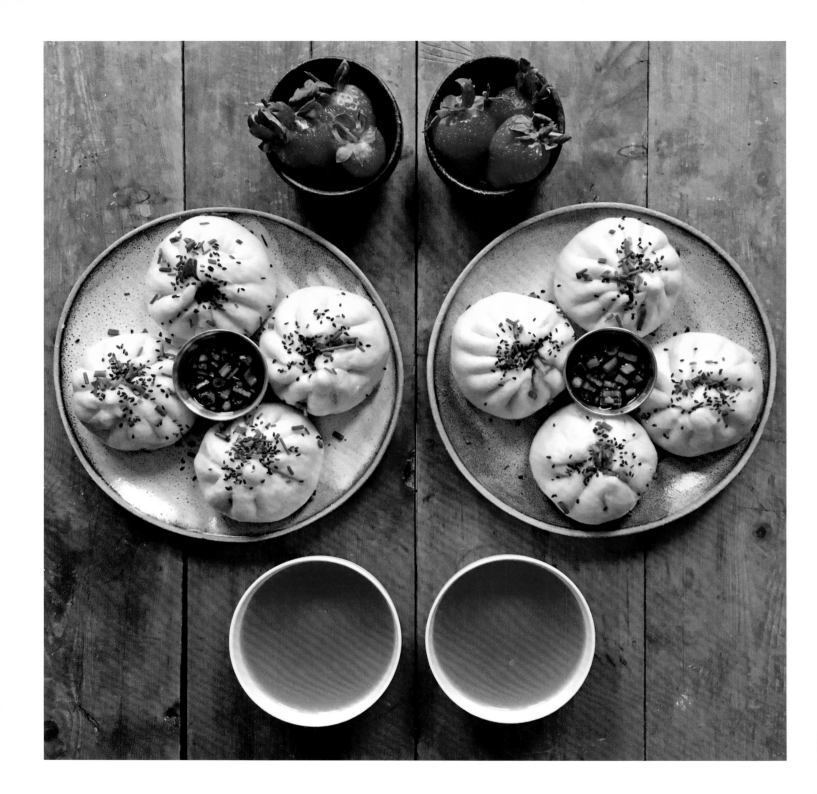

When I was a child, on weekends I would go into Liverpool city center with my family. On Seel Street was a small Chinese bookshop that, surprisingly, sold steamed bao buns. Try doing that in Waterstones. I vividly remember the glass cabinets and huge steamers full of them. Sadly, all traces of the shop are now gone but for me it began a love affair with the bao bun that has never faded.

Shengjian buns are a typical Shanghainese breakfast. The crispy bottom makes them robust and you'll typically get four in a portion, thrown into a plastic bag on the go before work or school starts, to get you through the day.

SHENGJIAN MANTOU
SHANGHAINESE BREAKFAST DUMPLINGS

Makes 8 big buns

For the Filling

3 dried shiitake
   mushrooms
¼ lb Chinese leaf cabbage
   (about 2 leaves)
1 tsp salt
⅓ lb pork mince
¾ cup scallion, finely
   chopped
2 cloves garlic, minced
2 tsp cornflour
1 tsp Chinese rice wine
1 tsp sesame oil
¼ cup water
1 tbsp light soy sauce
½ tsp white pepper

For the filling, soak the dried shiitake mushrooms in boiling water for 5 minutes until plump. Drain the liquid and chop finely.

Finely shred the cabbage leaves and place them in a bowl. Sprinkle the salt over them and toss with your hands for one minute. Leave to stand for 15 minutes, then give them a good squeeze and drain off the excess water.

Place the pork, cabbage, scallion, and garlic in a large bowl. Make your hand into a claw shape and, with a circular motion, stir everything together. Dissolve the cornflour with the rice wine and add, along with the oil, water, soy sauce, white pepper, and chopped mushrooms, to the pork mix. Combine thoroughly (with the same claw) and set aside. You can prepare this a day ahead if you prefer.

(continued on following page)

For the Dough

½ cup milk
1 tbsp sugar
1 tsp dried yeast
¾ cup plain flour
2 heaped tbsp cornflour
1 tsp baking powder
2 tbsp sunflower oil
4 tbsp oil for frying

Moving on to the dough, warm the milk, ideally to 100°F, and add the sugar and yeast. Give it a stir and set aside for 10 minutes to become bubbly.

Sieve the flour, cornflour, and baking powder together into a large bowl. Make a well in the middle and add the yeast mix and 2 tbsp oil. Bring it together into a dough and knead until it is smooth. Depending on how strong you are, this could be 5–10 minutes. Leave the dough to rest for 10 minutes.

Turn the dough out on to a clean surface and roll it into a sausage shape, 1 foot long. Cut the dough into 8 even pieces and roll each into a smooth ball. Take one at a time and, using a rolling pin, flatten it into a circle 4-5 in across.

Place 2–3 teaspoons of the pork filling in the center of the dough and bring up the sides, pinching at the top to seal the dumpling tightly. If you're looking for inspiration, there are some fascinating videos on YouTube on all the different ways they can be sealed. Cover with a tea towel to rest for 10 minutes as you complete the remaining tasks.*

Heat 4 tbsp of oil in a large frying pan over a medium heat. Put the kettle on too. Place as many buns as you can fit into the pan without overcrowding and fry them for 3 minutes. Be careful that the heat isn't too high; it's better to take your time than to burn them.

Pour ½ cup of freshly boiled water over the buns and cover with a lid. Check after 5 minutes, then, once the water has been

completely absorbed, remove the lid and cook for a further 3 minutes. Your dumplings should look fluffy white on top and dark golden brown underneath.

Serve immediately with black rice vinegar, chopped scallion, and a cup of something like an oolong or a smoky lapsang souchong.

*At this point you can freeze the buns – they won't take any longer to cook from frozen, either. Place them on a tray or plate lined with baking parchment with space between them, dust with some flour and freeze them. Then bag or store them with the date. You should eat them within a fortnight.

Hong Kong today is a dizzying hybrid of two cultures – contemporary mainland China and historic British rule. It comes as no surprise that Hong Kongers have discovered the joys of combining tea and coffee to create yuanyang. Super-strong and super-sweet, it is guaranteed to wake you up in the morning.

In another delicious if somewhat tannic concoction, very strong tea is mixed with evaporated milk. Also called "silk stocking" or "pantyhose tea," as it is made with what looks like a giant pair of tights, the ultimate aim is to get an incredibly smooth and silky mouthfeel. Perfect with some custard buns and Chinese red bean pastries. Try this if the thought of tea and coffee combined doesn't get you going.

YUANYANG AND HONG KONG MILK TEA

For the Yuanyang
¼ cup loose-leaf black tea, enough to make 3 cups
2½ cups strong black coffee (instant for an authentic experience)
½ cup evaporated milk
3–6 tbsp sugar or vanilla syrup

Put the loose tea in a large teapot with 3 cups of boiling water. After 4 minutes, strain the tea into a pan. Prepare the coffee; instant is authentic, but if you have an espresso machine that works well too. You'll need about 8 shots topped up with hot water.

Add the coffee to the pan, then add the evaporated milk and sugar to taste. Bring to a boil and pour back into the cleaned teapot to serve. Alternatively, chill and serve as a refreshing summer cooler.

To make Hong Kong Milk Tea, prepare the tea as in the yuanyang recipe but omit the coffee. Add the evaporated milk and sugar and bring to a boil in a pan. Strain through a fine tea-strainer and serve immediately.

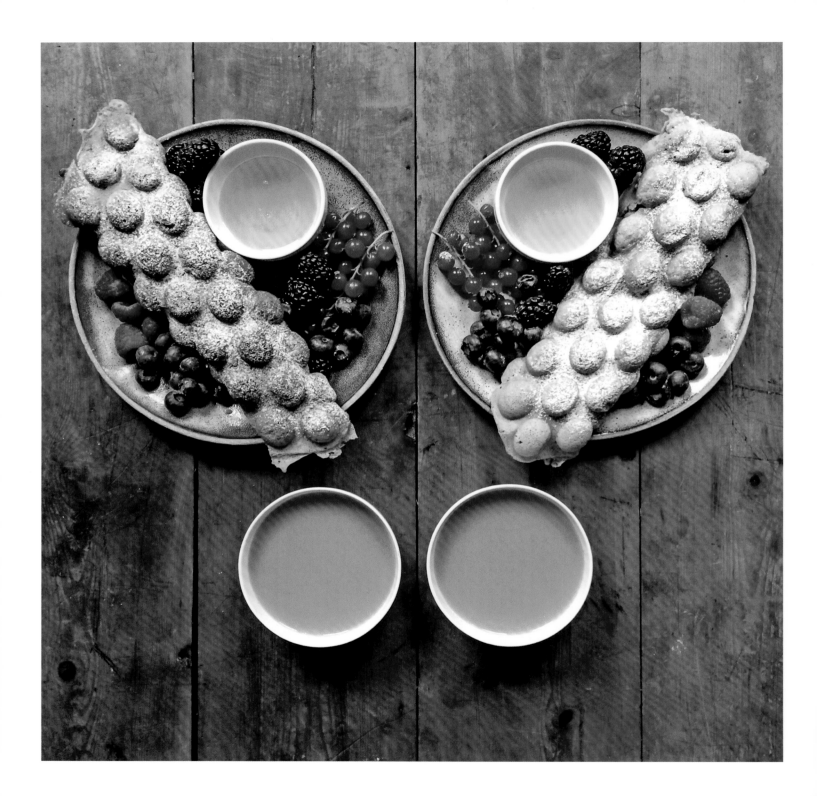

In Hong Kong, street food is serious business. Street hawkers and *dai pai dongs* (open–air food stalls) serve locals and tourists day and night. Egg waffles are perhaps the most unique and popular food to emerge from the city.

Strangely, though, the first encounter I had with them was at Beijing International Airport. Served with a disposable plastic glove (they're impossible to eat with chopsticks) and a cup of Hong Kong milk tea (see page 123), the texture is crisp and light with an aroma of custard.

You will need the right pan to make them. Mine is from Nordic Ware and is available online with international shipping. If you are in Hong Kong, then head to Shanghai Street, where you can pick one up for as little as $15. It is a must–have addition to the kitchen for any cook with an adventurous side.

MATCHA HONG KONG EGG WAFFLES

Makes 4 to 6 waffles, depending on the size of your pan

1 cup plain flour
2 tsp baking matcha – I get mine from Tombo
¼ cup cornflour
1 tsp baking powder
Pinch of salt
¼ cup instant custard powder (optional but nice)
3 eggs
⅓ cup sugar
1 tsp vanilla extract
½ cup evaporated milk
½ cup water
2 tbsp vegetable oil

In a bowl, mix together the plain flour, baking matcha, cornflour, baking powder, salt, and custard powder, if using.

In a separate bowl, put the eggs and sugar, and whisk until light and fluffy. Add the vanilla and, whilst whisking, incorporate the evaporated milk, water, and oil.

Mix the liquid with the dry ingredients until completely combined. Pour the mix into a jug and refrigerate for an hour. I've tried skipping this stage, but letting the batter rest makes a really major difference in the end. The gluten is more relaxed, giving a delicate rather than a chewy texture. Before use, bring the batter out of the fridge for a few minutes in order to bring the temperature up.

Separate the two sides of your waffle pan and preheat gently for 10 minutes.

On one side, using a quick circular motion, fill all the cavities to about 80 percent. Clamp on the other half of the pan and immediately flip the whole thing over. Cook for 2 minutes on each side.

Gently open the pan; the waffle will stick to one side. Flip out the waffle on to a cooling rack rather than a plate, as it will steam and become damp. The first one will always be a bit ugly–looking but you'll develop a knack.

Roll your waffles into cones or cover them with your favorite toppings. Fresh strawberries and chocolate sauce are a classic – as is a cup of Hong Kong milk tea (see page 123).

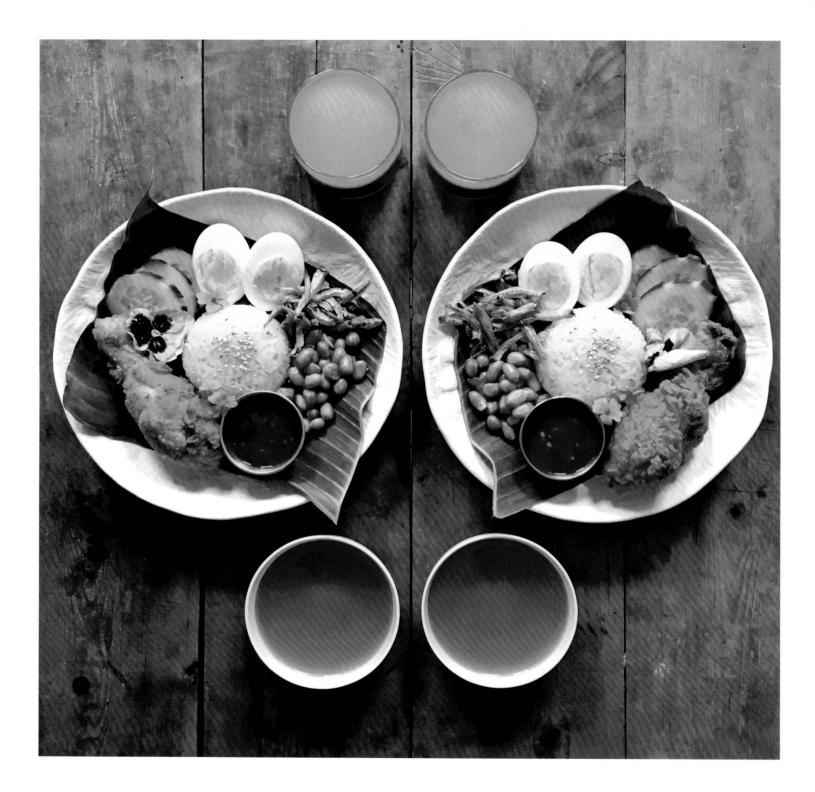

This literally translates as "fat rice" because of the way the rice is cooked with coconut milk, pandan leaf, and lemongrass. It acts as the fragrant canvas that, along with the spicy sambal, brings together heat but also freshness. No wonder it's one of the most popular breakfasts in Malaysia.

Street hawkers and roadside cafés sell nasi lemak to busy commuters, most commonly on a banana leaf but also in a folded parcel called a bungkus, which is both practical and beautiful. Only those with time to spare would sit and eat from a plate!

NASI LEMAK WITH SAMBAL
MALAYSIAN COCONUT RICE

The rest of the sides can be adapted to suit your tastes: the egg can be hard–boiled or fried, served with a beef rendang, grilled fish, or a piece of fried chicken, pickled or fresh vegetables.

It is, of course, a spicy way to start the day, which is something I love, especially when washed down with some fresh coconut water. It's a good contender for being one of the best hangover cures out there.

(continued on following page)

For the Sambal Chili Sauce

3–4 fresh red chili peppers, not bird's–eye or scotch bonnet (unless you're a sadist)

¼ cup oil

1 bulb garlic, roughly 15 cloves, minced

1 tbsp sugar

1 tbsp tamarind paste

1 tbsp fermented shrimp paste (optional; alternatively, add 1 tsp salt)

1 cup water

2 tbsp white wine vinegar

To make the sambal, finely dice the chili – up to you if you want to keep the seeds. If you do this in a food processor, make sure you pulse only a few times as you don't want a purée.

Put the oil, minced garlic, and chili in a cold frying pan, turn the heat up to medium and cook for 3–5 minutes until it starts to soften but not brown. Add the sugar, tamarind paste, and fermented shrimp paste with a third of the water and cook, whilst stirring, until the water has been absorbed. Add another third of the water and repeat until all the water has been used up.

Add the vinegar and take off the heat. Leave to cool completely.

Decant the mix into a sterilized jar. It will keep in the fridge for 2 weeks.

For the Nasi Lemak

4 pandan leaves, also called screwpine, available in Asian supermarkets
2 cups water
1 cup rice
½ cup coconut milk
1 stalk lemongrass, bruised
1 tsp fenugreek seeds
3 tbsp oil
⅔ cup raw peanuts
½ cup dried anchovies (Japanese chirimen are also delicious)
2 eggs
Slices of cucumber

Optional Extras

Fried chicken portion
Beef rendang
Grilled fish fillet

To make the nasi lemak, put the pandan leaves and water in a blender or food processor and blitz. Strain to remove any large pieces.

Wash the rice to remove as much of the starch as possible and drain completely. Add it to a pan with the coconut milk, pandan water, lemongrass, and the fenugreek seeds. Put the lid on and bring to a simmer over a medium heat for 15 minutes – don't be tempted to look at it or stir it!

After 15 minutes, quickly check to see if the rice is cooked. If not, give it a few more minutes. Then turn off the heat and leave the lid on so it steams. When it's ready, fluff it with a fork or chopsticks.

Place the oil and raw peanuts in a separate pan, and cook over a medium–high heat for 5–7 minutes until the peanuts turn a darker shade of brown. Remove them with a slotted spoon and drain on some kitchen paper.

Add the anchovies to the pan and cook for 7–10 minutes until crispy. Remove and drain on kitchen paper.

If you go with boiled eggs, then semi–soft, 6–minute–boiled is a great option, but fried might be easier.

Assemble all the ingredients on a plate with a big piece of banana leaf. For the rice, I line a cup with cling film to help get the perfect dome shape without the mess. Turn out the rice into the middle and surround it with peanuts, anchovies, egg, slices of cucumber, and any extras, like chicken, rendang, or grilled fish. Serve the sambal in a small dish or add a big dollop on top. Delicious accompanied by black tea sweetened with a teaspoon of condensed milk.

8 SWEET, SOUR, SPICE
THAILAND, INDIA, MYANMAR

This chapter has a different type of breakfast-to-go. Leave the endlessly chewy muesli bars at home: here the vada pav from Mumbai and moo ping from Bangkok reign supreme. Have no worries either about waking up to bland food in this time zone. Though the intention is never to shock your taste buds awake, they're definitely not food sadists. The aim is to coerce you gently into recognizing that there is something far more fabulous that you could be eating to start the day.

In the past year I have learned more about the diversity of Indian cuisine than any other. Rather than the heavy, cream-laden fare found in British supermarkets and in many of the less good Indian restaurants catering to so-called British tastes, the Indian subcontinent has been at the heart of global trade and civilization for centuries and this is reflected in the amazing food on offer. We have picked just a few of our favorites.

Whilst Thai cuisine has enjoyed global fame for many years, the rising star in this time zone is Myanmar, formerly known as Burma. Over the coming years you will certainly see more than just mohinga, the pungent stew of fish, vegetables, and noodles that is by far the most popular breakfast on the streets of Yangon.

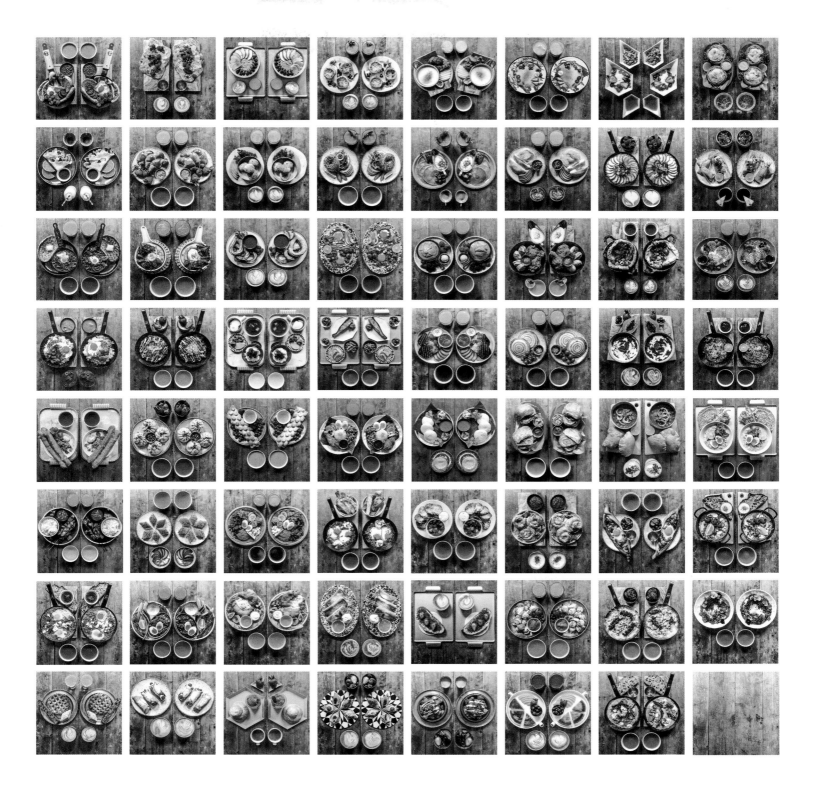

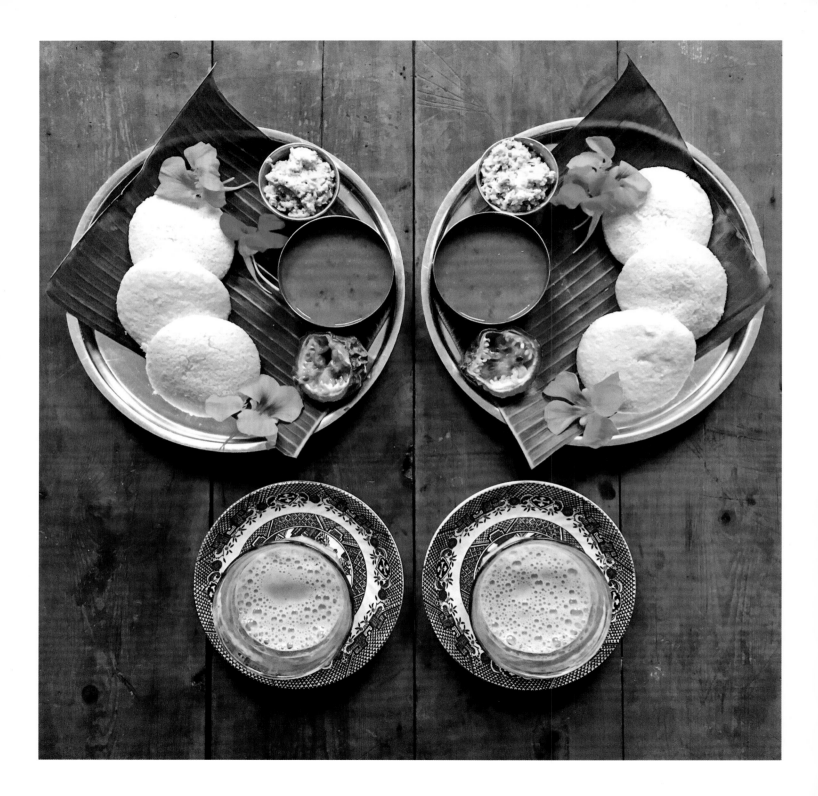

Mark and I adore India. In April 2015, we started in Delhi and worked our way south via Agra and through Rajasthan. We finished with a week in Goa, where I had the pleasure of meeting Greta, a fantastic cook who taught me how to make all sorts of delights from across the subcontinent.

Like a fluffy white flying saucer, idli are probably south India's favorite breakfast. They are simple to make from scratch but require some advance planning and either a sunny windowsill or warm oven to help fermentation.

Start early the day before by soaking the rice and dal. Serve with sambar (a lentil–based stew) and coconut chutney for an authentic breakfast, or you can slice them open for a gluten–free version of a Chinese bao bun and fill them with what you like.

Special idli rice, also called sona masuri, gives the best fermentation because it is short and high in starch. It is available only in specialist shops. However, I have had great success with pudding rice and carnaroli.

If you can't find a specialist idli pan, then you can use one of those easy egg–poaching pans with the four indents – they're practically the same thing.

IDLI SOUTH INDIAN FERMENTED RICE PANCAKES

Makes about 20 idli

3 cups rice (long-grain is fine)
1 tsp fenugreek seeds
½ cup water
1 cup black gram lentils (urad dal)
3 tsp salt
Oil for greasing the pans

Start in the morning of the day before you'd like to eat – as I said, some forward planning is required. In a bowl, mix the rice with the fenugreek seeds and cover with the water. In another bowl, put the urad dal and cover with water. Leave both bowls for a minimum of 5 hours.

The evening of the day before eating, drain the water from the rice but don't discard it. Put the wet rice in a blender and add ½ cup of the water. Blend until you have a smooth batter, adding extra water, a little at a time, until it flows easily. Decant this into a large bowl and repeat with the dal (start with ¼

(continued on following page)

cup of water this second time, as you should have some residual liquid in the blender).

Add the liquid dal to the rice with the salt and mix together using your hands. The bacteria on your skin will help kickstart the fermentation. Leave this covered overnight to ferment in a warm oven; I leave the oven light on. Depending on the time of year, this process will give different results, but you should have a huge, bubbling white mass.

The day of eating, give the batter a good stir. The consistency should be that of thick cream.

Prepare your idli pan by lightly oiling each of the sections with either a brush or a paper towel. Fill the bottom of the pan with water, making sure it doesn't touch the idli holder. Ladle in enough batter to reach just beneath the edge; you'll get some rise but not lots.

Steam the idli for 20 minutes with the lid firmly clamped on.

Remove the idli with a wet spoon, running it round the edge of each pancake. Repeat with the remaining batter. Serve with sambar and coconut chutney.

Leftovers can be transformed into idli fry, a delicious snack of deep fried idli served with a dip, chutney, or sauce of your choosing and a cup of tea.

There is nothing more satisfying than fresh masala chai – the flavorings you find in tea bags are nothing in comparison to using fresh whole spices.

Making your own masala powder is easy and allows you to customize your own blend. It also makes a lovely gift. My advice, however, is to make it in small quantities and often, as ground spices go stale much quicker than whole.

The only spice that isn't optional is the green cardamom which is the base of all masala mixes. That said, in developing your own blend it is helpful to grind all the spices separately, tasting just a pinch. Once you understand the different characters of each individual component, you'll be mixing like a master in no time. Just don't forget to write down your recipe so you can make it again next time.

MASALA CHAI SPICED TEA

For the Masala

1 tbsp ground ginger

15 green cardamom pods, black seeds removed

½ nutmeg

8 black peppercorns

2 cinnamon sticks – Saigon or Ceylon varieties are best, but cassia bark is also suitable

6 cloves

1 tbsp fennel seeds (optional)

2 star anise

For the Chai

1 cup milk – buffalo is traditional, but cow or non–dairy is also fine

1–2 tsp masala powder

2 tbsp sugar

3 tsp loose black tea

In a coffee or spice mill, grind all the spices individually. Add them to a jar, screw on the lid, and shake. Label and date.

If you plan to use your grinder for coffee again and don't want the taste to carry, grind a few batches of rice.

To make the chai, heat the milk in a pan over a high heat with the masala powder and sugar. Once it comes to a boil, turn down the heat and add the tea. Cook for 5 minutes and taste for sweetness.

Pass through a fine tea–strainer into cups. Leave for 1 minute to allow any masala powder debris to settle, and enjoy.

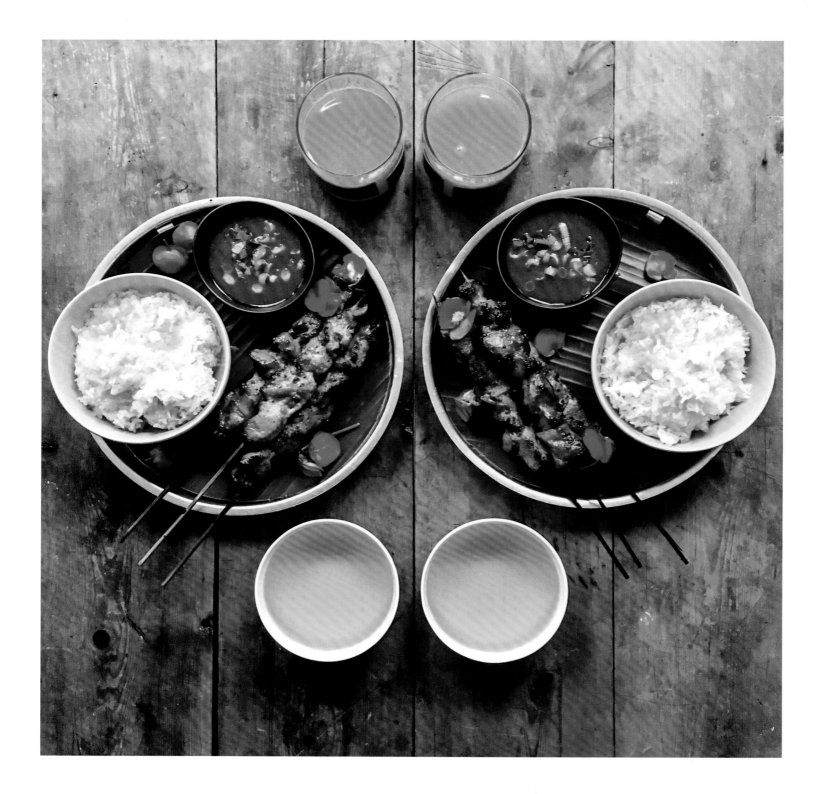

In Thailand, *moo* is pork, something I find hilarious as I always thought pigs said *oink*.

Awful dad jokes aside, this is quintessential Bangkok street food. A portion will typically set you back around $1. A few skewers of marinated pork with a bag of steamed rice and a pot of dipping sauce – what could be more delicious?

KHAO NIAOW MOO PING WITH JAEW
THAI GRILLED PORK SKEWERS, STEAMED RICE, AND A DRIED CHILI DIPPING SAUCE

For the purists out there, hunt down coriander root (or grow your own) and don't miss out on the toasted rice powder for the jaew. Pretty much everything else beyond that can be adapted to your own taste.

It is best to marinate the meat the night before, but it takes only a few minutes to cook.

(continued on following page)

Serves 4

For the Rice

1 cup rice – it must be labelled either sweet, sticky, or glutinous

Water

For the Pork

¾ lb pork shoulder or pork shoulder steaks

2 thumb–sized pieces of coriander root, or ¼ cup cilantro stalks

5 garlic cloves

1 tsp white peppercorns (or use black if you can't find them)

¼ cup grated palm sugar or light brown sugar

2 tbsp fish sauce

1 tbsp light soy sauce

1 tbsp oyster sauce

1 tsp baking soda

8 bamboo skewers

2 cups/13.6 oz can coconut milk

Put the rice in a bowl and cover with twice the amount of water; ideally this should be done the night before.

Cut the pork shoulder into bite–sized chunks.

In a pestle and mortar, smash together the coriander root, garlic, and peppercorns. Do this whilst thinking of someone for whom you have an intense dislike.

Scrape it out and into a large, re–sealable bag. Add the sugar, fish sauce, soy sauce, oyster sauce, and baking soda. Seal the bag and give it a squish so it is all combined. Add the diced pork and massage well for a few minutes. Think of someone you love at this stage.

Place the bag on a plate and pop it in the fridge for a minimum of 3 hours but over-night is best. Put the bamboo skewers in some water too.

For the Jaew

2 tsp toasted rice powder
  (see method)
3 tbsp fish sauce
2 tsp tamarind paste
1 tsp dried red chili flakes
1 tsp grated palm sugar or
  light brown sugar
2 scallions, finely sliced

For the jaew, you could buy toasted rice powder, but it's easier and far more economical to make it yourself; a coffee grinder achieves the best results but a pestle and mortar is fine too. Put ¼ cup raw uncooked Thai sticky rice into a coffee grinder and blitz to a powder. This will give you rice flour.

In a dry frying pan over a medium heat, add the rice flour and continually shake the pan or stir for 10 minutes. It will change from paper white to a golden yellow. Turn off the heat and continue to stir for a further minute. Once cool, store in a jar for myriad Thai dishes.

For the jaew, put all the ingredients in a jam jar, then screw on the lid and shake.

In the morning, remove the pork from the fridge and assemble your skewers – you want a good 4–5 pieces per stick. Brush each skewer on both sides with the coconut milk. Halfway through cooking you can add another layer of coconut milk for maximum caramelization.

Preheat your grill to 400°F. Cook the skewers for 10–15 minutes, turning occasionally.

For the rice, the traditional Thai method is to steam it in a cone–shaped bamboo steamer and pot, which doesn't cost much but isn't that common. I found mine in a Vietnamese supermarket, but they are available on eBay for as little as $7, or from SousChef with additional serving baskets.

To steam the rice, fill the metal pot with water and bring it to a boil. Drain the rice and add it to the bamboo basket. Place the conical steamer on top of the pot and cover with a pan lid. Cook for 10–15 minutes without touching or stirring it.

Turn off the heat and leave it for a further 5 minutes to steam.

Serve the pork skewers with rice and jaew on banana leaves whilst listening to All Saints' "Pure Shores."

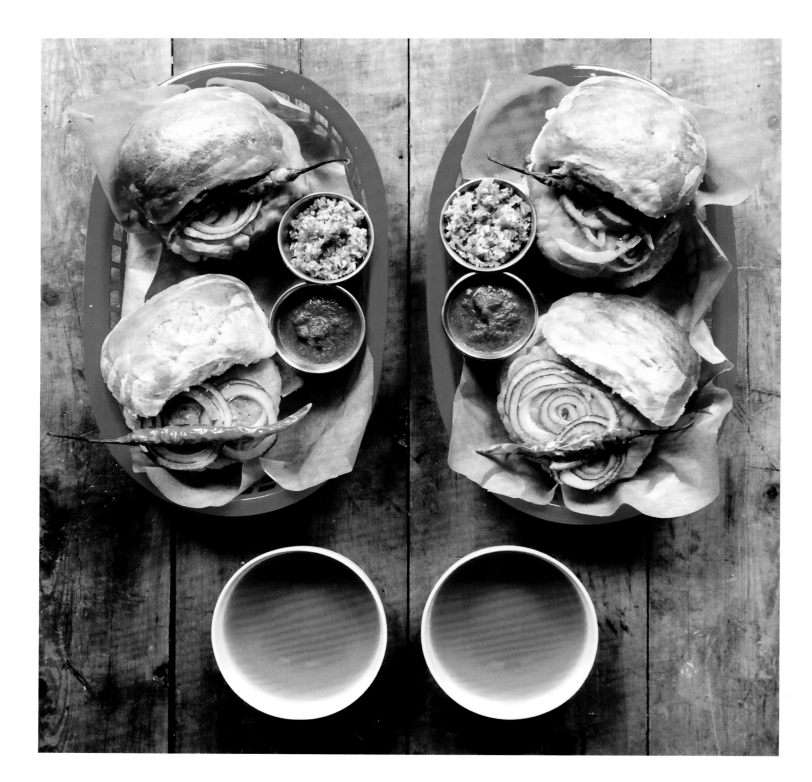

The king of Maharashtrian street food.

This is a spiced mashed potato patty, dipped in a chickpea flour batter and fried. It didn't cross my mind when I first tried it in Mumbai in 2015 that it was vegan, but it did remind me of the Bombay potatoes of my childhood, now evolved into something rather more otherworldly. Serve vada pav with delicious chutneys and sauces for the full experience.

VADA PAV SPICED POTATO BURGER FROM MUMBAI

We were only passing through on our way to Goa, but, like most people, we grabbed some to go with a cup of hot masala chai (see page 135). Mine was gone in about 30 seconds.

I like mine with an Ahmedabad twist, which involves frying the bread roll (pav) in garlic butter before adding the potato burger (vada), but you can skip this step if you prefer.

For ease and speed, I suggest using a soft white bap or dinner roll but insist on making my own chutney – a mini food processor will make light work of this for you.

(continued on following page)

Serves 4

For the Dry Teeka Chutney

½ cup raw peanuts
½ cup sesame seeds
2 tbsp oil
½ tsp asafoetida
½ tsp salt
1 tsp cumin powder
6 garlic cloves, minced
2 green chilis, chopped
¾ cup unsweetened desiccated coconut
2 tsp red chili powder

Prepare your chutneys first. They can be stored in the fridge for a few days.

To make dry teeka chutney, fry the peanuts in a dry frying pan over a medium–high heat for 5 minutes until they release their aroma. Remove and allow to cool completely. Repeat with the sesame seeds, and cool.

Put both the peanuts and sesame seeds into a food processor and blitz to a fine powder.

Put the oil in a pan over a medium heat. Add the asafoetida, salt, and cumin and cook for 1 minute. Follow with the garlic and green chili and cook for an additional minute.

Finally, add the coconut and red chili powder. Stir thoroughly until completely combined. Remove from the heat and leave to cool.

For the Green Chutney

½ cup cilantro
5 green chilis
Juice of 1 lemon
1 tbsp oil
¼ cup water

To make the green chutney, put all the ingredients except the water in a blender or mini food processor. Slowly add the water; you might need less if you have a particularly large lemon.

For the Vada

2 medium potatoes, or
   1½ cup leftover mashed
   potato
2 tbsp oil, plus extra for
   frying
6 curry leaves
2 tsp black gram lentils
   (urad dal)
1 tsp mustard seeds
¼ tsp asafoetida
2 tsp turmeric
1 tsp salt
Thumb-sized piece of
   ginger, peeled and
   minced
1 or 2 green chilis,
   chopped, plus extra for
   frying
1 tsp lemon juice
¼ cup cilantro, finely
   chopped
Finely sliced raw onion for
   serving

For the Vada Batter

2 cups chickpea flour (also
   called besan flour)
½ cup water, ice cold
1 tbsp rice flour (optional)

To make the vada, boil the potatoes until cooked, then peel and mash.

Put the oil in a frying pan over a medium–high heat. Add the curry leaves, urad dal, and mustard seeds. You might get some spitting, so be careful when you're adding them to the pan. Follow with the asafoetida, turmeric, salt, ginger, and chilis and cook for 3–4 minutes. Take off the heat and add the lemon juice. Pour the hot mix over the potatoes and combine with a fork. Add the chopped cilantro.

Split the mixture into 6–8 balls, depending on how hungry you are. Flatten them slightly. Heat enough oil that the potato balls will be submerged when frying. You want the surface to be shimmering like a mirage.

In a bowl, whisk together the chickpea flour and water. If you have rice flour it will make the batter a bit crispier.

Dip each vada into the batter and lower gently into the hot oil. Cook until the exterior is golden brown, then remove and drain on kitchen paper. Don't forget the mix inside is already cooked so it won't take too long.

To prepare Ahmedabad–style pav, gently heat some butter in a pan with 1–2 minced garlic cloves. Cut open the bread roll and place the inside face down in the pan. Fry for 1 minute then remove from the pan.

On one side of the pav, heap a teaspoon of the teeka chutney, on the other, smear a teaspoon of the green. Add 1 or 2 vada.

Serve with a fried whole green chili, slices of raw red onion, and a cup of masala chai (see page 135).

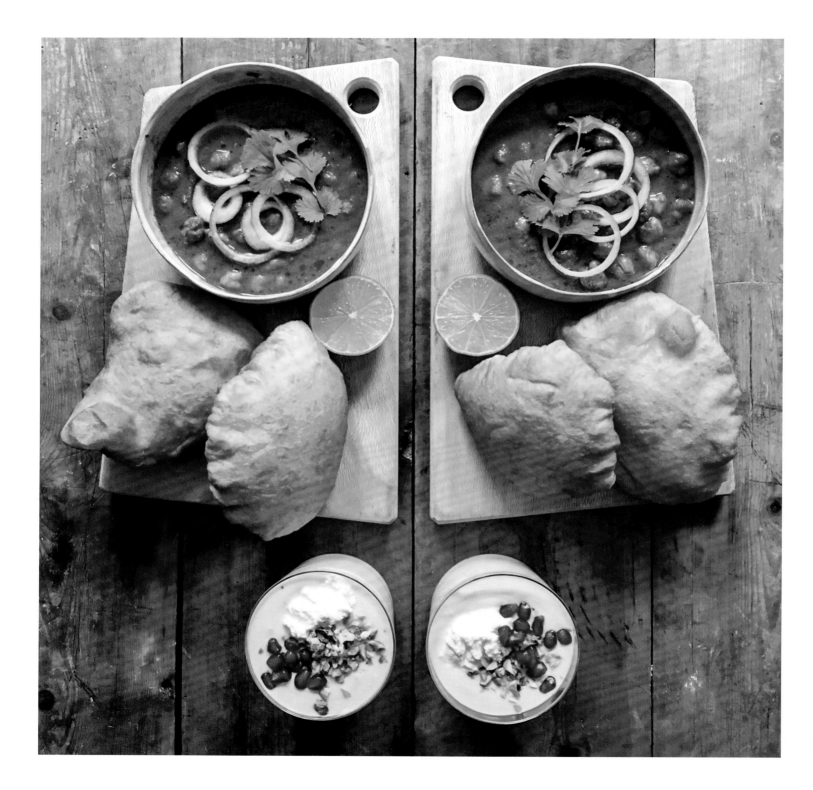

Blazing down the motorway in India, Mark and I stopped off for a mid-morning break at Highway Masala, halfway between Delhi and Agra. It wasn't very far into our journey, but it was the second day of our first visit to India so everything was a bit overwhelming.

The roadside diner was like a dream: the Formica tables, the plastic trays. We felt that Stanley Kubrick or David Lynch would really appreciate its beauty.

Browsing the breakfast menu, one item stuck out. Chole bhature, made of two massive balloons of hollow, fried bread with a spicy chickpea stew that is cooked with tea, all for the princely sum of 130 rupees, or $2.

What I find enlightening about food in India is the focus on vegetarian food as the norm, with everything else described as "non-veg." It doesn't mean that it's healthy in the slightest, however, or light. You certainly won't see a salad at Highway Masala.

CHOLE BHATURE CHICKPEA CURRY WITH PUFFED BREADS

Serves 2 to 3

For the Masala Blend
1 black cardamom pod
1 dried bay leaf
1 tbsp coriander seeds
5 black peppercorns
2 cloves
1 in cinnamon stick
1 tsp cumin seed
¼ tsp carom seed
1 tsp fennel seed
1 tsp amchur powder
   (dried mango powder)
2 dry red chilis

To prepare the masala blend, put all the spices and chilis into a large, dry frying pan over a medium heat and cook for 2 minutes. Stir the spices occasionally, making sure they don't burn. Remove from the heat and allow to cool completely. Using a coffee or spice grinder, mill the spices into a fine powder and set aside.

To prepare the chole put the dried chickpeas into a large bowl or pan with twice the volume of water. Add the baking soda and stir. Leave overnight or for at least 8 hours.

Drain the chickpeas and give them a quick wash. Transfer them to a large pan with 3⅓ cups water and the muslin tea bag. Put the lid on and boil for 1 hour or until the chickpeas are soft.*

In a second pan, heat the oil over a medium heat and soften the onion and garlic with a pinch of salt. Add the ginger and continue cooking for another minute. Add all of the masala blend to the pan and cook until you have a dark and heavenly scent. Add the tomatoes and stir well.

(continued on following page)

For the Curry

1½ cups dried chickpeas
Water, for soaking and boiling
½ tsp baking soda
2 tsp black tea, tied in a piece of muslin
3 tbsp oil
1 medium onion, finely diced
3 cloves garlic, minced
Pinch of salt
½ in fresh ginger, peeled and minced
2–3 tomatoes, finely diced

For the Bhature

Makes 6 breads
1½ cups plain flour
⅓ cup live curd or live yogurt, at room temperature
½ tsp salt
½ tsp baking powder
¼ tsp baking soda
1 tsp fine semolina
1 tsp sugar
3 tbsp water
Peanut oil for frying

Remove the muslin bag from the chickpeas. They should be stained a dark brown color from the tea. Tip this mix, water and all, into the spiced tomato mixture. Stir thoroughly and cook on a low heat for a further hour, possibly 90 minutes, until the chickpeas are tender but not falling apart.

Moving on to the bhature, there are a few tricks to doing this well: semolina (sooji) helps keep them crisp, the oil needs to be really, really hot (which is why I use peanut oil as it can hit 450°F before smoking), the amount of resting time is crucial and the technique you use to baste the top of the bhature with hot oil will help them puff up gloriously.

In a bowl, place the flour, yogurt, salt, baking powder, baking soda, and semolina, and combine.

Dissolve the sugar in the water and add this to the flour, combining well with your hands to form a dough.

Knead the dough for 10 minutes with your hands. Place the dough in a clean bowl, in a warm place, covered with a tea towel that has been soaked in warm water. Leave the dough for 2 hours (no less!) so that the live cultures from the yogurt start to ferment.

Divide the dough into 4 balls and coat each with a little oil. Cover with a damp cloth and leave for a further 10 minutes.

Heat your oil in a large pan to 425°F; if you have a temperature–controlled deep–fryer, even better.

Take one dough ball and roll it into an oval. You're looking for it to be around 2 mm thick.

Lower the dough into the oil and, using a slotted spoon, hold the bhature down for the first 10 seconds until it starts to expand. As soon as it's floating, start to baste the top with oil. The whole process will be very fast.

Place the bhature on kitchen paper to drain and repeat with the remaining dough.

The best way to eat this is to have a generous portion of the chole in a bowl, with a side of two bhatura. Garnish with thin slices of raw onion, cilantro, and wash down with a lassi (yogurt–based drink) of your choice.

*If you want to save time soaking in the future, you can soak a bigger batch, boil and then freeze them.

Chole Bhature

After years of isolation, Myanmar is beginning to get the recognition it deserves for delicious fresh food. I promise you that over the next few years, as more of us visit the currently unspoiled country of pagodas and pristine beaches, we will return with a thirst for Burmese food.

This fragrant catfish and vermicelli noodle dish, with a whole plethora of crispy, spicy sides, allows the eater to customize their bowl to perfection. It may seem the polar opposite of what we in the West might consider a morning meal, but for over 50 million people this is the breakfast of champions.

This recipe comes from the family kitchen of @freyacoote, who is also the founder of Yee Cho @yeechoburmese, a Burmese supper club that takes its name from her grandmother's nurse in Yangon, the former capital city Rangoon.

I have embellished her mohinga with additional recipes for kyethun kyaw (onion fritters) and pay kyaw (fried split chickpea fritters), which help lift the dish to heaven. I hope you enjoy it as much as Mark and I do.

For the Mohinga

1 tbsp rice flour

2 eggs

2 lemongrass stalks

1½ in piece of fresh ginger, peeled

4 tbsp smooth peanut butter

1 quart water

1 tbsp gram flour (also called besan flour)

4 tbsp peanut oil

16 garlic cloves, sliced

1 tsp turmeric

2 tsp chili flakes

2 white fish fillets, cut into chunks – ideally catfish but tilapia, cod, or haddock is fine

8 oz rice vermicelli noodles

1 chicken stock cube

8 shallots, sliced

¼ cup cilantro, chopped

MOHINGA BURMESE FISH AND NOODLE SOUP

To make mohinga place the rice flour in a dry frying pan and toast until browned and fragrant. Set aside to cool.

Boil the eggs for 8 minutes, then transfer to cold water. Once cooled, peel and cut into halves.

Pound together the lemongrass and ginger and set aside.

In a bowl, mix together the peanut butter and 1 cup of the water until smooth. Add the rice flour and gram flour to make a smooth paste. Add the remaining 3 cups water.

To make the kyethun kyaw cut the onions in half through the root and then slice finely into half–moon pieces. Set aside.

Combine the rest of the ingredients (except the oil) in a bowl until you have a smooth batter. Place in the fridge whilst you wait for the oil to heat up.

Heat the oil to 350°F.

Put the onion into the batter and coat thoroughly. Taking a small handful of batter–coated onion, gently drop it into the oil.

(continued on following page)

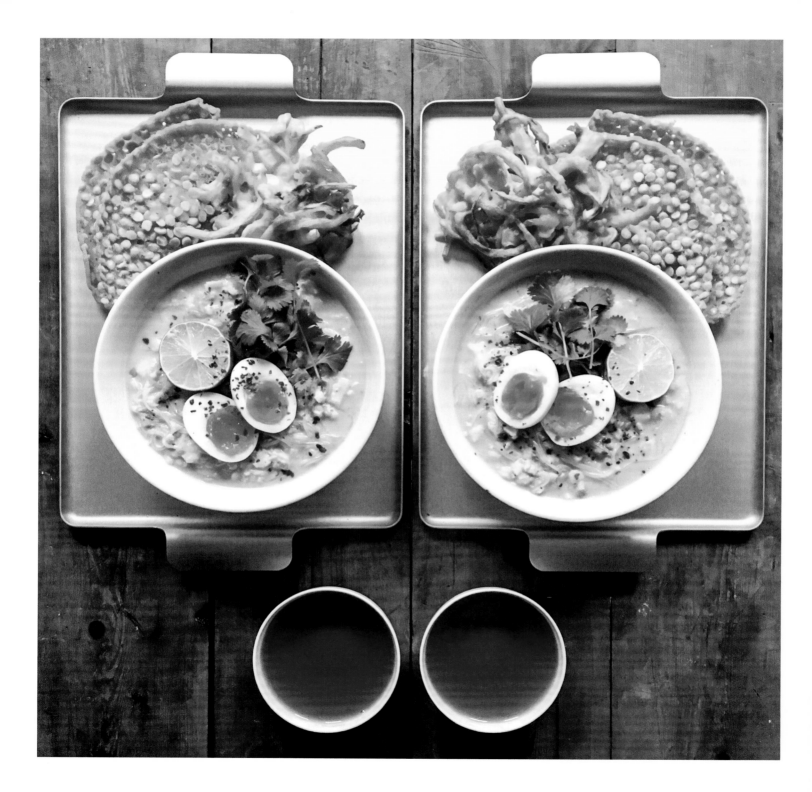

For the Kyethun Kyaw

2 large onions, or 5 shallots
1 cup rice flour
1 tbsp glutinous rice flour*
    (also known as sweet
    rice flour or mochiko)
3 tbsp self-raising flour
3 tbsp gram flour
Water, ice cold
2 quarts oil for frying

For the Pay Kyaw

1¾ cup chana dal (dried
    split chickpeas)
1 tsp turmeric
1 tsp salt
1 cup glutinous rice flour*
2½ cups water
¾ cup oil

Leave undisturbed for the first minute until it forms a crust. Then, using a slotted spoon, turn the fritter and continue to cook for another 2 minutes until golden brown.

Drain on kitchen paper and continue with the rest of the batter.

To make the pay kyaw soak the split chana dal overnight in water.

Combine the rest of the ingredients (except the oil) into a thin batter and add the drained chana dal.

Heat the oil in a frying pan over a high heat.

Each time you pour out a small cup of the batter, give the whole mix a good stir so that each pancake gets some of the chana dal, otherwise it will all sink to the bottom.

Cook the fritters until all the moisture has gone. Remove from the oil and drain on kitchen paper. Store them in an airtight container.

In a large frying pan or wok, heat the 4 tbsp peanut oil and add the sliced garlic for about 5 minutes. You want it caramelized but not burnt. Remove 1 tbsp of the garlic and set aside for later. Add the turmeric and continue to cook for 30 seconds. Add the pounded lemongrass, ginger, chili flakes and fish, and continue to cook until the mix is dry and the fish is cooked through.

Soak the vermicelli in some freshly boiled water until soft.

Add the peanut butter mix to the pan, along with the chicken stock and shallots, and continue to cook for a further 10 minutes. You may need to use extra water to thin out the soup.

Drain the vermicelli and divide between two bowls. Add two or three ladles of the soup and garnish with the boiled eggs, cilantro, the reserved fried garlic, kyethun kyaw, and pay kyaw.

*If you can't find glutinous rice flour, place some raw uncooked glutinous or sticky rice in a coffee or spice grinder and mill until you have a fine flour.

Jodhpur is a place like no other. Mark and I arrived just before dusk one day and, after settling in, we ventured out into the streets. Unbeknownst to us, it was Dhinga Gavar, a festival where unmarried women court suitors by "playfully" beating them with sticks and the rest of the crowd dress up as Hindu gods. That night we were beaten raw.

The next day, a short stroll to the Sardar Market brought the barrage of sound, smell, and color you would hope for when visiting a busy Indian city. It's exhilarating. If you ever visit, I recommend a trip to the Shri Mishrilal Hotel for a delicious makhania lassi. But now you can also make your own.

MAKHANIA LASSI JODHPUR'S FINEST WHITE BUTTER LASSI

So wonderfully thick that it comes with a spoon, it is garnished with fresh white butter (*makhan* is white butter in Hindi) and it's essential also to decorate with plenty of chopped nuts, like pistachio and cashew.

I have never seen fresh white butter in a shop, probably because of its short shelf-life, but if you have a food processor it is very easy to make your own. You can then transform it into homemade ghee, a vital component in Indian cooking.

(continued on following page)

For the Lassi
½ cup single cream
1 big pinch saffron
1 tsp green cardamom
　powder
2½ cups crème fraîche
⅓ cup plain yogurt
1 tsp rosewater
3 tbsp superfine sugar
Chopped pistachios for
　garnish

For the Makhan
2½ cups double cream
1¼ cup ice–cold water

Warm the single cream in a pan and add the saffron and cardamom powder. Leave to infuse and cool completely. It should be a vivid yellow color.

Combine the crème fraîche, yogurt, and rosewater in a jug and add the cooled saffron cream. Stir well and add sugar to taste.

Pour into a glass and decorate with a dollop of makhan (see below), some chopped nuts – I like pistachio – and a few strands of saffron.

To make the makhan, pour the room-temperature cream into a food processor and add ⅔ cup of the ice water. Mix on high for 2 minutes. Add the remaining water and continue on the highest speed for another 2 minutes.

The cold water will have bound to the water in the cream, leaving solid white butter. Remove the butter with a slotted spoon and mold into balls about the size of a cricket or baseball. Give them a good squeeze to get as much water out as possible.

Store in an airtight container. It will keep in your fridge for around 3 days but does freeze well.

To turn it into ghee, heat the makhan in a pan over a gentle heat, stirring all the time. Turn the heat up to medium and continue to stir. It will separate naturally after about 10 minutes, but lower the heat and take your time so it does not burn. You'll have a clear, golden liquid with white chunks floating in it.

Leave to cool completely, then, using a sieve, strain out the milk solids. Use the ghee for making parathas, roti, curries, and all sorts of Indian delights.

9 SIMPLICITY AND AUTHENTICITY
IRAQ, RUSSIA, ETHIOPIA, AFGHANISTAN

Last night's dinner becomes tomorrow's breakfast.

The joy of Ethiopian cuisine is its frugal nature. The transformation comes from last night's dinner, when you shred up the injera, adding any leftover wat or greens, and fry it with extra berbere spice to make a delicious fit–fit, another dish literally meaning "mixed together."

Afghanistan, thousands of miles away, sits between India and Turkey in its influences. On the Silk Road, the food is neither spicy nor bland. Roht is between bread and cake in texture, with a fine crumb and heavenly spices. I love it with a glass of milk.

The ancient recipe for Baghdad baid masus pre–dates modern borders. Perhaps this should be categorized as Safavid, Ottoman, or Jalayirid? Six hundred years or so after its creation, it's still a knockout.

Russia, the gargantuan nation that crosses more time zones than any other, finds comfort in a plate of simple pancakes. Now pass the vodka, please.

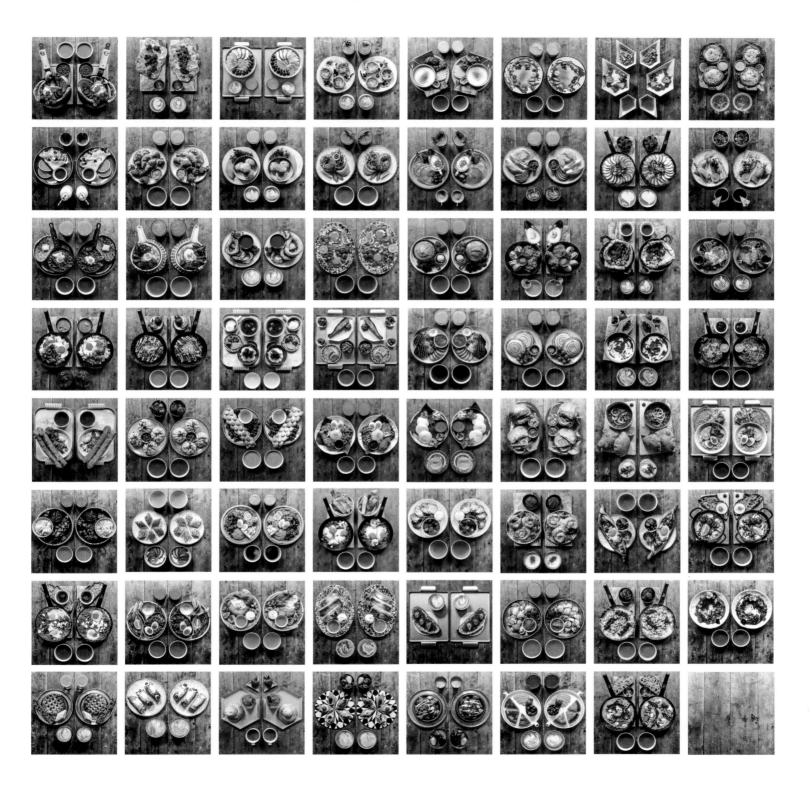

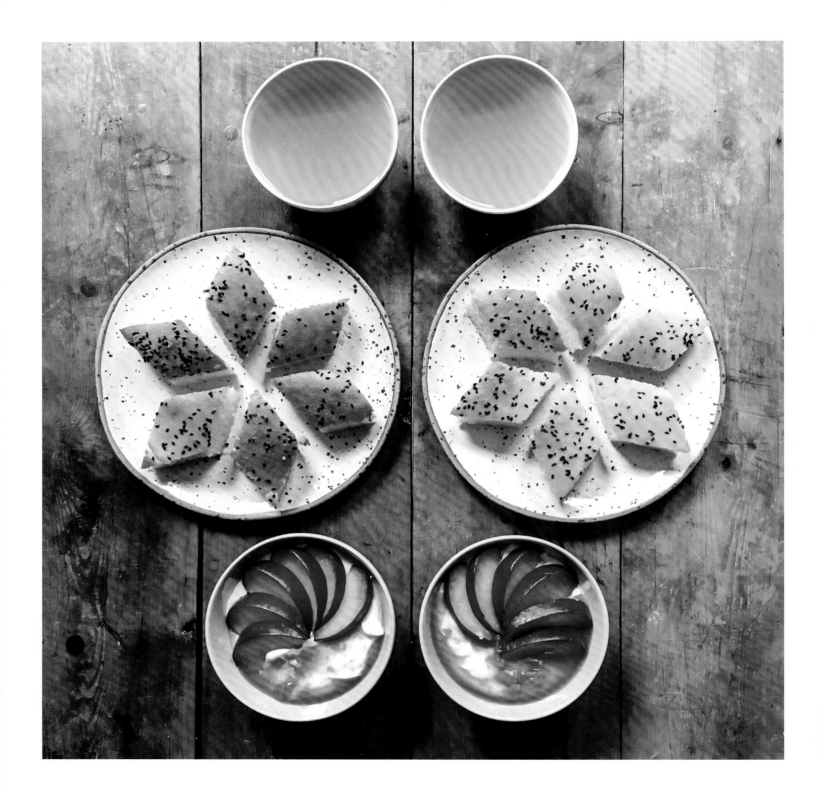

Also spelt rot or roat, this Afghani bread is incredibly simple to make and you probably have all the ingredients at home already (perhaps not nigella seeds, but they're easy to come by).

It's best enjoyed with dried apricots, fresh pistachios, yogurt, and tea, or simply on its own with a glass of milk. Any leftovers are delicious with loads of butter.

ROHT AFGHANI BREAD

Makes 1 loaf, serves 4 to 6

½ cup milk
1 tsp dried yeast
3 cups plain flour
¾ cup superfine sugar
12 cardamom pods, seeds
    ground
Pinch of salt
2 tbsp plain yogurt
1 stick melted butter
½ cup sunflower or
    vegetable oil
2 eggs
3 tsp nigella seeds

Warm the milk and add the yeast, give it a stir and leave to sit for a few minutes until frothy.

In a large bowl add the flour, sugar, cardamom, salt, yogurt, melted butter, oil, and eggs. Mix to form a thick batter and pour in the yeasty milk mix. Leave covered in a warm place for about 90 minutes or until it has doubled in size.

Preheat your oven to 400°F and line a 10 in square cake tin with baking parchment.

Gently stir the batter and pour into the prepared tin. Sprinkle liberally with nigella seeds and bake for 15 minutes or until golden brown.

Remove and leave to cool slightly before turning the loaf out and slicing it into large diamonds.

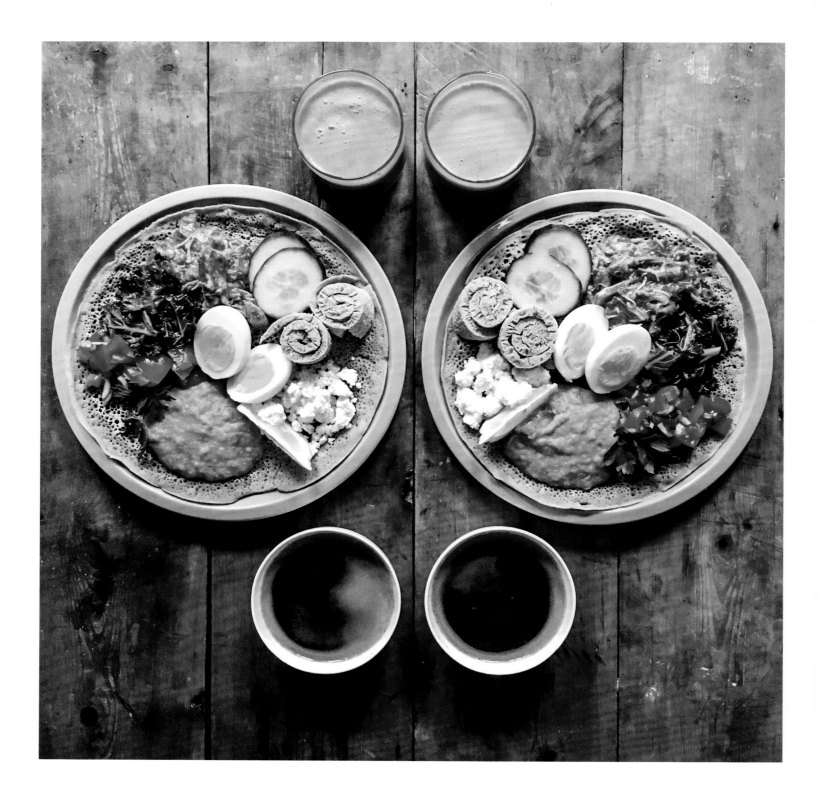

One of the world's smallest grains, teff is a bit of a wonder. Full of resistant starch and naturally gluten–free, it promotes sustainable farming, as it can be grown in drought or flooded conditions, protects against soil erosion, and yields results in less than 12 weeks. It also makes delicious injera. Most often a typical lunch or dinner, leftover injera and wat can be turned into a breakfast dish called fit–fit.

The process is like making a sourdough loaf, using wild yeast in the air to create a bubbling batter. Plan in advance as fermentation times can vary. I make a simple teff starter a few days ahead and feed it over three days before using it to make injera.

INJERA AND FIT–FIT
ETHIOPIAN PANCAKES AND LEFTOVERS

With a bouncy texture and slightly sour taste, injera are perfect for topping with classic Ethiopian stews (wat, see pages 160 and 161), ye'abesha gomen (see page 162), and ayib, a fresh cheese, and timatim (see page 163), a refreshing salad. The sourness of the dough pairs well with all sorts of sweet toppings too.

Fry leftovers with nitter kibbeh (see page 165), a seasoned butter, and extra berbere spice (see page 164).

(continued on following page)

Makes 6 to 8 pancakes

For the Starter
2 cups teff flour
1 cup water, filtered
    or bottled (this is to
    minimize chlorine, which
    is ever–present in tap
    water)

To make the starter: if you are familiar with making sourdough bread, this will be easy. You will need an airtight container and somewhere warm it can live. On top of the fridge is a good place.

On day one combine half of the teff flour and half of the water in your container. Stir well to make a batter and, with the lid open, place it somewhere warm for 24 hours. You may have some bubbles, but don't worry if you don't.

On day two, remove a tablespoon of the starter and discard. Add a further ¼ cup teff and ¼ cup water, stir well and leave the lid ajar for another 24 hours.

By day three you should definitely have some bubbles and a sour smell from your starter.

Remove a tablespoon and add the remaining ¼ cup teff and ¼ cup water.

By day four your starter should be ready to use. It can now live in the fridge but remember to bring it out once a fortnight and repeat the feeding process of removing a spoonful and adding fresh flour and water. Just remember to bring it to room temperature before using it to make pancakes.

For the Pancakes

2¼ cup teff flour

3 cups tepid water

1 cup teff starter

To make the pancakes, in a large bowl whisk together the teff flour, water, and starter. The bowl needs to be large enough for at least triple expansion of the liquid. Cover the bowl with a tea towel and stand it somewhere draft–free and warmish. Leave it for 24 hours, undisturbed and unstirred! It's tempting to poke it – don't. It should swell up and have the texture of a cartoon brain. You'll know what I mean when you see it. It should also have a slightly sour smell.

When it's ready, give it a stir with a whisk to knock it back like bread and decant into a jug for easy pouring.

Preheat a large, non–stick frying pan (or mit-ad, if you are fortunate enough to have one) over a medium heat. This is not like making a crêpe, unfortunately; there is no flipping involved either!

Start from the edge, pouring in a circle towards the center. Your injera should be thicker than British or French pancakes but thinner than American.

Cook for 4–5 minutes until lots of holes appear and the wet batter has cooked completely. The color will vary between a light and dark brown and the pancake will be flexible with a slight stretch. Place sheets of grease-proof paper between the injera once you've cooked them to prevent them from sticking.

Place one injera on a plate and top with as many toppings as you can cram on. Roll the rest up and serve on the side, using them instead of cutlery to scoop up the mélange of flavors.

Fit-Fit

Fit–fit literally means "a mixture" and is one of the most common breakfast dishes in Ethiopia and Eritrea. What you have left over from the night before will dictate what type of fit–fit you end up with on your plate.

In its simplest form, fit–fit is torn pieces of day–old injera, fried with onion, nitter kibbeh, the seasoned and clarified butter (see page 165), and extra berbere spice (see page 164) to taste.

Beyond that, the rest is up to you, depending on what you mix your injera with and what leftovers you have. Add some leftover doro wat (see page 161) and you have yourself a dish of doro fit–fit; any leftover mesir wat (see page 160) and you have a dish of mesir fit–fit.

Finish with a dollop of cooling yogurt and some fresh herbs.

This lentil stew should be thick enough to be scooped up with pieces of injera (see page 157), but keep an eye on it throughout cooking to make sure it doesn't become too dry, topping up with water if necessary so it doesn't burn. The consistency you are looking for is like hummus.

Feel free to swap red lentils for yellow to turn this into kik alicha, another classic topping for injera.

MESIR WAT ETHIOPIAN RED LENTIL STEW

2 onions
2 garlic cloves
¾ in ginger, peeled
3 tbsp oil or ghee
2 tsp turmeric
1 tbsp hot paprika
1 tsp cayenne pepper
1½ cups red lentils
2 cups water
Salt and pepper

Purée the onion, garlic, and ginger in a food processor.

Heat the oil or ghee in a large pan and add all the spices. Cook gently for 2–3 minutes, then add the onion purée. Cook for another 10 minutes until translucent.

Add the lentils and water and bring the pan to a boil. Cook for a further 30 minutes, stirring occasionally and checking to see if it needs another dash of water. Once done, add salt and pepper to taste and leave to cool slightly.

Serve with injera.

A popular accompaniment to injera (see page 157), doro wat is a fiery chicken stew that is also delicious with rice, couscous, or bulgur. It should be clear that this and the mesir wat (see facing page) are not themselves on the menu for breakfast in Ethiopia: the magic happens with the leftovers. This can be made 2–3 days in advance and refrigerated, which helps the flavors develop significantly.

DORO WAT SPICY ETHIOPIAN CHICKEN STEW

4 chicken thighs, skinned
 and boned
Juice of 1 lemon
5 tbsp ghee
1 large onion
1 tsp salt
3 garlic cloves, minced
¾ in fresh ginger, peeled
 and minced
3-4 tbsp berbere spice (see
 page 164)
1 chicken stock cube
½ cup white wine
1 tbsp honey

Put the chicken in a bowl with the lemon juice, massage together, and set aside.

In a food processor, purée the onion. Heat 2 tablespoons of the ghee in a pan and gently fry the onion with the salt until translucent. Add the garlic and ginger and another tablespoon of the ghee and continue cooking for a further 5 minutes.

Add the berbere spice and the remaining ghee. Dissolve the chicken stock cube in 1 cup boiling water. Add this to the pot with the wine, honey, and the chicken pieces. Check for seasoning. Stir well and turn the heat down to its lowest setting.

Cover and leave for 45 minutes, checking and stirring halfway through. Remove the chicken pieces and shred the meat with two forks. Return to the pot and stir well.

Serve with injera.

Kale makes the perfect substitute for collard greens in this quick and healthy dish. Serve alongside doro and mesir wat (see pages 160 and 161) on injera (see page 157), or have it on sourdough toast with a poached egg for a classic with a twist.

YE'ABESHA GOMEN SPICY KALE

2 tbsp ghee
1 tsp ground ginger
1 tsp hot paprika, or 1 tsp sweet paprika with ½ tsp hot chili powder
½ tsp ground cardamom
1 tsp cumin seed
1 tsp red chili flakes
3 garlic cloves, minced
1 medium onion, chopped
Juice of 1 lemon
2 cups kale, chopped

In a pan, heat the ghee over a high heat. Add the ginger, paprika, cardamom, cumin seed, and chili flakes and cook for 3–5 minutes until they are aromatic.

Add the garlic, onion, and lemon juice and cook for a further 5 minutes.

Finally, add the chopped kale and stir well. Cover with a pan and allow the kale to sweat down for 5–7 minutes. Stir well again and remove from the heat to cool slightly.

A refreshing and simple tomato salad to serve on injera alongside the spicy doro and mesir wat (see pages 160, 161 and 157).

This salad should be made fresh whether you decide to eat with the other toppings for lunch or dinner, or with leftover injera the next day for breakfast.

TIMATIM ETHIOPIAN TOMATO SALAD

¼ cup olive oil
2 tbsp white wine or cider
   vinegar
Juice of 1 lemon
2 garlic cloves, minced
1 tsp berbere spice
   (optional; see page 164)
4 ripe tomatoes
1 jalapeño, de-seeded
½ medium onion

In a small bowl, mix together the olive oil, vinegar, lemon juice, minced garlic, and berbere spice until well combined.

Roughly chop the tomatoes and finely chop the jalapeño and onion. Mix well in a bowl and pour the dressing over. Leave for 5 minutes, then serve.

This spice mixture is the cornerstone of Ethiopian cookery. It's available from specialist suppliers but it's easy to make your own to your personal tastes.

It's sweet, intensely spicy, and incredibly versatile. Add it to shakshuka (see page 179) or scrambled eggs for extra *zhush*; a dash in a Bloody Mary or sprinkled over chopped strawberries is a revelation.

The added bonus is that you will probably have a lot of the spices already in your cupboard (#winning) and the rest are available pretty much everywhere. A spice or coffee grinder will make light work of pulverizing it into a powder, otherwise you can use a pestle and mortar – but I'd suggest getting comfy first.

The mix will keep for 3 months in a jar.

Makes 1 jar of spice

For the Whole Spices
1 cinnamon stick (about 4 in long)
5 cloves
5 allspice berries
1 tbsp coriander seed
1 tbsp cumin seed
1 tsp ajwain/carom seed
1 tsp whole black peppercorns
Seeds from 5 cardamom pods
1 tsp fenugreek seeds
5 dried red chilis (substitute chipotle for a less spicy alternative)

For the Ground Spices
2 heaped tbsp sweet paprika
½ tsp ground ginger
½ tsp dried oregano
1½ tsp hot cayenne pepper
1 tsp nutmeg
1 tsp turmeric
1 tsp salt

BERBERE CLASSIC ETHIOPIAN SPICE

Smash the cinnamon stick into shards and put them into a cold, dry frying pan with the rest of the whole spices.

Bring the pan up to a medium heat. Jiggle the pan about to stop the spices from burning; you want them to toast slowly to maximize the flavor. After 3–4 minutes the aroma should be quite intense. Pour the spices into a dish and leave to cool completely.

In a spice grinder, put the toasted whole spices and the ground spices and zap. Check after a minute, but keep going until no large pieces remain.

Spoon into a jar, label, and date. Don't forget to taste a pinch to see how spicy you've made it, otherwise you might blow your head off later.

This seasoned and spiced butter will transform otherwise ordinary dishes into authentic Ethiopian ones. Similar to ghee, the butter is heated to clarify the milk solids from the fat, which can be used in cooking at incredibly high temperatures.

Fenugreek is the only spice that you can't skip; after that, the aromatics and level of spice are up to you. As nitter kibbeh keeps in the fridge for a very long time, it is best to make this in large quantities. You'll find plenty of uses for it.

NITTER KIBBEH ETHIOPIAN SPICED BUTTER

½ tsp ground fenugreek
½ tsp ground turmeric
½ tsp ground cinnamon
½ tsp grated nutmeg
2 cloves
2¼ lbs unsalted butter
4 cloves garlic, sliced
1¼ in fresh ginger, peeled and diced
½ onion, diced

Put all the spices in a dry frying pan on a medium heat. Toast them for around 5 minutes or until they become aromatic. Remove from the pan and set aside.

Dice the butter into cubes and add this to a heavy pan on the lowest heat. Melt the butter but do not let it brown.

Once it has completely melted, bring the butter up to a high heat until it starts to bubble. Add the garlic, ginger, and onion and cook for 2–3 minutes. Add the toasted spices and lower the heat so that you have a gently bubbling, buttery liquid. Leave for 30 minutes without touching or stirring.

The bottom of the pan, where the milk solids are, will be golden brown. The top, where the clarified butter is, will be clear and yellow. Take off the heat and leave to cool for a further 30 minutes.

Slowly, through clean cheesecloth, pour off the top layer, leaving the sediment behind. Use a spoon to remove any solids that slip past you. Store in a jar or airtight container. It will keep in the fridge for 6 months.

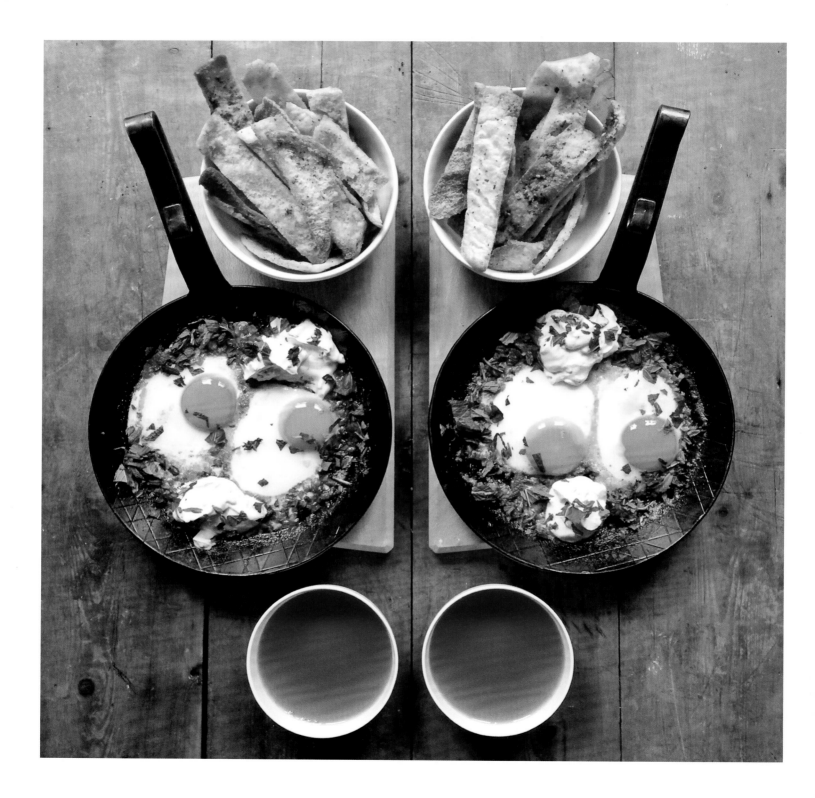

If, like me, you love shakshuka (see page 179) but have had it a few too many times, then give this one a try: eggs fried in a spiced cumin and coriander butter, with finely diced celery and onion, served with my twist – crispy pita chips and a herby labneh to dip.

The recipe is an adaptation of one I came across in the wonderful book *How to Milk an Almond, Stuff an Egg, and Armor a Turnip* by David Friedman and Elizabeth Cook, a truly fascinating book that is also available online. The original recipe for baid masus or special eggs includes gum mastic, saffron, and vinegar, with the disclaimer, "Some people like this; others do not like anything that has enough mastic to taste."

It is fascinating how particular flavors remain the same or change over time. I personally find mastic in the original recipe a bit odd. The taste of pine and cedar, however subtle, reminds me of bathroom cleaner and I am firmly leaving it out.

2 pita breads
Olive oil
3 tsp za'atar
½ stick butter
2 celery stalks, finely chopped
1 medium onion, finely chopped
1 clove garlic, grated or finely chopped
1 ½ tsp cumin
1 ½ tsp coriander
1 tsp hot paprika or chili powder
4 eggs
¾ cup labneh (substitute a scant ¾ cup cream cheese mixed with a tablespoon of yogurt if you're struggling to source this)
Fresh chopped mint, parsley, and cilantro
Juice of 1 lemon

BAGHDAD BAID MASUS
SPECIAL EGGS FROM BAGHDAD

Preheat your oven to 350°F.

Open up the pocket of each pita and split each into two so that you have four ovals. Cut each into strips. Place them on a baking tray, drizzle with olive oil, and sprinkle with za'atar. Bake for about 15 minutes until crunchy and brown around the edges.

Heat the butter in an ovenproof frying pan over a medium heat and add the celery, onion, garlic, cumin, coriander, and paprika. Cook this for 10–12 minutes until soft.

Crack in the eggs and when they are just about set on top, put the pan in the oven with a lid on. The oven should still be hot (from baking the pita) but not switched on.

In a bowl, mix the labneh with the freshly chopped herbs and lemon juice. Remove the eggs from the oven and season to taste with salt and pepper.

Serve from the pan at the table, with dollops of the herby labneh and pita chips for dipping.

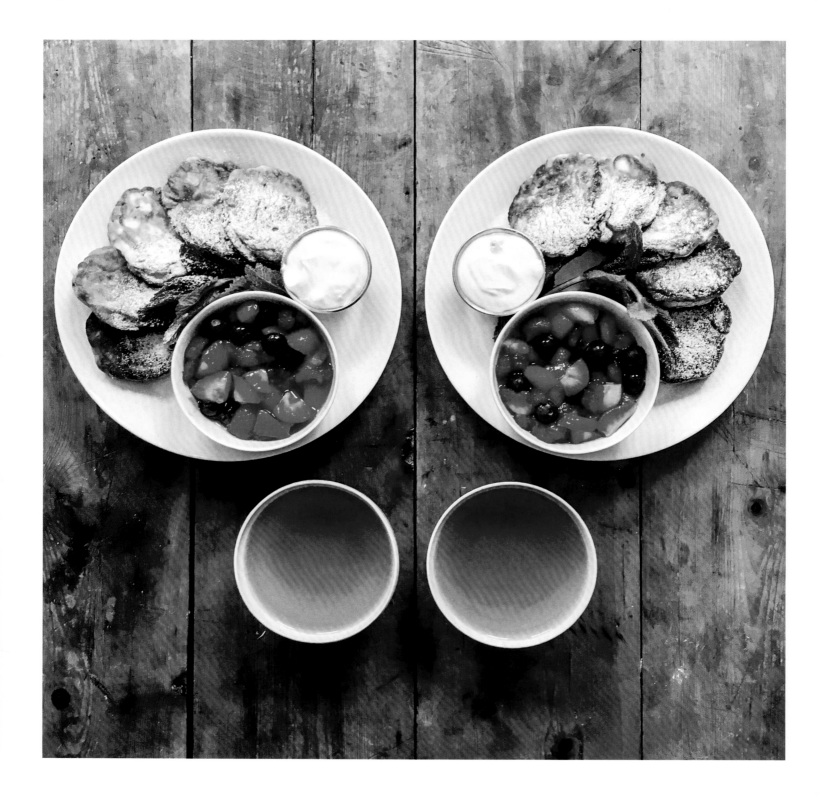

I've had a lifelong relationship with quark, the fat-free soft cheese. When I was young, I would go along with my mum to Slimming World and watch as people got weighed and everyone applauded them for how well they had done. Quark, then and now, is well known amongst dieters around the world.

These delicious little pancakes from Eastern Europe and Russia are most certainly not for those on a diet. Creamy quark cheese, raisins, sour cream, and jam . . . All that's missing is Kate Bush singing "Babooshka" in the background.

If you've never heard of, or can't find, quark, it's actually really easy to make and you can find the instructions at the end of this recipe.

SYRNIKI RUSSIAN PANCAKES

Serves 2-4

1 cup quark
3 eggs
1 cup flour plus ¾ cup for dusting
½ tsp salt
¼ cup superfine sugar
1 cup raisins
1 tsp baking soda
1 tsp white or cider vinegar
½ stick butter
¼ cup sunflower oil

To Serve
Sour cream
Jam of your choice
Soft fruit
Powdered sugar

Put the quark in a bowl and break it up with a spoon. Add the eggs one at a time and combine well. Add the flour, salt, sugar, and raisins, and stir. You should have a fairly wet batter. In a small cup, quickly stir together the baking soda and vinegar, then add it to the batter.

Heat a frying pan over a medium–high heat with the butter and oil.

Spread a dusting of flour on a smallish plate or bowl. Dollop a dessertspoon of the batter into the flour. Sprinkle flour on top and, with some flour on your fingers, pick it up and shape it into a rough, flattened pancake.

Gently place the pancake in the pan and repeat with the next. I cook no more than four at a time, but do so moving clockwise around the pan, adding, flipping and removing the cooked pancakes once they are ready. Lower the heat if necessary and cook them for 4 minutes on either side.

Serve with sour cream, jam or fruit, a dusting of powdered sugar, and hot black tea.

Quark
Put 12 pints whole and preferably unhomogenized milk in a pan, add ¼ cup lemon juice and leave it to sit overnight. The next day it will have soured. Gently heat the milk to no more than 110°F until it starts to separate.

Strain the liquid through a cheesecloth, gathering it together like a giant tea bag, and leave it to drip over a bowl for 10 hours.

You will be left with a semi–soft, slightly dry white cheese with an acidic flavor. It will keep refrigerated in an airtight container for a maximum of 3 days.

10 A QUESTION OF IDENTITY
EASTERN EUROPE, TURKEY, ISRAEL, EGYPT, LIBYA, THE BALKANS

Israeli cuisine is a culmination of the differences in the Jewish diaspora. It draws influence from a global palette and continues to define itself today. Blintzes, the filled and fried pancakes from Eastern Europe; shakshuka, eggs cooked in a tomato sauce from Tunisia; and many others not listed in this book, such as zhug, hummus, and even chicken soup – all form part of the Israeli identity as much as they do that of their country of origin.

Turkey and the Balkan states, once part of the Ottoman Empire, are joined together by one ingredient, butter. Pide and burek, whilst seemingly unconnected, are brushed liberally with melted butter.

In a stark contrast, Egypt is positively healthy; a bowl of ful is likely to keep you going for several hours and with a few tweaks can make a nutritious and delicious vegan dish.

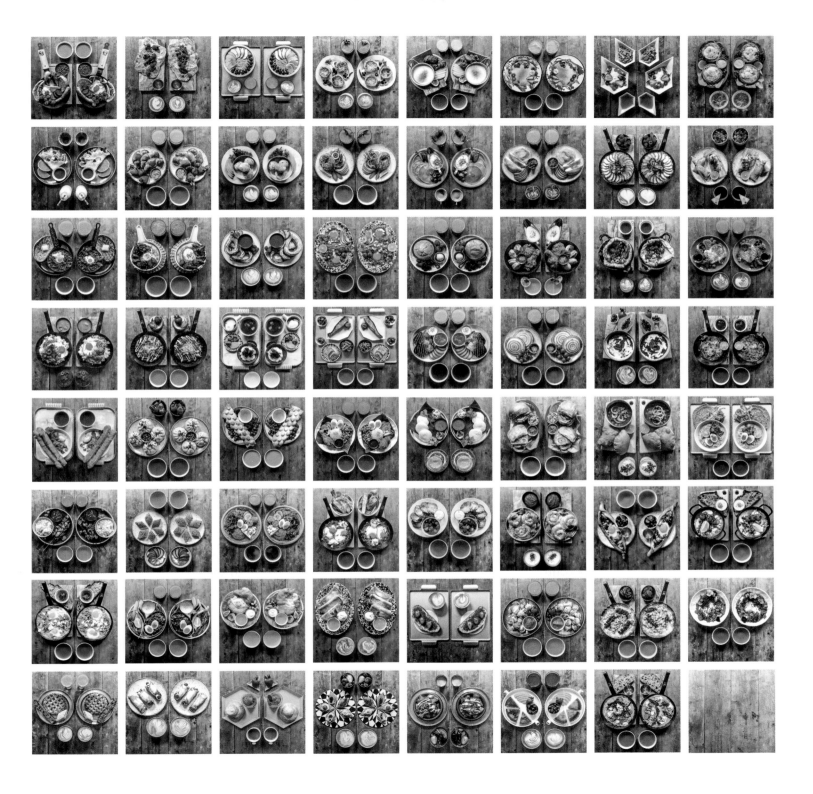

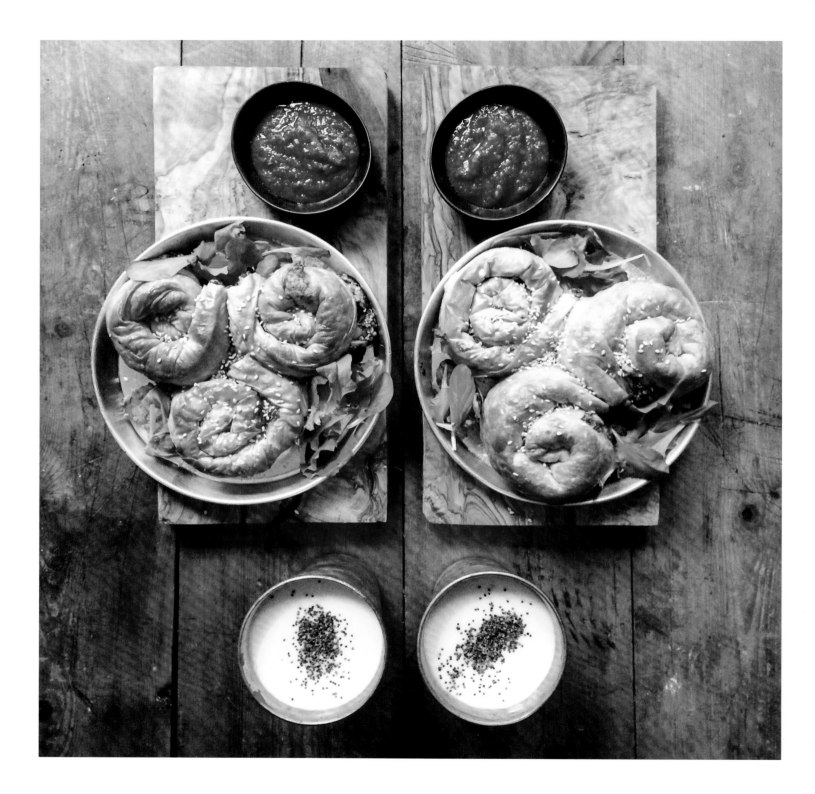

In 2012, on our first holiday together, Mark and I went to Venice and worked our way round the coast to Croatia to see my old flatmate, Daniela. Whilst waiting for a boat to take us to the island of Cres, we had a walk around the small yet chic city of Rijeka.

Near the main port is the Velika Tržnica, also known as "the Belly of the City." We had stayed in a small hostel the night before and were out in search of breakfast.

They came in all shapes and sizes. Sweet and savory fillings. Sleep–inducing carb–fest or light as a feather. Burek is a spiral of flaky pastry filled with pure buttery pleasure.

Filo pastry is an art and requires a calm disposition to make well. Unless you've done it before and are happy with the process, I don't expect anyone to make their own, given the quality of shop–bought filo.

BUREK FILLED PASTRIES FROM THE OTTOMAN EMPIRE

Serves 3, though possibly only 2 ½

2 cups spinach
2 cups feta
1½ cups cottage cheese, drained
Zest of 1 lemon
1 egg
Salt to taste
1 packet filo pastry – you'll need about 6 sheets
1½ stick butter, melted
Sesame seeds and poppy seeds to decorate

Preheat your oven to 400°F and prepare a baking tray with parchment.

In a food processor, blitz your spinach until finely chopped. Decant into a large bowl. Crumble the feta into the spinach along with the cottage cheese, lemon zest, egg, and salt.

Prepare some damp tea towels to cover your filo as you work.

Place a single sheet like a landscape painting in front of you. Brush lightly with butter. Apply ⅙ of the spinach mix across the bottom half – it won't look like much. Roll from the bottom away from yourself until you have a long sausage.

Roll the sausage into a spiral, but not too tightly, otherwise the pastry will tear. Place on a baking tray and brush liberally with melted butter. You could keep adding to the spiral to make a giant burek, but only if you're a massive show-off.

Bake for 25 minutes until golden brown. Sprinkle with sesame or poppy seeds and serve with drinking yogurt or salty ayran (see page 174).

This salty and sometimes sour yogurt drink from Turkey is refreshingly drinkable when summer is unbearably hot. It might seem strange that a salty drink would quench your thirst, but that's exactly what it does.

It pairs deliciously well with barbecued meats and fish, and in particular all types of burek (see page 173).

For maximum flavor, in this recipe I use sea salt rather than free-flowing table salt. My personal favorite is from Halen Môn Sea Salt Company from Anglesey in Wales. They also produce a sea salt with vanilla that is out of this world and particularly good sprinkled on hot chocolate.

AYRAN SALTED YOGURT DRINK

½ tsp or a big pinch of sea salt
1 cup ice–cold water
1 cup thick yogurt
Fresh mint leaves
Poppy seeds

In a jug, dissolve the salt in the ice–cold water and add the yogurt. Stir well and taste for saltiness.

Pour into tall glasses and garnish with mint leaves or poppy seeds

My friend John Gregory–Smith @johngs is something of an expert when it comes to Turkish cuisine. One evening he took me to Antepliler on Green Lanes in north London for the best pide that the capital can offer. Dare I say it, it's better than pizza.

In Turkey, every home, village, and region has their favored techniques and toppings for pide. Surprisingly, the dough takes only 30 minutes to prove, making it a serious candidate for a good weekend breakfast. Add any topping you like, crack in an egg halfway through, and then brush liberally with melted butter.

It's also a good contender for curing the worst hangover.

PIDE TURKISH PIZZA

Makes 4 pide

1 tsp dried yeast
1 tsp sugar
2½ cups strong bread flour or 00 flour (typically used for pasta)
1 tsp salt
1 tbsp olive oil
½ cup cold water
1 stick butter, melted

In a jug, combine the yeast, sugar, and a few tablespoons of warm water. Leave to sit for 10 minutes.

In a large bowl, combine the flour, salt, and olive oil. Add the yeast mix and work everything together with your hands, slowly adding the water until you have a ball. You may not need all the water.

Tip the dough out on to a lightly floured work surface and knead it for 5 minutes until smooth.

Oil the bowl and the dough and leave covered for 30 minutes.

Now prepare your fillings.

For the spinach filling, finely dice a medium onion and fry gently in a pan with olive oil, 1 tsp cumin and 1 tsp caraway seeds for 10 minutes. Add 7 oz spinach leaf and wilt for a few minutes. Take off the heat.

For the lamb filling, put a good glug of olive

(continued on following page)

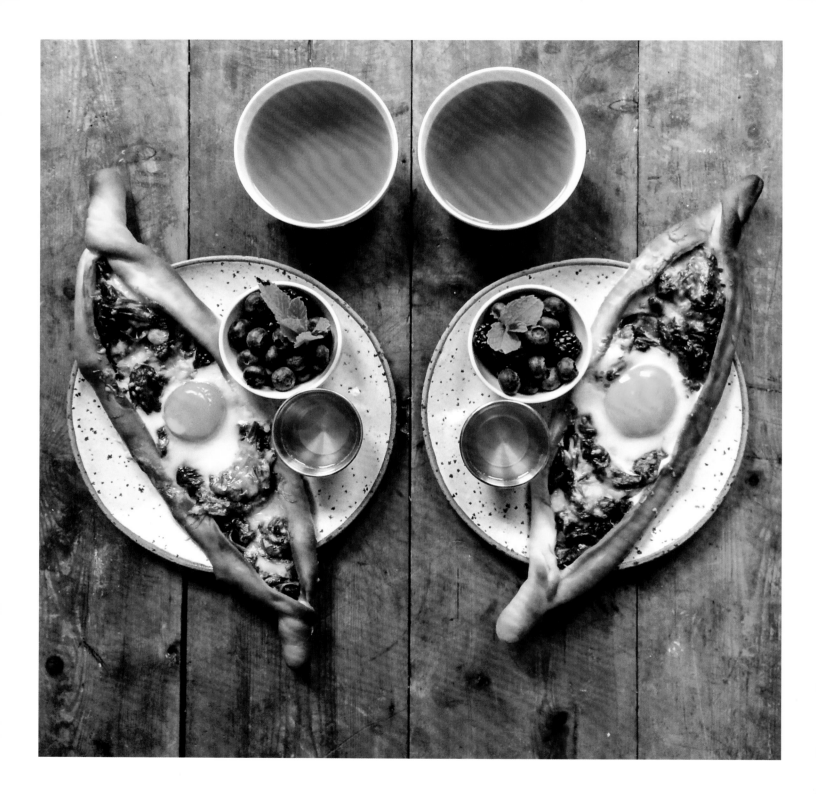

Filling Suggestions

Spinach with cumin, caraway, and a salty cheese like Beyaz peynir or feta, and an egg

Minced lamb with garlic, yogurt, pomegranate, and fresh mint

Turkish beef pastrami, called Pastırma, with cheese and egg

oil into a frying pan and add 1 tsp cumin, 1 tsp ground coriander, 1 minced garlic clove and ½ tsp chili powder. Cook for 3 minutes on medium heat so your spices are really pungent. Add ½ lb lamb mince, 1 tsp fresh thyme, the zest of 1 lemon, and season with salt and pepper. Cook for 15 minutes and take off the heat.

For the Pastırma filling, simply grate your cheese of choice and roughly chop the Pastırma.

To assemble the pide, preheat your oven to 400°F and line a baking tray with parchment.

Place the dough on a floured surface and knead it again for 20 seconds. Cut the dough into 2 equal pieces. At this point you could freeze half and use the other piece to make two far more sensibly sized pide, but in for a penny in for a pound.

Roll each half into a long boat, around 16 in long and 4¾ in wide. Poke it all over with a fork and transfer it carefully to the baking tray. Repeat with the second half.

Add your fillings, leaving a ¾ in border around the edge. I like to fold the edge over, but you could also crimp it with your thumb and finger to create a raised border. Twist the ends of the pide to a point so that the whole thing resembles a boat shape.

Bake in the oven for 12–15 minutes until golden brown. Brush with plenty of melted butter and serve.

For the spinach filling, I layer the spinach first, top with cheese, and add an egg halfway through the cooking time.

For the lamb, I dot a few teaspoons of yogurt over the lamb and add the pomegranate and fresh mint after it has finished cooking.

For the Pastırma, I just use the cheese on its own for the first half of cooking and add the Pastırma and egg halfway through.

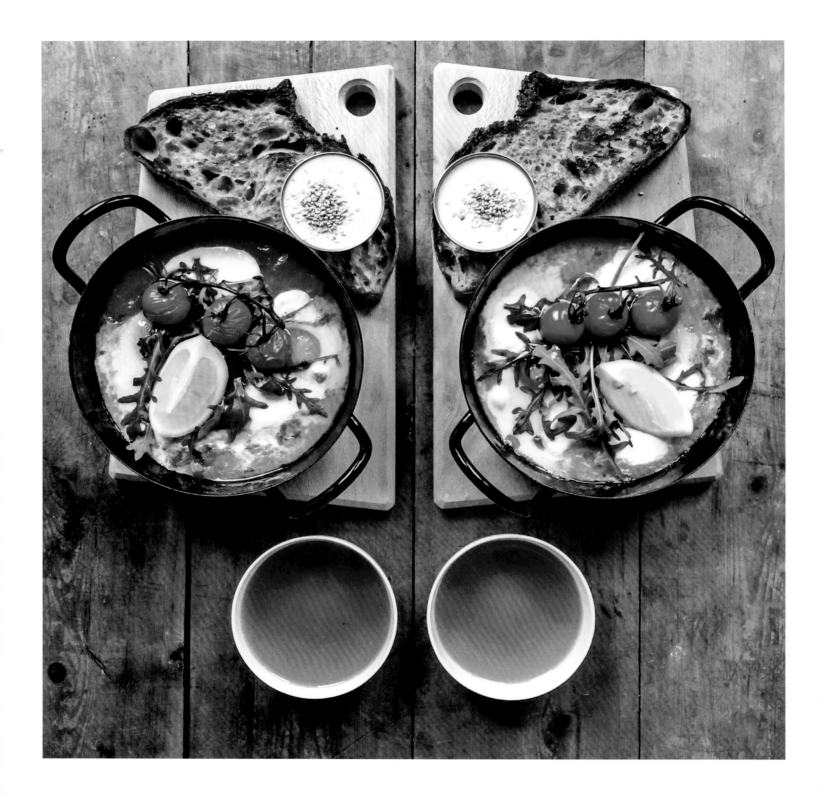

Created by Tunisian Jews, shakshuka has made its way on to the menus of many of London's cafés and restaurants. Some of my favorites are served in Ottolenghi's Nopi and The Good Egg, a little place in north London.

The simplest of dishes really, eggs cooked in a tomato sauce is also sometimes the easiest recipe to get wrong. The flavors should be rich and nuanced, not watery and acidic. This is largely down to the tomatoes you use. My advice is to avoid "salad tomatoes," which are devoid of flavor.

Much like a good bolognese, this is always much better the day after. With that in mind, I make the tomato sauce in advance, meaning that when it comes to Saturday morning, a delicious hot pan of shakshuka is as quick and easy as breaking some eggs.

The tomato sauce will sit happily in the fridge for 3 days.

SHAKSHUKA BAKED EGGS IN TOMATO

For the Tomato Sauce
6 fresh ripe tomatoes
1 onion
2 red peppers
3 tbsp olive oil
2 garlic cloves, minced
2 tsp berbere spice
   (optional; see page 164)
2 cups/13.6 oz can plum
   tomatoes
2 tsp tomato purée

For Serving
4 eggs
3 tbsp tahini
Lemon juice
1 garlic clove, minced
Pinch of salt
Labneh or thick Greek
   yogurt
Fresh parsley
Crusty bread

To make the tomato sauce, cut a cross into the bottom of the fresh tomatoes and submerge in a bowl of freshly boiled water. Leave for 1 minute, drain, and peel the skins off. Roughly chop and set aside. Finely chop the onion and de–seed, then slice the red peppers.

In a pan with a suitable lid, on a medium heat, gently fry the onions and pepper in the olive oil until soft, then add the garlic. Make sure your heat isn't too high – burnt garlic is gross. Add the berbere spice and cook for 5 minutes.

Add the tinned and fresh tomatoes and the tomato purée, then gently simmer for 45 minutes with the lid on. Stir every 10 minutes.

Season to taste, leave to cool completely, and refrigerate.

The morning you want to eat shakshuka, warm the sauce in a frying pan or skillet (individual or sharing). Once it is hot, make indents with a spoon and crack an egg into each. Cover with a lid and cook on a medium heat for 5 minutes. The white of the egg should be just set with a runny yolk.

In a small bowl, mix the tahini with the same amount of cold water and whisk. It will loosen in consistency and become lighter in color. Season with lemon juice, garlic, and, salt to taste.

Serve with dollops of labneh or yogurt, chopped parsley, plenty of crusty bread, and lashings of tahini.

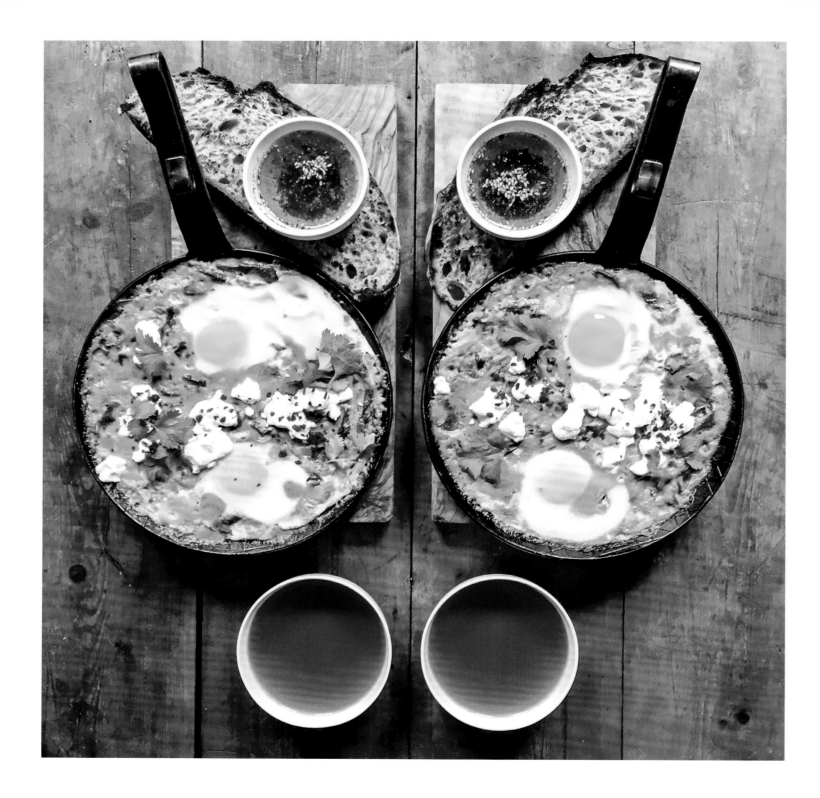

You may already be familiar with shakshuka, the dish of eggs cooked in a rich tomato sauce. If not, then don't worry, there's a recipe on page 179.

But green, you say? Yes, green! Other than having a salad at breakfast, how can you cram a lot of vegetables into your diet without having a dreaded green juice? It's also a wonderful and thrifty way to use up any leafy vegetables that might be on the turn in the fridge.

Packed with herbs, greens, and a hidden surprise underneath the eggs, this is the answer. With an earthy sweetness and mellow, spicy kick that truly wakes you up in the morning, it might just convince you to change sides.

You'll need a hand or standing blender and a shallow ovenproof dish or skillet.

GREEN SHAKSHUKA EGGS BAKED IN GREENS

1½ cup frozen peas
¾ cup trimmed green beans
Salt
¼ cup oil
1 tsp caraway seed
1 tsp cayenne or hot chili powder
½ tsp nutmeg
1 leek, finely sliced
1 cup kale or spinach
Juice of 1 lemon
¼ cup fresh mint
½ cup hummus – shop-bought is absolutely fine
4 eggs
½ cup feta or goat's cheese (optional)

To serve
Olive oil
Za'atar
Toast
Pul biber or chili flakes

Add the peas and green beans to a bowl of boiling water with some salt. You don't want to cook them too much, just defrost them.

Heat a frying pan over a medium heat, put in the oil and caraway seed, cayenne, nutmeg, and a pinch of salt, then cook for 1–2 minutes. Add the sliced leek and continue to cook for a further 5 minutes or until soft.

Preheat your oven to 400°F.

Add the kale or spinach and cover with a lid for 2–3 minutes so that it wilts. Drain the peas and beans and add them to the blender. Add the lemon juice and fresh mint. Blitz until smooth. Put this back in the pan with the rest of the mix and stir well. It needs to be almost like a thick soup. Adjust with water if it is too thick.

Smear the hummus on the bottom of your ovenproof serving dish or skillet in a thin layer. Spoon in the green mix – it should look like a swamp or lagoon. Crack in the eggs, cover with a piece of aluminium foil and bake in the oven for 15–20 minutes until the eggs are set.

Crumble feta and chili flakes over the eggs and serve with a small side dish of olive oil with za'atar and toasted bread.

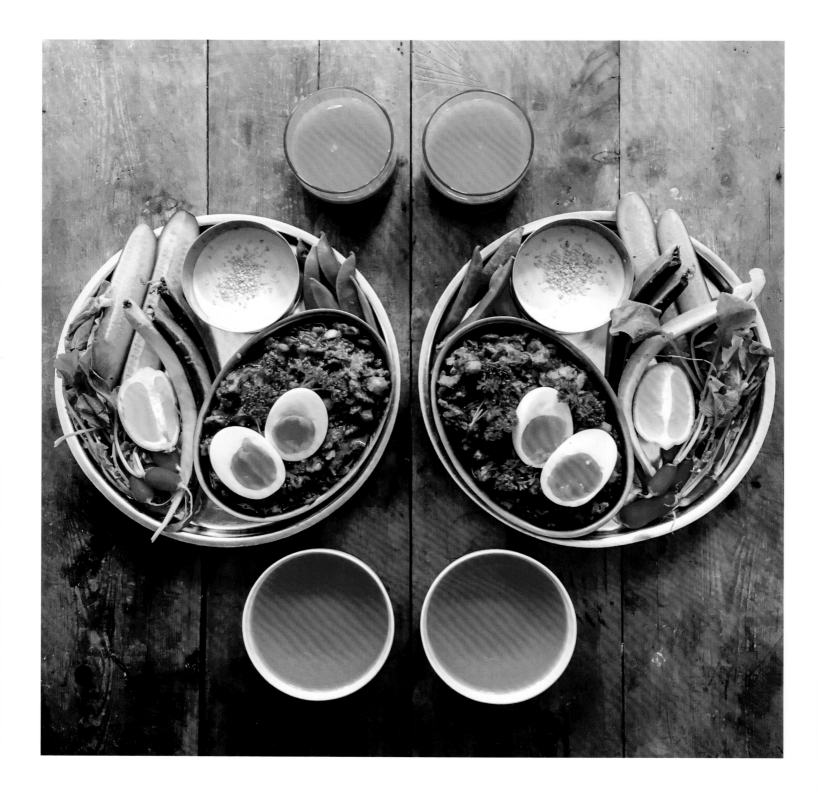

Ful medames ticks a lot of boxes. It's filling but not heavy, cheap as chips, easy to make, exotic, and, most importantly, Mark says it's delicious.

You can serve it as a breakfast dish, but in Egypt, where it is most popular, you will find it on the table at lunch and dinner too. Serve it with some fresh or pickled vegetables like carrot, onion, or turnip, or, if you can't find any, then add some white wine or cider vinegar to the dressed herbs for a bit of bite.

Tinned broad beans in the UK are most often the green variety, which means they are fresh and have never been dried. These can be eaten raw in a salad but, whilst they're not bad, they're not what you're after for this recipe. I personally recommend the dried variety. With cooking, they gently break down, giving thickness and body to the dish; they're happy to sit in the cupboard for a very long time; they're cheaper ounce for ounce compared to tinned; and they absorb the flavors of whatever you combine them with.

Start by soaking 1⅓ cup dried beans in water with ½ tsp baking soda overnight. The next day boil them in fresh water for 45 minutes or until tender. You could soak even more and freeze the rest once they are cooked to save time should you wish to cook this again.

1⅓ cup dried broad or fava beans
½ tsp baking soda
1 tin chickpeas
2–3 cloves garlic, minced
1 small red onion, diced
Juice of 2 lemons
4 tomatoes, chopped
½ tsp cumin
½ tsp turmeric
1 cup olive oil
2 tbsp tahini
Pinch of salt
¼ cup fresh parsley, basil, cilantro
1 scallion
3–4 radishes
2 tsp white wine or cider vinegar (optional)
2 hard–boiled eggs (optional)

FUL MEDAMES EGYPTIAN BEANS

Soak the broad beans overnight with ½ tsp of baking soda. Boil in fresh water for 45 minutes and drain again. Add the chickpeas (you can save the chickpea water and use it as an egg–white substitute called Aquafaba) and put them in a pan with 1 cup water over a medium heat. Cook for 10 minutes whilst stirring.

Add the garlic and onion with half the lemon juice, 2 of the chopped tomatoes, the cumin and turmeric. Continue to cook for another 10 minutes.

Using a wooden spoon or masher, give the beans a good mush to help thicken the mix. Add half of the olive oil and taste for seasoning.

Take off the heat and leave for 5 minutes whilst you get on with the rest.

In a small cup, mix the tahini with about ¼ cup ice–cold water and stir. It will loosen in thickness and turn lighter in color. Add salt and a dash of the remaining lemon juice for flavor.

Roughly chop the herbs, scallion, the remaining 2 tomatoes, and the radishes and place in a bowl. Dress with the tahini mix, remaining olive oil, and a dash of vinegar, if using.

To serve, place two full ladles of the beans in a bowl and top with a generous amount of the tahini, sliced hard–boiled eggs, an extra drizzle of olive oil, and pickled or fresh vegetables.

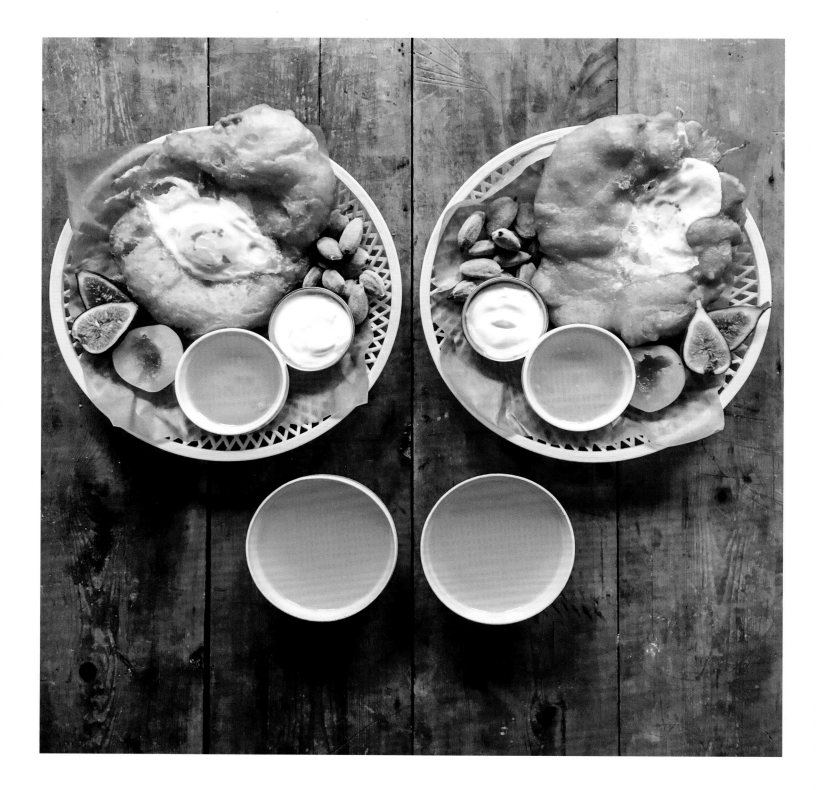

Sfinz, from Libya, is where doughnut meets deep–fried pizza. Compared to your average doughnut, they're huge. They don't have a hole in the middle and they're eaten only on a Friday (probably not such a bad thing, considering my waistline right now).

Libyans also have these along with green tea, which is the perfect combination to complement their delicate and fluffy white interior.

Despite the Friday rule, I would be tempted to make these a weekend treat and that's because they take a good 3 hours, if not more, to make from start to finish, and even I don't fancy getting up that early!

Serve either savory with a fried egg or sweet with date molasses, honey, and qashta cream (also known as Puck Cream – it's a cream cheese that comes in a tin and is available in some supermarkets and Middle Eastern shops).

SFINZ LIBYAN DOUGHNUTS

Makes 4 sfinz

1 tsp dried yeast, or 2 tsp
   fresh yeast
2 tbsp superfine sugar
1 cup warm water
2 cups bread flour
1 tsp salt
1 tsp baking powder
2 tbsp olive oil
1 cup milk
Oil for deep frying

In a small bowl, mix the yeast and sugar in ¼ cup of the warm water and leave until it starts to bubble.

Mix all the dry ingredients together in a large bowl and add the yeast mixture. Then add the olive oil, the remaining water, and the milk. The dough will be very sticky, so oil your hands and knead it together for 5 minutes. Scrape down the sides and shape the dough into a ball. Leave it covered to rise in a warm place for an hour or until it has doubled in size.

When it has risen, knead the dough again for a minute and leave for a further 30 minutes to rise a second time.

Brush a large baking tray with oil. Divide the dough roughly into 6 pieces and shape each into a ball. Place on the oiled tray and leave for 15 minutes covered in cling film.

Preheat your oil – you want it hot so it sizzles.

Using an oiled plate, take one ball of dough and flatten it out – the edges should be thicker than the center, much like a pizza.

Put the dough into the hot oil. Once it floats, flip it over to cook the other side. If you are adding an egg, crack it into the middle of the sfinz and, using a spoon, gently submerge the sfinz so that it cooks evenly.

Drain on kitchen paper, keep warm, and repeat with the other sfinzes. It is best to roll each sfinz like a wrap and enjoy them hot.

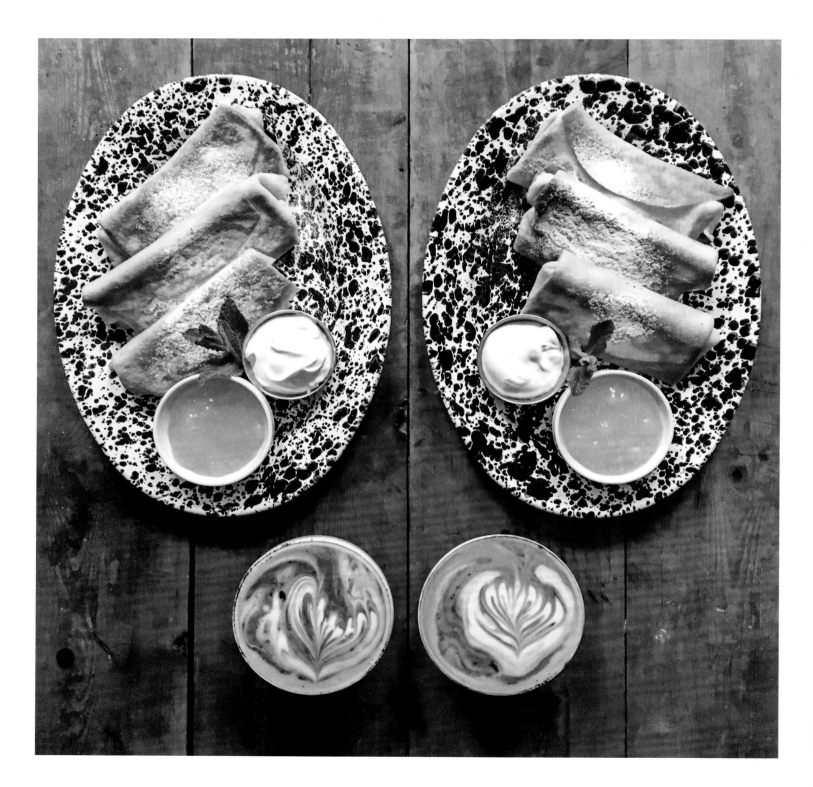

"A moltsayt on a
tsimes iz vi a mayze
on a moshl."

"A meal without a
sweet dish is like a
story without
a moral."

—**Yiddish proverb**

One of the cornerstones of Ashkenazic Jewish cooking, this blintzes recipe is an adaptation from the seminal and irrepressible book *Love and Knishes* by Sara Kasdan, which has come to me via my friend @felicityspector.

Blintzes are super–soft crêpes, filled with a cheesecake–like filling, folded and fried. The original recipe asks for "dry cottage cheese," which I was unable to find, or at least I couldn't work out if it was just regular cottage cheese found in the UK with some of the liquid drained off or something more exotic. Either way, with standard ricotta these make a delectable dessert as well as a delicious breakfast.

This is seriously comforting food, and particularly appetizing with sour cream and apple sauce.

BLINTZES FILLED JEWISH PANCAKES

For the Crepes
1 cup plain flour
1 cup sparkling water or
  seltzer
4 eggs
½ stick butter, melted
Pinch of salt
¼ cup boiling water

For the Filling
½ lb ricotta cheese
¾ cup powdered sugar
1 tsp vanilla extract
1 egg yolk

For Serving
½ stick butter
Apple sauce
Sour cream

In a large bowl, whisk together the flour and sparkling water, then add the eggs one at a time, followed by the melted butter and salt. Leave to rest for 10 minutes.

In a separate bowl, mix together all the ingredients for the filling and return it to the fridge for 30 minutes to firm up.

Add the boiling water to the pancake batter and whisk thoroughly. The boiling water helps the blintzes keep their softness and pliability later when rolling.

Preheat a non–stick pan and pour in enough batter to cover the surface.

Cook the blintz until it is just done but not browned. It is also important not to flip it. Remove and stack the pancakes on a plate.

Repeat until all the batter is gone. This can be done a few hours in advance of assembling the next stage.

To fill, take each blintz and place 2 heaped teaspoons of the filling roughly at the six o'clock position. Smush it down a bit with the back of the spoon. Fold in the left and right sides of the blintz to near the center and, from the bottom, roll it all the way to the top. It should resemble a spring roll or a burrito.

Preheat the pan again on a low heat and add the butter. Once it has melted, turn up the heat to medium and put in the filled, rolled–up blintzes. Fry them on each side for 4–5 minutes until golden brown.

Serve immediately with warm apple sauce and sour cream.

11 NOT QUITE CONTINENTAL
NORWAY, ITALY, AUSTRIA, ALGERIA, SPAIN, THE NETHERLANDS, DENMARK

Scandinavian flavors come loaded with seeds and grains, whether a crispbread or a bowl of leftover rye porridge, but the Scandi breakfast would be lost without a glass of aquavit or Gammel Dansk at 8 a.m.

Italians are masters of the light breakfast, saving their bellies for lunch. The great savior is the island of Sicily, where mornings are so ferociously hot in the summer that granita is necessary to cool you down.

Across the Mediterranean in Algeria, breakfast is simpler still: m'shewsha is an eggy honey pancake that is faintly similar to a custard tart but without the crust.

My personal favorite, and I am most certainly biased in this judgement and make no apologies, is the Netherlands. They eat chocolate on bread (!) and it's not just the children who are addicted to it.

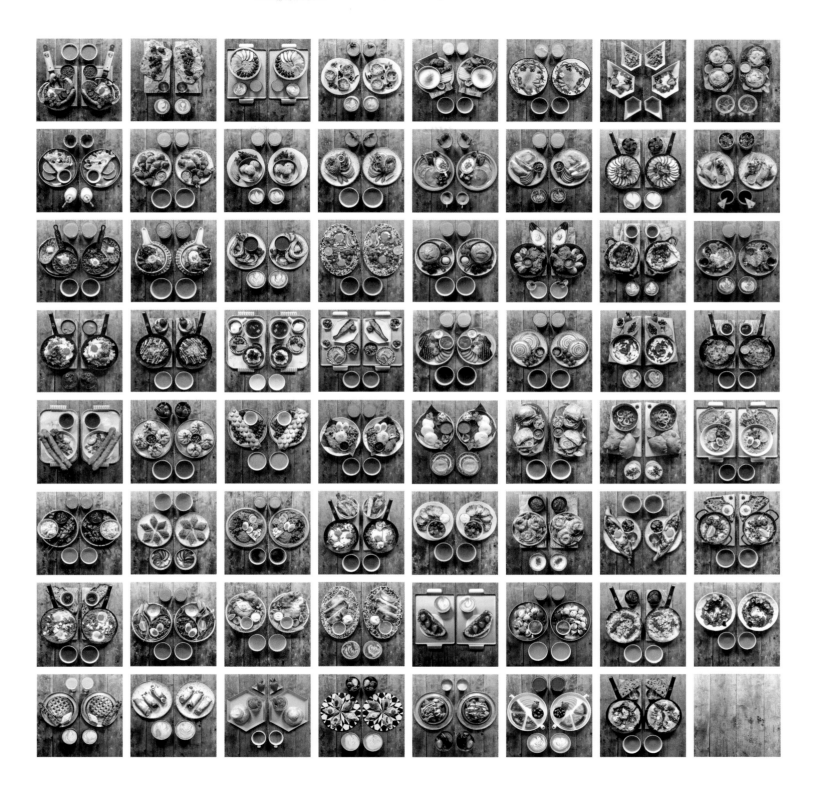

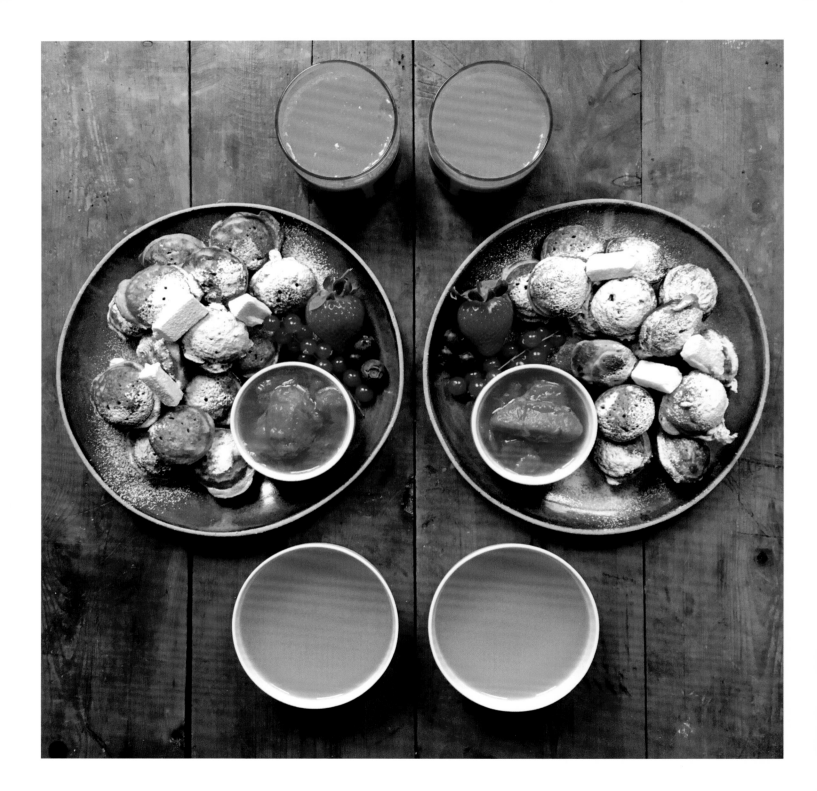

In the Netherlands these sweet little pancakes are not on the menu at breakfast. But that doesn't mean they shouldn't be. I often and gleefully inhale them by the dozen straight from the pan, served with soft salty butter and plenty of powdered sugar.

After several ruined poffertjes pans (all non-stick), I finally invested in one made of cast iron and I would advise you to do the same. The first batch is always the cook's treat, but with some practice you'll be popping perfect poffertjes every time.

You'll also need a squirty plastic bottle (a cleaned-out ketchup bottle is perfect) and a funnel for this recipe, as it makes the whole process much quicker and cleaner!

POFFERTJES DUTCH PANCAKES

Makes 30 poffertjes, although it's never enough

2 cups milk
1 tsp dried yeast
2 cups buckwheat flour
1 cup plain flour
Pinch of salt
1 egg
Oil for frying

Warm the milk in a pan or microwave for a minute. Add the yeast, give it a stir, and leave for 5 minutes to dissolve and start bubbling.

Mix the buckwheat, plain flour, and salt in a bowl and pour in the yeasty milk. Crack in the egg and use a whisk to combine everything until smooth.

Cover the bowl with a tea towel and leave in a warm place for 45 minutes. It will start to bubble and increase in size like a loaf of bread.

Using a funnel, pour the mix into your plastic bottle.

Gently preheat your pan until it is hot and brush each of the indents liberally with oil. I fill the outer ring first and wait 30 seconds before filling the inner; this is to give enough time to flip the outer without the inner overcooking.

Using a kebab skewer or cocktail stick, loosen the edge of each pancake and flip. This will take some practice but gets easier, I promise.

Serve with butter, powdered sugar, and some of my Earl Grey and plum compote (see page 10).

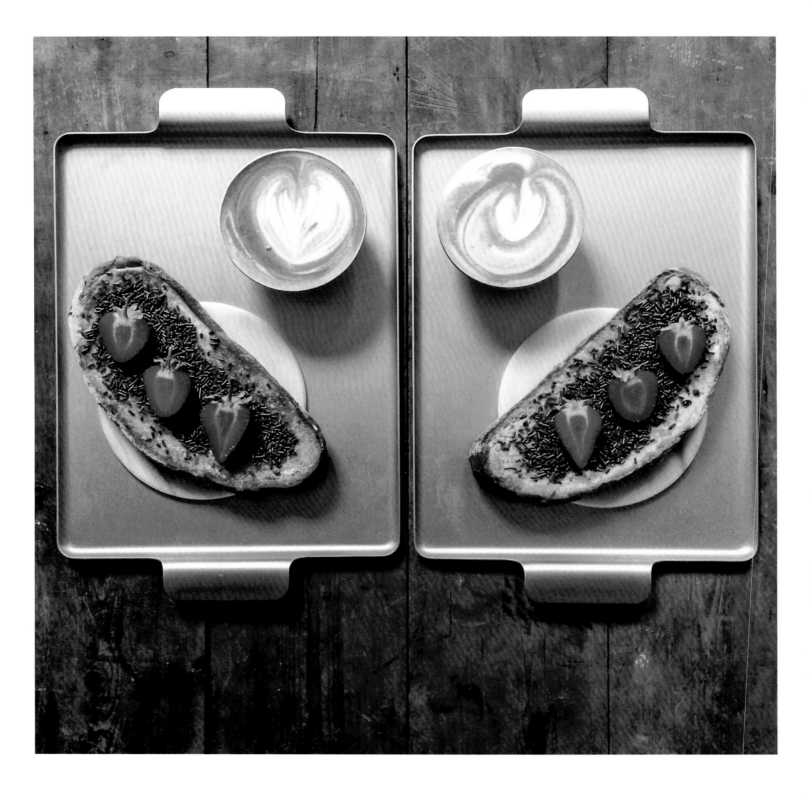

The true secret of the happiest people in the world starts at breakfast and it's not avocado on toast.

When I met Mark it wasn't just love at first sight, but love at first bite. Dutch cuisine is one of my favorites (and one of the most unappreciated), and when I think of Dutch food I instantly think of fabulous Old Master paintings in museums: a grandiose spread of cheese, ham, and maybe a dead pheasant in the corner.

ONTBIJT A DUTCH BREAKFAST

Today you'll find that breakfast in the Netherlands is probably chocolate sprinkles, or hagelslag, on buttered bread. (Although I have added a recipe for poffertjes, small puffy pancakes, in this book, these days it is really more street food than breakfast.) I prefer my bread toasted and my butter salted, but it's important not to deviate too far from its perfect simplicity.

This is not a recipe, but an exercise in true happiness. Toast your bread and butter generously whilst it is still hot. Sprinkle with a thick layer of hagelslag (the De Ruijter brand is the best) and eat immediately. Make sure you have a plate under your chin, otherwise you'll make a mess.

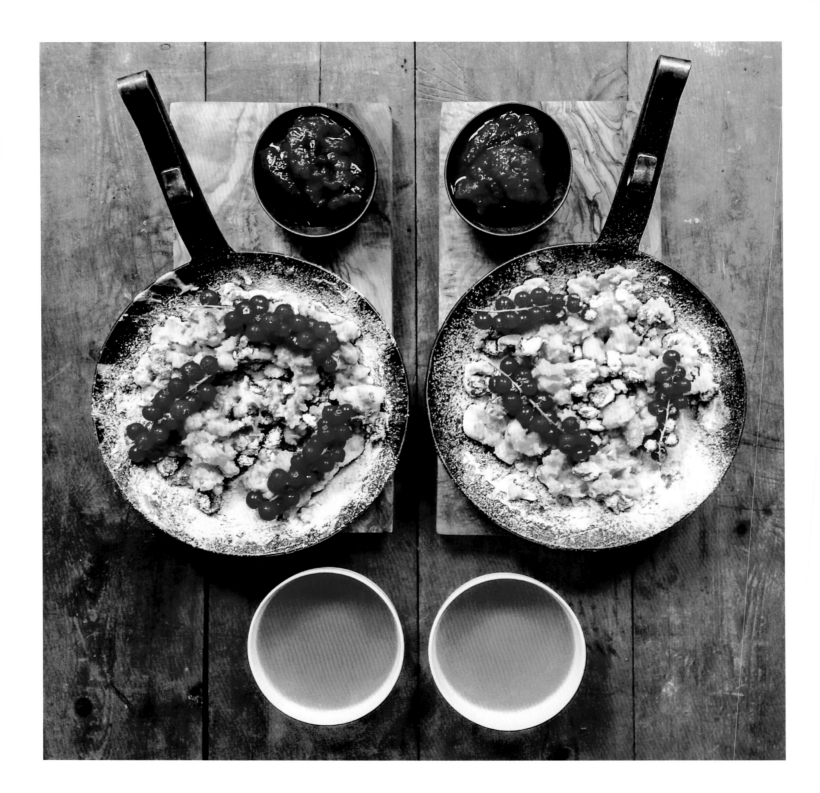

I first tried the favorite pancakes of Kaiser Franz Josef I of Austria, also known as "the Emperor's Mess," after an Austrian friend came to stay and kindly left us with a goodie bag of treats. One item was a ready–mix of Dr. Oetker Kaiserschmarrn.

I have no shame in using packets of ready–mix (butterscotch Angel Delight being one of the great pinnacles of 20th–century gastronomy) but, sadly, the doctor does not deliver his Kaiserschmarrn to London – so I learned to make my own.

The light, fluffy blobs of shredded pancake, with an alpine avalanche of powdered sugar on top, is perfect for that person who can't help but make a mess in the kitchen. My version, made completely from scratch, uses ghee in order to produce the best crispy bits.

KAISERSCHMARRN THE KAISER'S FAVORITE PANCAKES

4 eggs
1 cup flour
Pinch of salt
2 tbsp superfine sugar
1 tsp vanilla extract
Zest of 1 lemon
1 cup milk
⅓ cup raisins
½ stick ghee or butter
Powdered sugar (lots)

Separate the eggs and place the yolks in a bowl with the flour, salt, sugar, vanilla, lemon zest, milk, and raisins, and mix into a batter.

In a separate clean bowl, whisk the egg whites into soft peaks and gently fold them into the batter.

Using a frying pan approx. 1 foot across, warm the ghee until melted. Pour the batter in and leave to cook on a medium heat, untouched, for about 5 minutes.

Using two spoons, rip the pancake apart into small, bite–sized chunks. Continue to cook for a further 3–5 minutes, turning the pieces to crisp the torn edges.

Serve with absolutely loads of powdered sugar and your favorite jam.

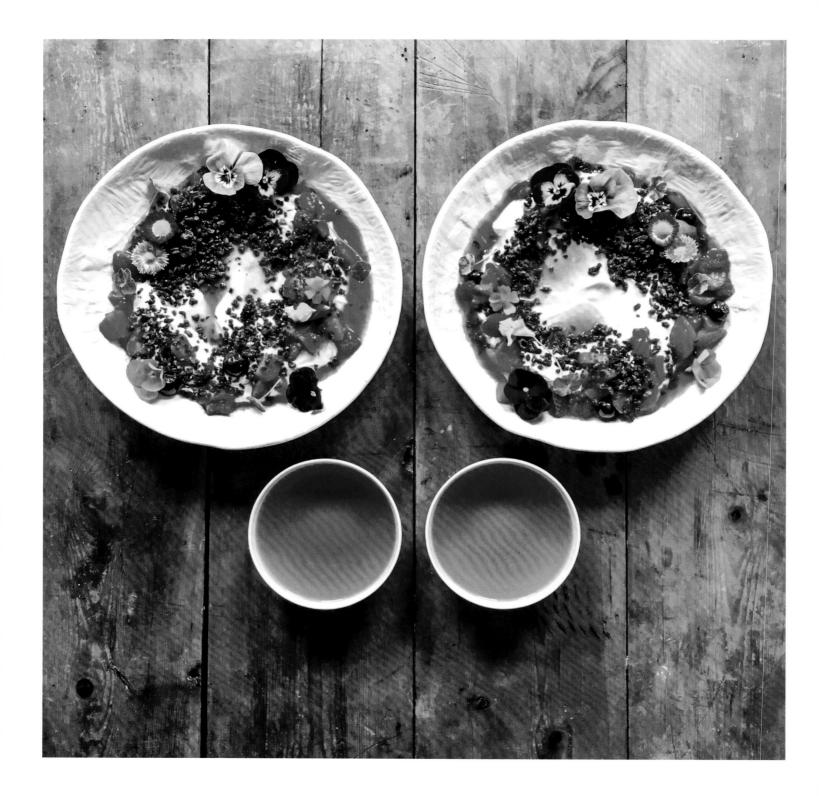

This recipe tells me a lot about Denmark – a tiny country, overflowing with so much rye bread that they can't finish it all. Those silly Danes. They're always trying to explain the concept of hygge to me, whilst I try to explain the meaning of the word please . . .

A very thrifty solution to the excess of rye is to pop it into a food processor, blitz it into a crumb called drys and eat it with ymer, a type of sour yogurt, and fresh fruit.

The second bake in this recipe is key to bringing out the natural sweetness of the rye, but I do like to add some brown sugar too. Feel free to experiment as well. I've added orange peel, honey, nuts – all with varying success. This recipe is for the pure, unadulterated variety.

YMERDRYS DANISH RYE BREAD WITH YOGURT

3 cups dark rye bread (or whatever you have left over)
2 tsp brown sugar
2 cups ymer or yogurt
2½ cups mixed soft berries

Preheat your oven to 350°F.

Tear the rye bread into chunks and put it in a food processor along with the sugar and any other flavorings you've decided on. Blitz until it resembles rubble.

Spread evenly over some baking paper on a baking tray. Bake for 15 minutes but give it a jiggle at around 7 minutes, for even cooking, then check again at 10 minutes.

Remove from the oven and allow to cool slightly. I like mine still a bit warm. Serve with yogurt and fruit.

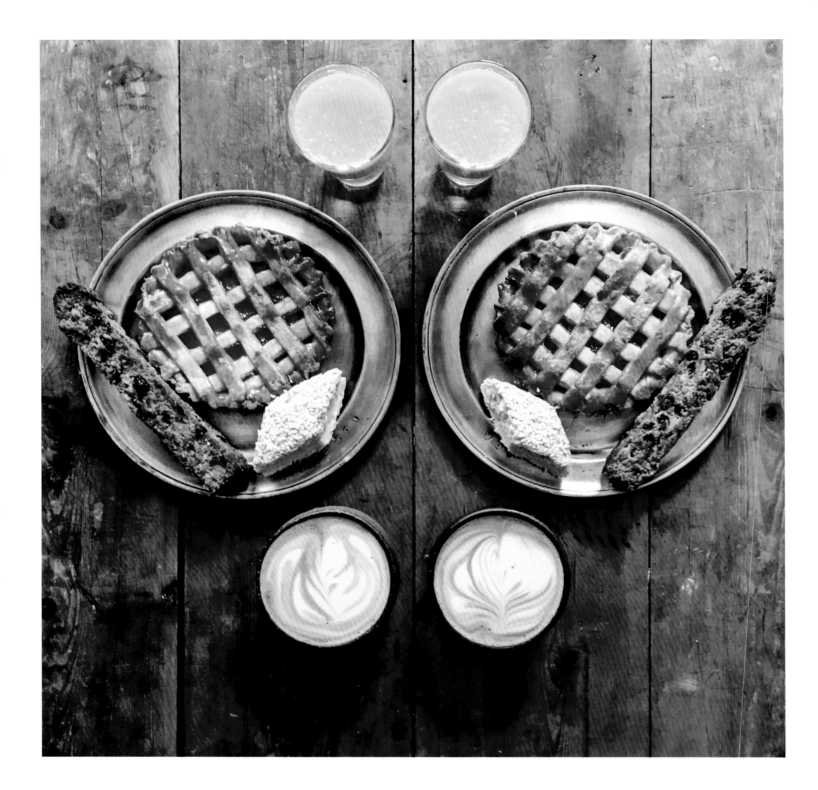

In Italy, it's not uncommon to have a slice of cake or some cookies with coffee for breakfast; those who are smart save themselves for lunch.

From region to region the selection is incredibly diverse. Whole supermarket aisles are dedicated to biscotti, merende, torte, and dolcetti. Compared to the UK or the US, a few cookies and an espresso can seem a very meagre breakfast indeed, especially when it's out of a bag.

PRIMA COLAZIONE BREAKFAST IN ITALY

Surprisingly, however, in the early days of SymmetryBreakfast, I gained a fan in South Carolina – Gretchen Honeysett Lambert of @nunziataspizzelles, an architect–turned–baker. A few messages were exchanged and, a few weeks later, all the way from South Carolina, a large, carefully wrapped box of biscotti arrived, both traditional and flavors of her own invention. The contents were gone in a matter of minutes. I needed more, but South Carolina is a little too far to go, even for something that delicious. A tricky situation indeed.

The only solution was to make my own. Here are two recipes as recommended by Gretchen – giugiuleni and Marsala biscotti – plus one of my favorites, albicocca crostata (apricot tart). This can be found in bars and cafés the length of Italy. Almost absurdly, it's probably the most substantial item to appear on the menu before midday. The recipe is surprisingly simple and, if you fancy a real Italian experience, swap the apricot for Nutella.

A top tip is to pop your bowl into the fridge about an hour before starting to cook and to handle the dough as little as possible.

(continued on following page)

For the Giugiuleni

Makes between 24 and 36, depending how big you make them

2½ stick butter, softened
½ cup superfine sugar
1 egg
2 tsp anise extract, available in specialist shops or online
1 cup milk
3 cups plain flour
½ cup potato starch
½ tsp baking powder
Pinch of salt
½ cup sesame seeds

For the Marsala Biscotti

Makes between 24 and 36, depending how thickly you slice them

1½ cups currants
1 cup Marsala wine
½ stick butter
1½ cup superfine sugar, plus extra for sprinkling
2 eggs
4 cups plain flour
2 tsp baking powder
½ tsp salt

To make the giugiuleni, preheat your oven to 350°F and line a baking tray with parchment.

Cream together the butter and sugar. Add the egg and anise extract and combine thoroughly.

Whisk in the milk, then gradually add the flour, potato starch, baking powder, and salt until you have a soft dough.

Spread the dough out on the baking tray – you want it at least ¾ in thick. Cover with the sesame seeds and gently press them into the dough.

Bake for 15–20 minutes – the sesame seeds should be golden brown. Remove from the oven and leave to cool for 1–2 minutes before cutting into diamonds and leaving to cool for a further 15 minutes. Transfer to a wire rack. Once completely cold, store in an airtight container.

Biscotti are possibly the most well known of all Italian biscuits. These twice–baked biscotti are flavored with traditional Sicilian Marsala wine. If you can't find any, try using port or dessert wine. They are delicious with a morning espresso or a Fernet Branca on the rocks in the evening.

In a small bowl, soak the currants in the Marsala and leave for 2 hours.

Preheat your oven to 350°F and line a baking tray with parchment.

In a bowl, cream together the butter and

sugar, then add the eggs. Drain the currants but don't throw away the wine. Add the boozy currants to the sugary butter and combine well.

Slowly add the flour, baking powder, salt, and a few tablespoons (probably 3–4) of the Marsala until you have a soft dough.

Divide the dough in half, roll each half into a sausage about 8 in long and then flatten it. Brush with the remaining wine and sprinkle liberally with sugar.

Bake for 20 minutes until golden brown. Remove from the oven and leave to cool for 30 minutes.

Using a sharp knife, cut each of the loaves into ¾ in–thick slices. Lay them out flat in a single layer across a fresh baking tray with new parchment. Bake for a further 15 minutes.

Allow to cool completely and store in an airtight container if not eating immediately.

For the Albicocca Crostata

Makes three individual 5-in tarts or one 9-in tart

1½ sticks cold butter
3 cups 00 flour (typically used for pasta)
1¼ cup powdered sugar
Pinch of salt
Zest of 1 lemon
3 egg yolks, plus 1 whole egg
2 cups apricot jam

To make the albicocca crostata, rub together the butter and flour in a bowl until you have breadcrumbs. Add the powdered sugar, salt, and lemon zest. Add the egg yolks and bring the mix together into a dough.

Form it into a ball and wrap it in cling film. Refrigerate for 45 minutes.

Preheat your oven to 350°F. Remove the dough from the fridge and split it evenly into three. Roll each piece out to fit a 5-in loose–bottomed tart or flan tin. Trim off the excess dough and gather it up into a ball.

Roll it out again and, using a knife, cut it into ¼-in–wide strips. A crimped ravioli cutter creates a very pretty effect.

Pour the apricot jam into the tart and, using the strips, create a lattice over the top.

Beat the whole egg with a tbsp of cold water and brush all over the pastry.

Bake the crostata for 45 minutes, checking at 30, until it is golden brown all over. Remove and leave to cool completely. Serve with a cappuccino.

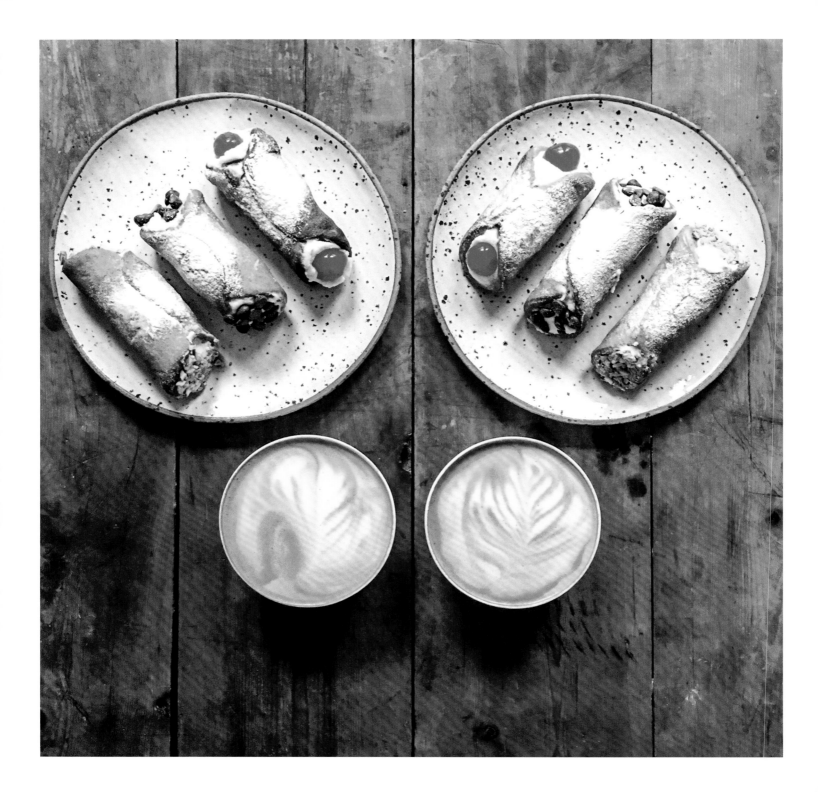

"Leave the gun,
take the cannoli."
—**Peter Clamenza**,
The Godfather, 1972

One of my most memorable holidays with Mark was to the tiny island of Favignana off the west coast of Sicily. I insist that you look it up and, if possible, take a trip.

Ice cream is a key fixture of Sicilian breakfasts (an excuse in itself to go), but in the mornings you might also find a cannoli on the side of your cappuccino. A delicious tube of deep–fried pastry, filled with sweet ricotta and decorated with glacé fruit, it's utterly delicious.

Although small, it's pretty indulgent – but you have to remember why Sicilians, and Italians in general, have such small morning meals. In Italy, lunch is king. If you've got a special lunch date fixed with friends or family, the last thing you want is to fill up at breakfast. This is how Italians live every day. Breakfast is a speedy espresso al banco (whilst standing) with a biscotti and, occasionally, a cannoli – quite literally, *la dolce vita!*

You'll need to invest in some cannoli tubes to make this. I tried to think of a substitute but there really isn't one. I bought mine online very cheaply. A diameter of ¾ in is perfect for this recipe.

Shop–bought ricotta in the UK has too much moisture compared to what is available in Italy. I find straining it using a 20 x 20 in piece of unbleached cheesecloth will mean your cannoli stay crisp longer.

CANNOLI SWEET RICOTTA–STUFFED PASTRY

Makes 12, possibly 10 cannoli

For the Fillings
½ lb ricotta
1 cup powdered sugar
Glacé cherries
¼ cup pistachios, shelled
   and finely chopped
⅓ cup dark chocolate,
   chopped

Put the ricotta into a bowl and break it up with a spoon until it is soft. Put it in the middle of your cheesecloth and bring the corners together and tie securely with string or an elastic band. Give it a good squeeze to get some of the water out. Put the bag in a colander and place that over a bowl. You need to put some pressure on top of the ricotta – I use a pan filled with cans – and leave it for at least an hour.

Remove the ricotta from the bag, place in a bowl and add the icing sugar. Stir well and refrigerate.

In another bowl, combine your flour, ground coffee, salt, powdered sugar, and lard. With your hands, rub the mix until you have breadcrumbs.

Add the Marsala and vinegar. Depending on your flour and the time of year, factors like air pressure and humidity may mean you need another slosh of wine. Combine until you have a dough, then knead for 5 minutes until it is smooth and elastic. Wrap and refrigerate for 30 minutes.

(continued on following page)

For the Cannoli

2½ cups plain flour

1 tsp ground coffee

1 tsp salt

2 tbsp powdered sugar

2 oz lard

2 tbsp Marsala or port (this helps relax the dough, so it's important not to skip!)

2 tbsp cider vinegar

2 quarts peanut or sunflower oil for frying (a very high smoke point is important)

1 egg white

If you have a pasta machine then use it – a uniform thickness will mean the cannoli cook evenly. Otherwise, use a rolling pin.

Remove the dough from the fridge and cut it into four. Roll each quarter on a lightly floured surface until it's 3/4-1 in thick. Using a 5 in cutter, cut circles out of the dough. Pile them up with a dusting of flour between each. Heat about 2 quarts oil in a pan over a high heat until it reaches 375°F.

Whisk the egg white in a small bowl.

Lay the first circle of dough on a clean surface. Place the cannoli tube in the middle and bring one side up over the tube. Brush with some egg white and bring the other side up. Press gently to secure.

Lower the whole cannoli, with the metal tube inside, into the oil and cook for 2–3 minutes until golden brown and with a blistered texture. Remove from the oil and drain on kitchen paper.

Carefully, using a tea towel in one hand and tongs in the other, slide out the metal core and dip it in some cold water. Dry the tube completely and repeat the process until all the dough has been used up.

Once the cannoli have cooled completely, store in an airtight container until you are ready to serve. If you fill them before you are ready to eat, they will go soggy.

Using a teaspoon, fill the cannoli with the ricotta mixture and smooth off the ends. Decorate the ends with either half a glacé cherry, a sprinkle of green pistachio, or pressed into chocolate chips.

Serve immediately with coffee – either cappuccino or espresso.

Catania is an ancient and beautiful city on the east coast of Sicily at the foot of Mount Etna, the tallest active volcano in Europe. Mark and I sat all night with a drink and watched the flashes of lava in the darkness. The impending doom does little to faze the local population. Tomorrow could be your last day on this Earth, so why not enjoy it?

With that in mind, it seems less strange that granita (similar to a sorbet) with a brioche is a common breakfast during hot Sicilian summers, almond and lemon being two of the most popular and refreshing flavors.

So, when I got an email a few years after our visit from Sophia, owner of @nonnasgelato and producer of Italian–inspired gelato on Broadway Market, just a few minutes' walk from where we live in Hackney, I was very excited.

This Sicilian breakfast was enjoyed on the many family trips that Sophia made as a child to visit her nonna, but now it has a British twist with the summer classic strawberries and cream.

"Some serve the granita inside the brioche like a sandwich but I prefer, like many Italians, to dip my deliciously soft brioche in the granita and cream. Paired with a strong espresso there's even more options for dipping!" – Sophia from Nonna's Gelato

GRANITA CON BRIOCHE GRANITA AND BRIOCHE

For the Granita
4 cups strawberries, rinsed and hulled
⅓ cup sugar
1 cup water
1½ tsp fresh lemon juice

To make the granita, cut the strawberries into pieces and combine with the sugar. Leave to stand at room temperature for at least 1 hour but up to 4.

Put a non–reactive shallow metal or glass container in the freezer.

Place the strawberries and water in a blender and purée. Add the lemon juice and strain out all the seeds. This is important for a smooth granita.

Pour the mixture into your container in the freezer. After 30 minutes the mixture will begin to freeze; you need to check and stir every 30 minutes whilst it freezes to break up any ice crystals that form. It should take around 2 hours of scraping and mixing for the granita to be ready to serve.

The granita can be kept in the freezer until you're ready to eat it. Make sure any larger crystals that have formed are broken up before serving, or, alternatively, run the mixture through a blender.

(continued on following page)

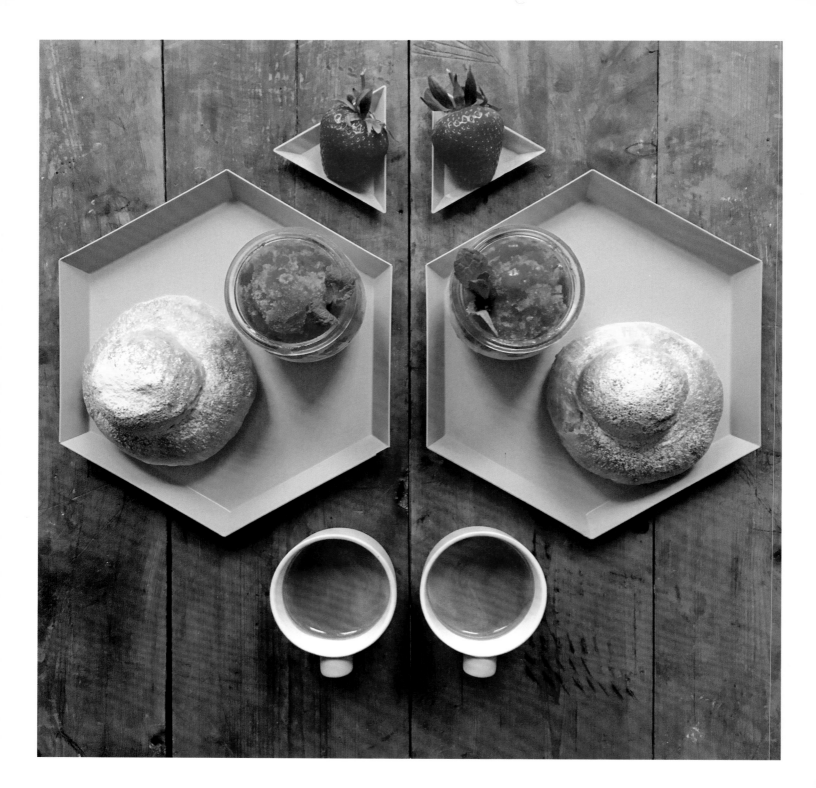

For the Brioche

9 cups bread flour
1 cup sugar
4 tsp salt
1⅔ cups milk
2 tbsp dried yeast
2 sticks butter, melted
4 eggs

For the Whipped Cream

1 tsp vanilla extract
½ cup double cream

To make the brioche, place the flour, sugar, and salt in a mixing bowl or stand mixer with a dough hook. Warm the milk to 100°F and add the yeast. Set aside for 10 minutes.

Add the milk and melted butter to the dry ingredients a little at a time until the dough is very sticky and clings to the sides of the bowl. Add three eggs, one at a time, and combine well. Knead the dough for 5 minutes in a stand mixer or for 10 if by hand.

Cover the dough with a damp cloth and leave it to rise in a warm place overnight or until the dough has tripled in size.

Preheat your oven to 400°F.

Divide the dough into 10 pieces. Take one of the dough balls and pinch off about a quarter of it. Roll the two pieces into balls and place the smaller piece on top of the larger, a bit like a snowman. Brush with a beaten egg and bake for 20 minutes or until golden brown.

To make the whipped cream, add the vanilla extract to the cream and whisk together until thick.

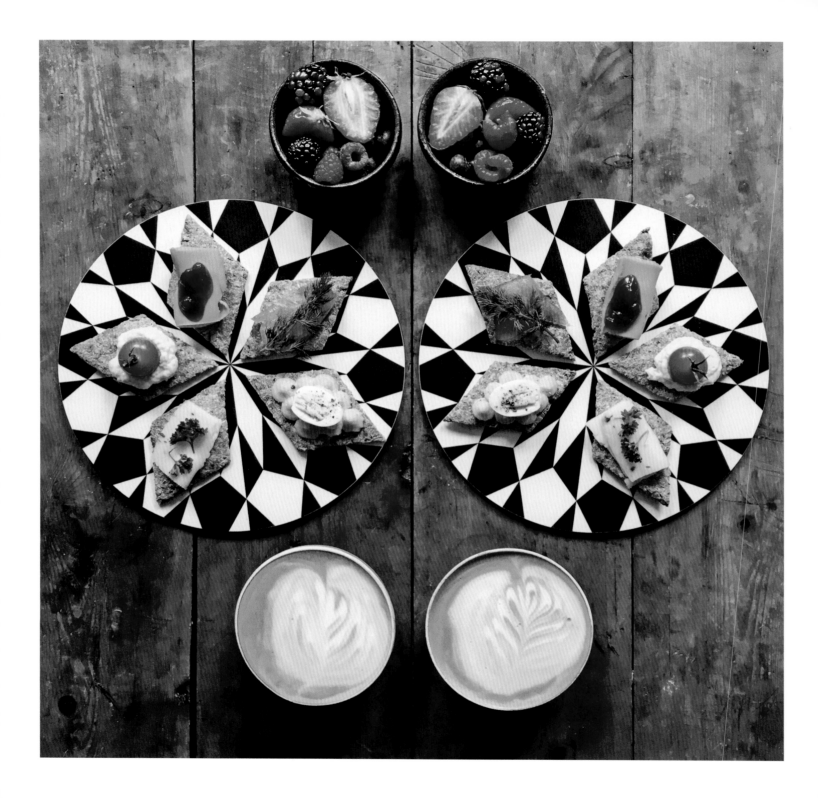

Norway has produced some questionable foods over the centuries. Amongst them canned whale meat and lutefisk (cod fish soaked in lye, an industrial chemical used in making batteries), which are both considered uniquely Norwegian and distinct from the cuisine of its Scandinavian neighbors.

But Norwegian traditions are thrown into question when none of my or Mark's Norsk friends like the taste, or have ever even tried, a steaming plate of rotting fish, preferring to eat svele, or waffles, with brown cheese and jam. I don't blame them!

On my first skiing trip to Norway with Mark, I quickly realized that I am not built for the sport and spent the rest of the week at the spa, in the kitchen, and at the local après-ski bar, pretending I had sore thighs.

Whilst trying to be productive, I came across this recipe in a Norwegian cookbook, had a guess at what it said and ended up with some pretty delicious crispbreads. It can be adapted endlessly, with different aromatics, seeds, nuts, or flours thrown in to create your favorite knekkebrød.

KNEKKEBRØD NORWEGIAN CRISPBREAD

Makes 1 giant crispbread, or 3 smaller ones

1 tbsp barley malt extract
3 cups water
1¼ cup dark rye flour
1¼ cup wholemeal flour
¾ cup sunflower seeds
½ cup sesame seeds
¼ cup linseeds
¼ cup flax seeds
⅓ cup oats
⅓ cup chopped walnuts
1 tsp salt

Optional Flavorings
Sea salt, fresh rosemary, caraway seeds, dried onion, nigella seeds, sesame seeds, pumpkin seeds, Everything Bagel seasoning (see page 49).

Preheat your oven to 320°F.

Dissolve the malt extract in the water. In a large bowl, combine all of the dry ingredients. Add the sweet water, use your hands and get stuck in. You should have a sloppy dough.

Prepare some baking parchment so that it fits your baking tray. It is easier to roll this dough directly on the paper and transfer this to the tray than to take the dough to the baking parchment.

Take a third of the dough and, using a spatula or spoon, press it out across the paper.

Place another sheet of baking paper on top and roll the dough underneath to about 3 mm thick.

Peel off the top sheet. Transfer the bottom sheet to your baking sheet.

At this point you can add any additional flavorings: sea salt, caraway seeds or fresh rosemary are all delicious.

If you want a giant crispbread to break into shards, then bake it for 1 hour. If, however, you want something more uniform, designed so that your leftovers fit your lunchbox perfectly (which is quite satisfying), then bake for 15 minutes, remove from the oven and cut to the desired size and shape, then continue to bake for another 45 minutes.

Repeat with the rest of the dough.

Once cooked, turn the oven off and remove the crispbreads for 30 minutes until the temperature drops. Return them to the oven until it is completely cold to ensure maximum crispness.

Store in an airtight container.

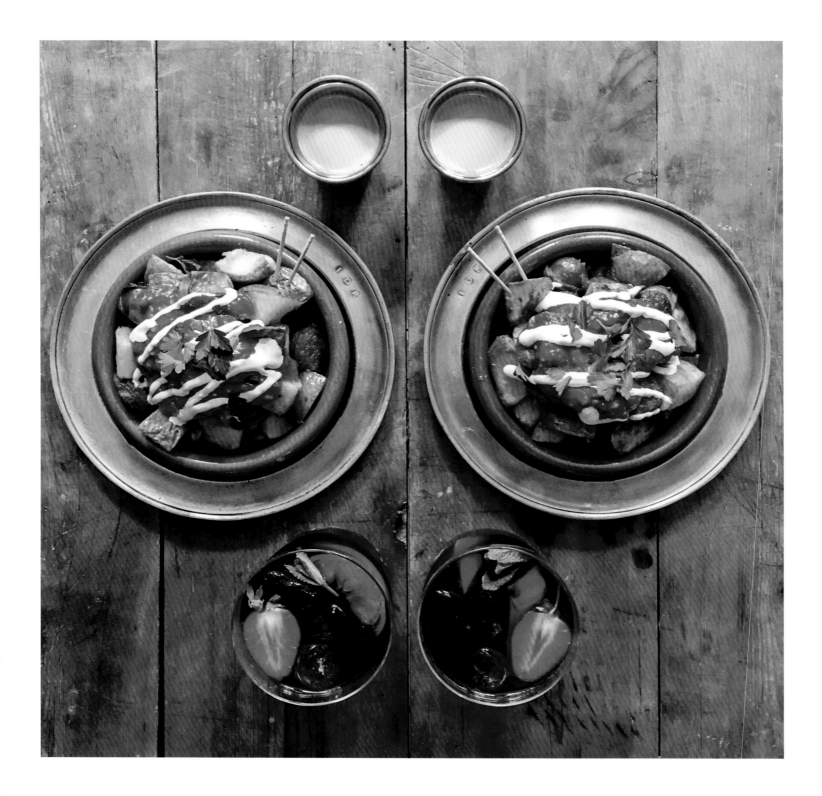

This is one of those "it's not really breakfast" recipes that some people may well question, but it's included here because it's one of those "the first thing Mark and I ate after waking up after a heavy night in San Sebastián around midday kind of breakfasts."

A delightful combination of carbs and spice, washed down with sangria if you're up to it, it just needs some sausage, perhaps, to finish it off.

Chorizo is an obvious choice for a Spanish classic, but if you come across any sobrasada or morcilla then you are on to a truly epic dish. Finish it with an extra dusting of sweet paprika, and, despite the fact that aioli is traditional, I prefer a squeeze of Japanese mayo.

My hangover tip would be to use half a jar of Dolmio with some added hot sauce, paprika, and garlic paste. No one will be any the wiser.

PATATAS BRAVAS SPANISH SPICY POTATOES

1½ cups new potatoes
1 cup olive oil
1 small onion
2 cups/13.6 oz can
    chopped tomatoes
1 tbsp hot sauce or
    Tabasco
½ tsp salt
1 tbsp sweet paprika
1 cup chorizo or sobrasada

Preheat your oven to 400°F.

Cut the potatoes into bite–sized pieces, substantial rather than bitsy. Add to a roasting dish with half the olive oil and coat the potatoes evenly. Roast for 45 minutes.

To make the sauce, finely chop the onion and fry until soft in the remaining olive oil. Add the tomatoes, hot sauce, salt, and paprika. Bring to a boil and then simmer for 30 minutes.

If you are adding chorizo, slice however much you want for two people and gently fry it in a pan. If you are opting for sobrasada, leave it until you start assembling later and dot with a few nuggets.

Start with a pile of the crispy potato and sausage and add a liberal amount of the spicy tomato sauce and paprika. Finally add the aioli or mayonnaise and eat with a cocktail stick for maximum authenticity.

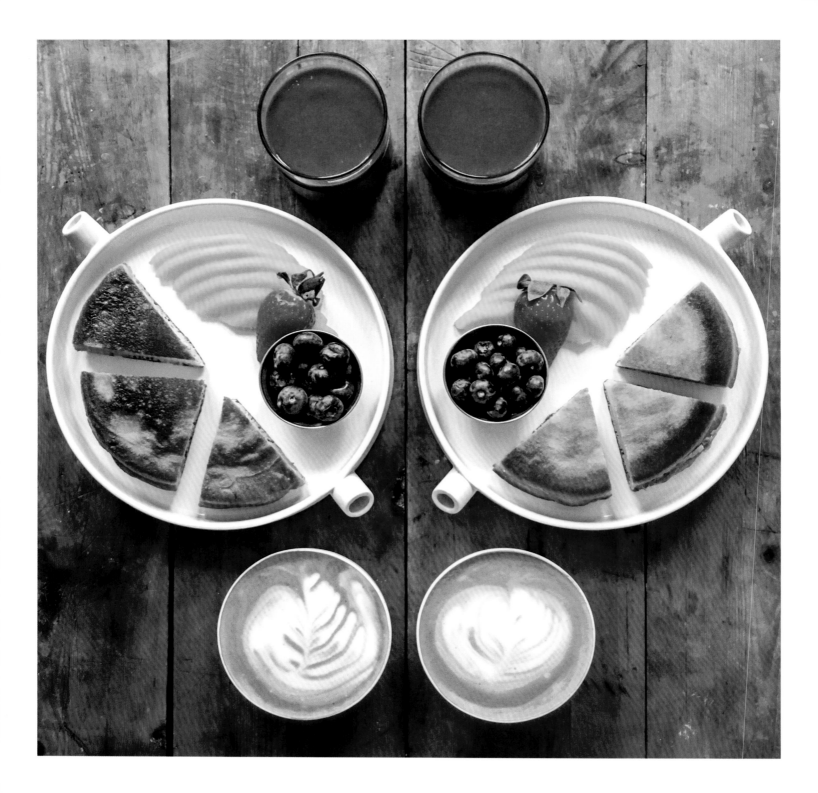

Common across Algeria, this is one of my favorite never–ever–gonna–fail breakfasts. Everything is mixed in a blender and then cooked in one pan. I would recommend the sweetness of coffee to balance out this eggy custard honey beauty. Or at least a double espresso.

M'SHEWSHA ALGERIAN HONEY PANCAKE BREAD

Makes one 9-in skillet to serve 2

5 eggs
½ cup oil or melted butter
¼ cup fine semolina
½ cup plain flour
2 tsp baking powder
1 tsp vanilla extract
Pinch of salt
1¼ cup honey

Put all the ingredients except for the honey into a blender and mix into a smooth batter. Pour the batter into either a cold cast–iron skillet that is well seasoned or a non–stick pan and put on a medium–low heat. After about 15 minutes it will have risen and come away from the sides.

Slide it on to a plate, place the pan over the top and flip. Cook for a further 10 minutes.

Warm the honey in a separate pan or micro-wave and pour over your m'shewsha. Cut it like a pizza into 8 pieces and serve warm. Alternatively, if you have smaller individual cast–iron pans, then this will do 2–3 servings.

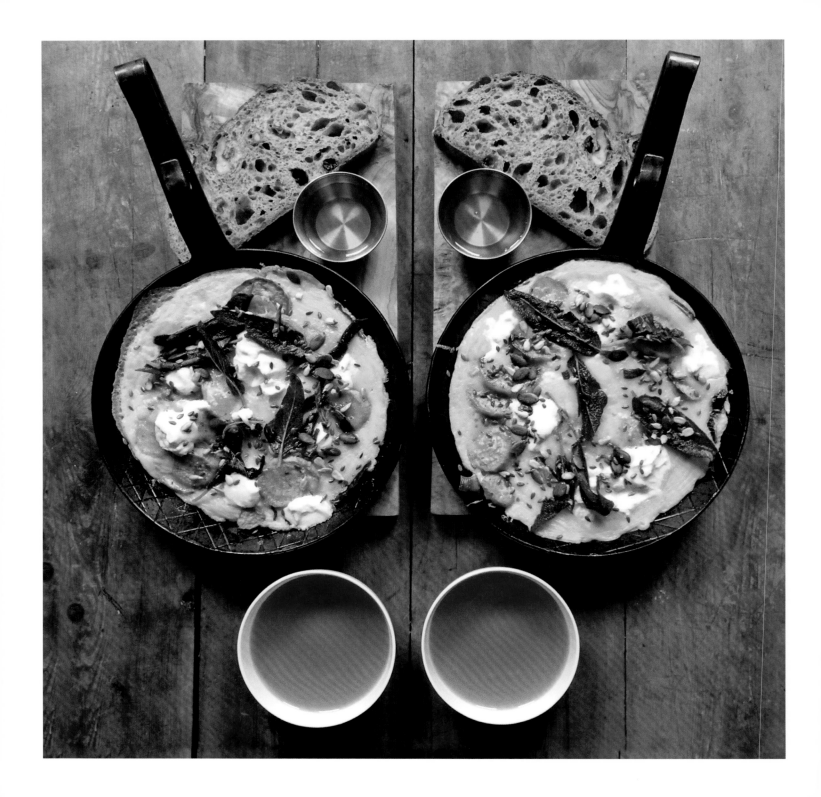

"Is there anyone who does not know how to make a frittata? Is there anyone in this world who has not in his life made some sort of frittata?"
—**Pellegrino Artusi**, *La Scienza in Cucina e l'Arte di Mangiar Bene,* first published 1891

Italian in origin, literally meaning "fried," the frittata today is distinct from the folded French omelette or the Spanish tortilla. This was not so much the case in Artusi's day, when almost any pan-fried beaten egg could be described as a frittata.

Artusi is the grandfather of Italian cookery writing. His work *Science in the Kitchen and the Art of Eating Well,* self-published in 1891, was the first book to include recipes from all 20 Italian regions and later came to define Italian cuisine. His legacy is still felt today.

He suggests a diverse range of frittata, from a simple *frittata in zoccoli,* with prosciutto, or one of my favorites, *frittata di riccioli per contorno,* a side dish of frittata cooked paper-thin with spinach, and sliced into long ribbons like taglierini.

Today, things are slightly more relaxed. Add any filling you fancy, beat some eggs in a deepish frying pan and then slowly cook until just set. Easy peasy.

This version uses soft goat's cheese and just a scant grating of Parmesan, but anything will almost certainly work.

If you are looking for more inspiration to jazz things up, check out @ellypear for her daily frittata updates.

FRITTATE DIVERSE FRITTATA

2 small-medium sweet potatoes
4 tbsp olive oil
1 small red onion
4 eggs
½ cup soft goat's cheese
¾ cup Parmesan, grated
½ stick butter or ghee
Sage leaves
3 tbsp mixed seeds or nuts – I used a mix of linseed, pumpkin, and sunflower
Drizzle of olive oil

Preheat your oven to 400°F.

Peel the sweet potato and slice it into discs just less than ½ in thick. Arrange them on a baking sheet and drizzle with 2 tbsp of the olive oil, season well and roast in the oven for 20 minutes.

Finely slice the onion. In a skillet or pan that can go in the oven, heat the other 2 tbsp oil and cook the onion on a medium heat for about 5 minutes. Add the cooked sweet potato and combine.

Crack the eggs into a bowl and whisk briskly. You want the yolk and white to be fully combined. Pour this over the potato and onion mix and turn down the heat

to its lowest. Cook for 5 minutes until the edges start to set, then break up the goat's cheese and dot it across the surface with the Parmesan.

Turn down the oven to 300°F and bake the frittata for 12–15 minutes or until just set.

In a frying pan on a high heat, heat the ghee until hot, then add the sage leaves. This may splutter, so take care, and cook until the leaves are crispy.

Remove the frittata from the oven and leave to rest for 5 minutes. Add the sage leaves to decorate and sprinkle liberally with seeds. Serve with a slice of bread drizzled with some olive oil.

12 COCKTAIL O'CLOCK
EYE-OPENER, APPETIZER, REFRESHER, STIMULANT

We've explored the idea that it's always breakfast time somewhere in the world, but what you mustn't forget is that it's also always cocktail o'clock.

The issue of alcohol in the morning is slightly contentious. My dad would call me a lush for having a drink before midday, but for many, whether it's Christmas morning, a birthday or just a long time since you've seen an old friend, a cocktail over breakfast is the best.

Like a digestivo to settle your stomach at the end of a meal, a cocktail can pucker your lips and get you salivating before the food even arrives.

The recent shift towards health at all costs means we've lost the joys of pairing food with alcohol. Something sharp and citrusy goes beautifully with the richness of Eggs Benedict, or, for an occasion where you might be hosting a party, nothing is more fabulous than a punch filled with color.

All cocktails serve 1 unless otherwise specified.

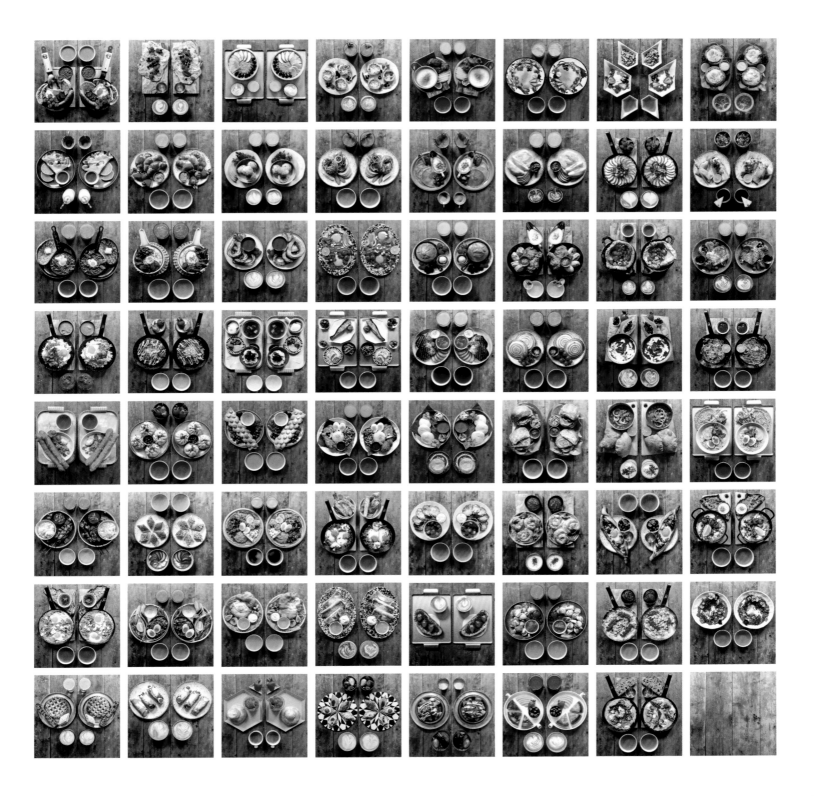

If you've ever sat at a bar and watched someone make cocktails, it can be quite mesmerizing.

Sugar dissolved in water – seems stupid even to mention it. It's not really a recipe, but it will unlock so many cocktails you might have otherwise glossed over in favor of something that involves just a base and a mixer. Once you have this simple sugar syrup recipe in your repertoire, you'll impress anyone who happens to pop by for a China Club, French 75, or a Pisco Sour.

SIMPLE SUGAR SYRUP

1 cup granulated white sugar (brown sugar is also great for a hint of caramel)
1 cup water
Orange, lemon, or lime zest (optional)

In a pan, heat all the ingredients together until the sugar has dissolved. Leave to cool and decant into a squeezy bottle with a stopper.

Store in the fridge for 3 weeks.

My friend Adrianna @seeadrianna is the only person I know who is actually from Dalston but has her roots in New York and Italy. Her two best hangover cures are: a can of ice–cold Fanta, or the dubious yet fabulous Oyster Shooter.

Oysters and vodka together – it shouldn't work, but it does. If you are truly hanging and have someone else to make these for you, then they are a joy. It's like a Bloody Caesar in bullet form.

If you really do have a hangover and you don't want a hospital visit, take extra care when you are shucking.

OYSTER SHOOTERS

1 freshly shucked oyster with its juices
1 shot ice–cold vodka
Tomato juice (optional)
Tabasco
Lemon juice

Place the oyster and its juices in a chilled glass, pour the shot of vodka over and do the same with the tomato juice, if using. Add Tabasco and lemon juice to taste. Serve immediately, down in one.

As the name suggests, this cocktail is meant to resurrect you after a big night. In the modern world, we know that more alcohol the morning after the night before does little to cure a hangover – that's a great big urban myth that cheers us up and spurs us on but doesn't do much for the liver. But that doesn't mean that certain "cures" can't be delicious in their own right – whether they're doing us any good or not is irrelevant.

The Corpse Reviver No. 2 is a wonderfully well-balanced cocktail, spritely with a hint of the macabre – the ghost-like veil of the Green Fairy. Absinthe, also known as la Fée Verte, originated in Switzerland and is a deeply misunderstood spirit. You are mistaken if you believe that it sends you mad or turns you into a criminal, none of which is true – Van Gogh was mad anyway.

Once the healing powers of the Corpse Reviver start to wear off, or if you wake up after noon, you might be willing to follow on with a Death in the Afternoon (see page 228) to keep the good times rolling!

CORPSE REVIVER NO. 2

A splash of absinthe or
    pastis
1 oz gin
1 oz Cointreau or triple sec
1 oz Lillet Blanc
1 oz lemon juice
Ice

Place your martini glass in the freezer for a few minutes before you start making your cocktail.

Put the absinthe in the chilled glass and swirl it around to reduce the temperature. Set aside.

In a cocktail shaker, put the gin, Cointreau, Lillet Blanc, and lemon juice. Add a handful of ice and stick on the lid. Shake for 10–15 seconds until the shaker becomes too cold to handle.

Discard the absinthe, leaving a thin coat on the inside of the glass. Using a strainer, pour the cocktail into the glass, but do not stir.

Serve immediately.

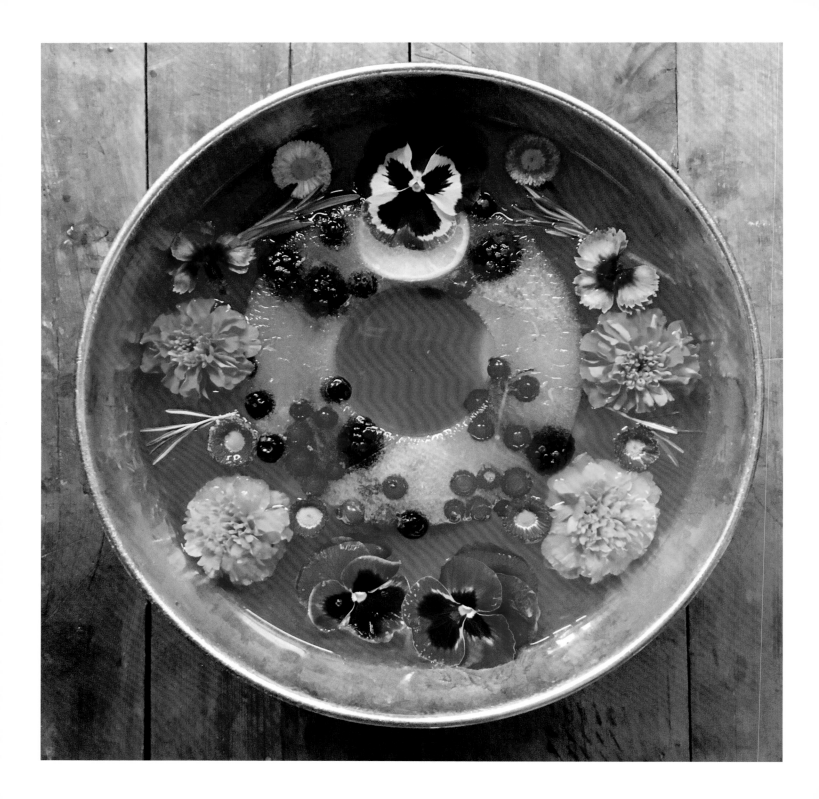

"Punch not only tastes good, it's good for you – specifically, for your intellectual development."
—**David Wondrich**,
Punch: The Delights (and Dangers) of the Flowing Bowl

I love punch. It's convivial and is made to be shared.

Like a tea bag versus a pot, there is no love or joy in making punch for yourself; you must make a batch. It's perfect for when you have a group of friends over for a lazy brunch on the weekend, or if you're celebrating something momentous.

Punches have been around for a very long time. The word itself, meaning "five" in Sanskrit, is reflected in traditional recipes containing just five base ingredients: alcohol, sugar, lemon, tea, and spices.

From India and Southeast Asia, punch made its way to the United Kingdom in the early 17th century. The Prince Regent, George IV – the original 18th–century party boy – had to take it just a little bit further to produce a glamorous drink that would impress his crowd. Surprisingly, the flavor combination is fabulous. I'm sure his parties were too.

Remember the punch bowl is the social point of contact, much like an office water cooler. When you go back for seconds or thirds, stop and have a chat with whoever is there.

REGENT'S PUNCH

Serves 8 to 10

For the Punch
2 tsp loose green tea
½ cup simple sugar syrup (see page 218)
1¼ cups white cognac (it's rare; use regular cognac otherwise)
⅔ cup dark rum
⅔ cup arrack (the distilled sap of the coconut flower, not to be confused with arak; alternatively use whiskey)
⅔ cup pineapple syrup*
½ cup maraschino
1 bottle champagne

I would advise putting the punch bowl where you plan to serve from, as it will be very heavy once full!

You'll need to make the citrus ice block the day before. Peel the lemon or lime and slice thinly, saving the peel for later. Layer the slices inside your tub or airtight plastic container with rosemary branches and redcurrants. Fill your container with cold water and freeze until solid.

To make the punch, put the green tea in a teapot with 3⅓ cups boiling water and ¾ cup cold. Leave to infuse for 7 minutes; you want it much stronger than if you were drinking it straight. Strain the tea into your punch bowl.

* You can buy pineapple syrup now. Monin is a popular brand. But it's also easy to make yourself. Take one small ripe pineapple, or half a large one, and peel, core, and chop into small cubes. Prepare the simple sugar syrup (see page 218) and add the pineapple whilst the sugar is still hot, then cover and leave for 24 hours. When cold, mash the mix and strain through a sieve. Add 2 oz vodka as a preservative. It will keep for a month in the fridge.

(continued on following page)

For the Ice Block

1 lemon or lime

Few branches of fresh rosemary

Redcurrants

Large savarin ring, bundt tin, or any plastic tub

Add the lemon or lime peel and leave to infuse as it cools.

Add the rest of the ingredients except for the champagne, and stir.

Just before your guests arrive, run some cold water around the outside of the citrus ice block to loosen it and gently lower it into the punch. Pop the champagne and pour over. Give the punch a gentle stir and leave to mingle for another 15 minutes.

Your punch is completed. Now smile and enjoy.

When you first start dating someone, there are some standard questions you need to get out of the way quickly: where they're from, what they like and dislike to eat, whether or not they'd ever consider owning a caravan (in which case the deal's off), and how many cats are too many cats. Mark and I discovered early on in our relationship that we are both summer babies, we like to cycle everywhere, and that both our mothers are named Yvonne.

Now it's probably not the most fashionable name today – I don't know anyone under the age of 20 named Yvonne – but in 1950s Glasgow and The Hague, Yvonne was the new black.

Likewise, peach schnapps. Though not so in vogue today, it is connected to the name Yvonne through six degrees of separation. The name comes from the word "yew," as in the tree historically used to make bows for archers. And the most famous brand of peach schnapps is Archers – et voilà!

Served short in honor of our vertically challenged mamas.

I WANT MY MAMA

Ice
1 oz peach schnapps
1 oz white rum
1 oz King's Ginger (whiskey infused with ginger)
1 oz lime juice
½ tsp vanilla extract
Few dashes of angostura bitters
Star anise for garnish

Put a handful of ice into a cocktail shaker. Pour in all the ingredients except the star anise, put the lid on tight, and shake vigorously until it becomes very cold in your hands. Strain into a chilled martini glass.

Garnish with a single star anise whilst listening to Carmen Miranda sing "Mama Yo Quiero."

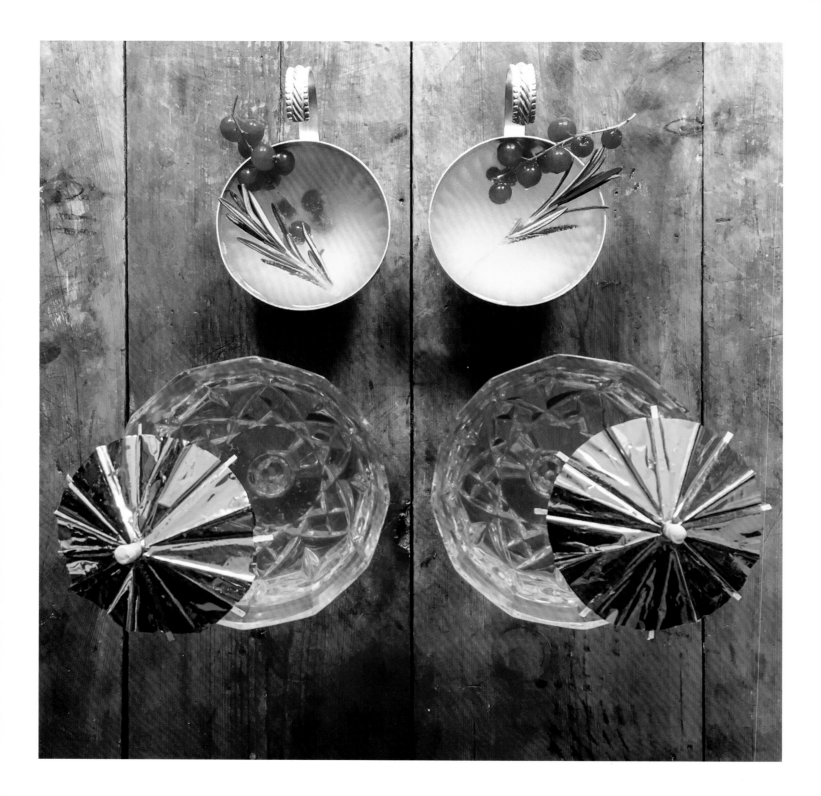

In the kindest possible way, my mother is completely mad. It's because she's Glaswegian. Living in England for the past 30 years has suppressed some of the Scottishness in her, but she still eats porridge with salt.

In her native Scotland, where "how" means "why," sausages are square, and a thing called "pizza crunch" exists (please Google this), you can understand why I sometimes approach food with reckless abandon.

Growing up there was always Irn-Bru in the house – a fizzy drink that's right up there with Coke in Scottish households but is pretty popular all around the world too, particularly where there's a Scottish population. It's a wonderful, toxic orange color (the line is that it's made from rusty girders*) and the flavor is difficult to describe. It simply tastes of Irn-Bru.

Now you must remember, the purpose of drinking alcohol in the morning is only to be abstemious – that is, to do so moderately. But just try telling that to the Scots.

*Just to be clear, there are no girders in Irn-Bru.

GIRDERS

1⅔ cups Irn-Bru (not diet)
¼ cup whiskey – just make sure it's Scottish
5 shakes of angostura bitters
Any fizzy white wine

In a pan, bring the Irn-Bru to a boil and reduce down to around ½ cup; this should take about 45 minutes and can be done up to a week in advance. Leave to cool and pour into a jug or squeezy bottle.

Pour the whiskey and Irn-Bru reduction into a champagne coupe and stir until combined. Add the bitters and top with fizzy white wine.

Garnish with a cocktail umbrella.

Alternatively, if you don't have time, a mix of half Irn-Bru and half whiskey will give you courage to face the day.

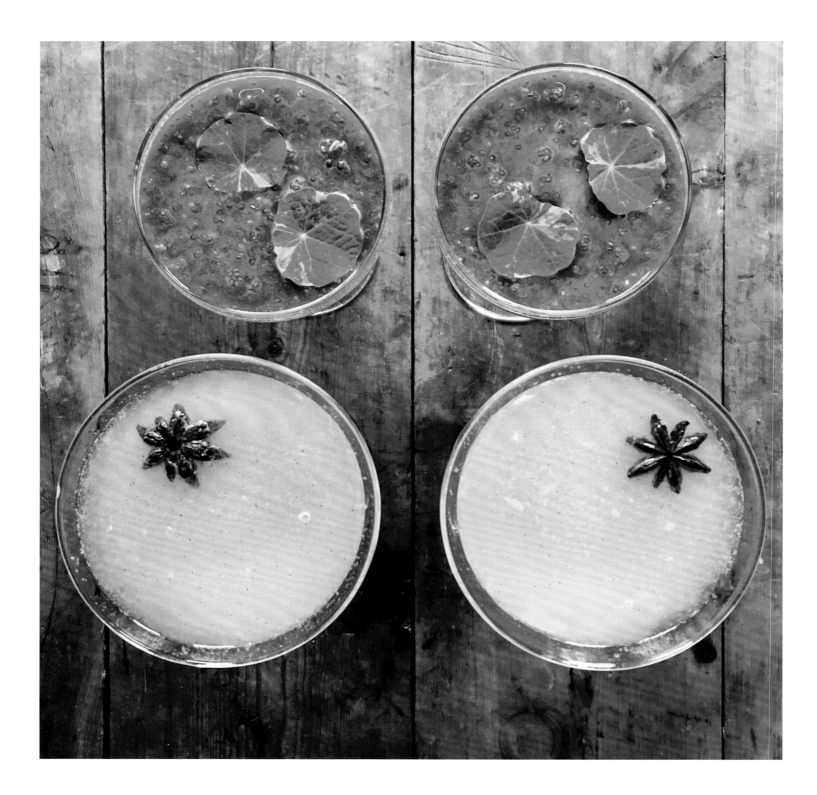

Kermit the Frog is the inspiration for this cocktail (laugh all you want). In September 2015 the despicable Kermit, dumped Miss Piggy for a new, thinner, and sexier girlfriend called Denise. Along with most people of a certain age, I was completely shocked and slightly saddened by Kermit's abhorrent behavior. Was this some silly PR stunt? Did my childhood just unravel? The most brilliant American showbiz relationship in history was over. Poor Miss Piggy can't karate-chop her way out of this.

There are a few things in this world that I just can't stomach. I've never had a taste for olives, but in this recipe we're talking green juices and chia seed. A friend describes drinking green juice as like drinking a lawn mower. I find chia disgusting; it has no texture that I can describe pleasantly. Both are supposedly good for you, but if I'm looking out for my health by searching out green or gloop, I think I'd rather have salad or, in this case, a cocktail.

Whilst this cocktail is named after Kermit, the scumbag, I hope that in drinking it you think of Miss Piggy and the revenge she could take on her former lover by putting him through the juicer.

DIRTY KERMIT

Serves 2

4 tbsp dried chia seeds or
   basil seeds
Juice of 1 lemon
5 stalks celery
½ cucumber
1 Little Gem lettuce, or ½
   iceberg
1 cup fresh spinach, with
   a few leaves saved for
   decoration
Juice of 1 lime
¼ cup vodka, cold

In a small cup, soak the chia or basil seeds with the lemon juice and 1 cup warm but not hot water. Set aside for a few minutes.

In either a juicer or blender, process the celery, cucumber, lettuce, and spinach, and add the lime juice. Pour into a jug.

Add the vodka and stir in the swollen chia or basil seed, keeping back 1 tsp for garnish.

Pour the juice into a tall glass and decorate with a single spinach leaf – which the more fanciful amongst us might think of as a lily pad – and a spoonful of the chia seed on top . . . for the frog spawn.

I am referring to having a drink in the morning. Some people are repelled by the thought of alcohol before lunch, but, fortunately for me, I do not know such people. Most people I know really enjoy a breakfast cocktail tipple.

Death in the Afternoon (which, of course, we're drinking in the morning) is deceptively strong. Hemingway suggested drinking three to five slowly, but I should imagine one would suffice before midday.

I like to float the absinthe on top of the champagne. It creates a beautiful effect that will certainly impress your guests and quite probably yourself too.

DEATH IN THE AFTERNOON

1 lemon
1 oz absinthe
Champagne

Using a potato peeler or channel knife, slice a 2–3 in piece of lemon zest. Squeeze it into your champagne flute to release the oils and rub it around the top of the glass. Drop the peel inside.

Pour the champagne into the glass until it is about three quarters full.

Hold the bowl of a teaspoon upside down just above the surface of the champagne. Pour the absinthe on to the back of the spoon and into the champagne. This will stop it from going straight to the bottom of the glass.

Serve immediately.

Milo is the unassuming malty chocolate beverage that is familiar to so many Australian children. Now it's all grown up in this deliciously rich and malty concoction that has a serious coffee kick. A simple espresso martini with an Antipodean twist, it's perfect if your smashed #avotoast isn't doing it for you.

MILO MARTINI

1 heaped tsp Milo or, at a push, Ovaltine

1 shot cold espresso, or 1 heaped tsp instant espresso powder

1 oz Kahlúa

2 oz vodka

1 oz simple sugar syrup (see page 218)

Ice

In a cup, dissolve the Milo with a few teaspoons of cold water to make a paste. Do the same with the instant espresso if you are using it.

Put all the ingredients into a cocktail shaker and, with the lid on, shake vigorously.

Pour gently into a martini glass and garnish with a sprinkling of Milo.

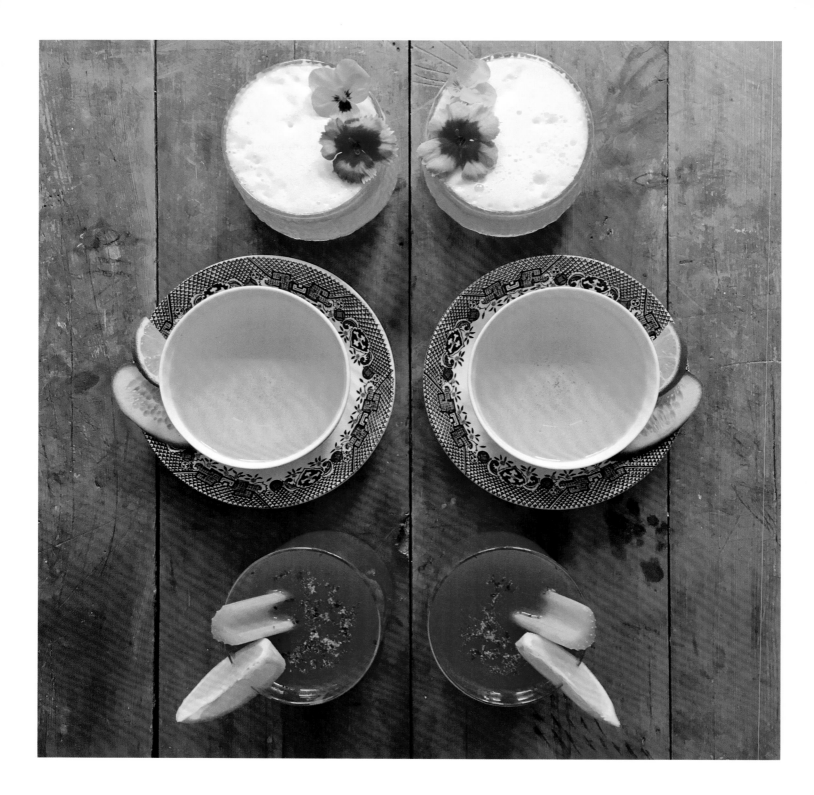

I've never met a Bloody Mary I didn't like. Whilst it's likely that the story of its invention in the 1920s at Harry's New York Bar in Paris is true, it cannot be confirmed. The one thing that is known is that it found fame at the King Cole Bar in New York, with Ernest Hemingway being one of its biggest fans.

Until I sat down to write this recipe, I realized that I have never actually measured out a single cocktail in my life! Although I have consumed many, many cocktails, their construction has always been on an ad hoc basis – and that's worked perfectly well. Until now. And the Bloody Mary in particular is deceptively complicated.

With so many variations to play around with, you could add a slug of clam juice for a Canadian twist, making it into a Bloody Caesar, switch the Worcester for Henderson's Relish, or Sriracha for when the Tabasco bottle is shaken dry. It's easy to find your personal preference.

BLOODY MARY

Serves 3 to 4

1¼ cups vodka
¾ in knuckle of fresh horseradish, or 1 tsp grated from a jar (optional)
1 quart tomato juice
1 tbsp Tabasco or any hot sauce
1 tbsp Worcestershire sauce, Henderson's Relish, or A1 steak sauce
1 tsp salt (celery salt, if you're fancy)
1 tsp freshly ground black pepper
Juice of 1 lemon
1 lemon, cut into wedges for garnish
Celery stalks, for garnish (mandatory)
Ice

Start by putting the vodka in the freezer at least an hour before making your drink. Good–quality vodka shouldn't freeze, so you could do it the night before. You could also put the jug in the fridge beforehand too.

If using fresh horseradish, slice it into matchsticks, roughly 10–15 pieces, and poke it into the bottle of vodka, then shake gently. If you are using grated horseradish from a jar, then add 1 tsp to the bottle and give it a good shake. Leave to infuse for 30 minutes.

Pour the tomato juice, Tabasco, Worcestershire sauce, salt, pepper, and lemon juice into a large jug. Stir gently until the salt has dissolved, then pour in the vodka. Use a sieve to make sure none of the horseradish goes into the jug.

Serve in high–ball glasses with a wedge of lemon, a stalk of celery, and some ice.

Most people would never expect a gin and tonic to be a suitable beverage for a morning meal. If you're familiar with Hogarth's *Gin Lane* etching in the Tate's collection, then you know why gin is referred to as "Mother's Ruin."

Gin, a cousin of Dutch jenever, is flavored with juniper – from which it takes its name – along with other botanicals like anise, coriander, liquorice root, or grains of paradise, a type of African pepper.

Infusing alcohol is incredibly easy and transforms classic drinks into revolutionary new ones. Infused with top-notch Earl Grey tea, flavored with oil from the bergamot orange grown in Calabria, Italy, new flavors are added to the botanicals in the gin.

Use the best loose tea you can get your hands on and ditch the tea bags. Your tastebuds will thank you.

G&TEA

2 oz dry gin
1 tsp Earl Grey tea
Soda or tonic water (ice cold)
Wedge of lime

It is best that your gin is room temperature as it infuses, so make sure you take it out of the fridge good and early, if that's where it's been lurking. Mix the loose tea and gin together and set aside for 5 minutes.

Strain the gin through a fine-mesh cocktail sieve or tea-strainer into a high-ball glass. Top with the desired amount of soda or tonic and garnish with lime.

If you want to make a whole bottle of tea-infused gin (or any other spirit), then it's recommended that you leave the infusion for longer, rather than increasing the amount of tea proportionally.

3 cups of alcohol with 1 oz of tea for 20 minutes will yield the same results, but I would definitely suggest experimenting. Different gins have different flavor profiles which suit different teas.

I am sick to death of pavlova. How many times have I made a hollandaise or mayonnaise and then, without even pausing for thought, used the egg whites to make a pavlova? It's time to move on.

If you have friends over or you're taking the time to treat yourself (it's important), then knocking up a cocktail with egg whites is my idea of heaven, whether it's breakfast time – there is, after all, Earl Grey in this – or any other time of day. Its frothy and silky softness, combined with a sour underbelly, is a wonderful contrast to something like Eggs Benedict.

The sugar syrup is easy to make and lasts for a few weeks (see page 218). It also has the added benefit of making you look like a professional bartender.

EARL GREY WHISKEY SOUR

2 oz whiskey
1 tsp loose-leaf Earl Grey
Ice
1 oz simple sugar syrup
   (see page 218)
1 oz fresh lemon juice
1 egg white

Combine the whiskey and loose tea in a cup and leave to infuse for 30 minutes.

In a cocktail shaker, place 3–4 ice cubes and add the infused whiskey, sugar syrup, lemon juice, and egg white. Firmly clamp on the lid and shake the dickens out of it. Pass through a fine–mesh cocktail strainer into a chilled coupe.

Serve with a maraschino cherry.

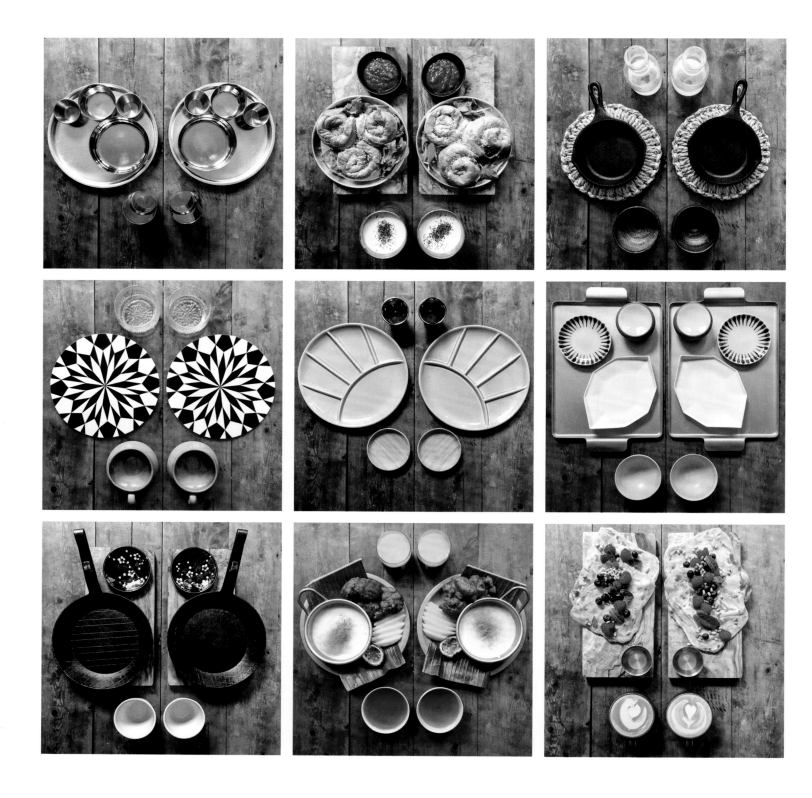

Beyond any doubt and with the utmost authority, I can confidently say that carefully presented food not only looks good but also enhances the enjoyment of eating and dining. Our perception and understanding of flavor begins with where and how we have encountered flavors before and the feelings we associate with those memories.

Never could I have imagined how surprising a chocolate cake could be until we visited Mugaritz, one of the world's best dining experiences in the Basque region of Spain.

As strange as it sounds, the chocolate cake was served, smeared, on what resembled a human hip joint, made entirely out of rock hard sugar. I spent at least a minute examining the dish, turning it round, savoring the moment, taking several photographs on my phone and being (and I dread the word) "mindful" of what I was eating.

Mugaritz is a wonderful example of extreme plating. In any other situation, I would have immediately understood or been able to approximate from memory the flavor, texture, and ultimately whether I would enjoy a piece of chocolate cake before it had passed my lips. At Mugaritz, they are careful not to let your own prejudice of food cloud your judgment.

From the greatest restaurants in the world to our own kitchens, there are many ways you can be playful with the dining experience. Whilst there is a lot of confusion (and cynicism) about what constitutes thoughtful plating these days, I have seen some of the very worst attempts to create theater. Restaurants that serve a full English breakfast in a dog bowl, or onion rings artfully arranged on salvaged plumbing should just stop it, there is no place for style over substance.

I love that breakfast in many American diners, comes with a large wedge of orange on the side. A palette cleanser not too dissimilar to how many Chinese people end their meal. I appreciate the gesture that has gone into such a minor detail.

Why should you care about the color or size of the plate when you're making dinner for the family, a loved one, or even yourself? Simply because we all need more love in our lives, not less. Food can be designed to promote conversation and sharing simply by the size in which its prepared or way it's served. The recipe for Regent's Punch on page 221 is a perfect example.

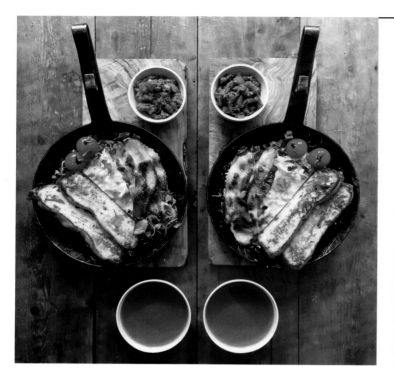
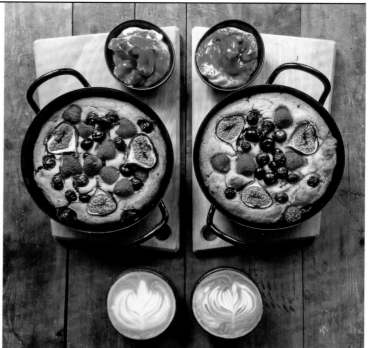

Above, I've tried to illustrate how the same dish, in this case cornbread, plated and prepared in different ways, using different colors and textures, can make food more or less appealing to us. I'm not saying that one is better than another; it's up to you to decide. How you might garnish your dish, with fresh herbs or edible flowers can make your eyes glow with delight.

Since I started SymmetryBreakfast, I have grown quite a collection of tableware from around the world and I have a slight obsession with individual cast iron pans, keeping your food hot whilst you upload a photo online and simultaneously allowing the cook to customise with minimal effort the spice or seasoning to each person's preference.

If you want to start growing a collection of tableware for yourself, I would highly recommend starting with a catering wholesale supplier, thrift store, or your grandmother's attic. Often you can buy single items (or, in my case, pairs) and they sell all manner of interesting pieces for a great price.

Until I started to write this book I had never measured a cocktail at home. A slosh of this and a glug of that and most of the time I've created something drinkable and sometimes wonderful.

Home cooking (and making cocktails), despite what anyone will tell you, is not an exact science. If you've ever made the same recipe twice with differing results then you'll know there are other factors involved than just your ingredients and what a recipe tells you to do with them.

If you wanted to be pedant, you'd weigh your eggs, test the gluten content in the flour, and count the number of stirs – perhaps important in patisserie but not so important at six in the morning.

Home cooks in China do not weigh rice; instead the number of people eating dictates the quantity. A pinch of salt will vary dramatically if you have unusually large hands or perhaps you have some wonderful Amalfi lemons rather than the more ubiquitous Eureka variety, how much juice is the right amount? Only trial and error will give you the answer.

In the UK, it is the law that packaged or loose goods are sold in metric weight, with the exception of pints in pubs, milk, and precious metals. Perhaps you feel a US cup is the most sensible way to measure your flour. My parents would be more inclined to weigh in imperial units. Me, I just eyeball it, a skill that has taken years of cooking and failing to get right with a 10 percent or thereabouts, margin of error.

But, if you've ever seen the film *Father of the Bride*, the scene where George Banks played by the brilliant Steve Martin goes on a rant about the "superfluous buns" at the supermarket before being arrested has stayed with me for years.

Banks revolts when he realizes that hotdogs are sold in quantities of 8, yet the buns come in bags of 12. This must be a conspiracy! He could just buy 3 packs of dogs and 2 bags of buns but hopefully you'll understand my next point.

Buttermilk across the five largest supermarkets in the UK comes in 284 ml pots; that's exactly 1 US cup. To me, using this as the fixed point, or multiples thereof in a recipe makes total sense, you purchase one pot giving you zero waste. There is nothing I despise more than a food writer who ignores or simply does not know what is available to the general public and asks for 350 ml buttermilk in a recipe. You then have to buy two pots with an almost useless amount leftover.

A friend of mine (who has also written a cookbook) has a recipe that requires "half an egg" as if there would be some adverse reaction to the finished dish if it were used in its entirety. I think that it is complete madness to believe it would.

I know you, Americans, love using cups and I must admit I love cooking with cups too, but it must be said that neither system of weight or volume is perfect. I take the standard and internationally accepted conversion that 1 US cup is 240ml of water in volume; however, neither of the sets I own are exact.

The honest truth is that it really doesn't make much difference. My advice would be to purchase both a set of scales and a set of cups and beyond that, everything else is a bonus. Cooking is a learning curve and I taught myself how to sharpen a blunt knife with the help of YouTube and numerous mishaps and disasters – it's all part of the fun and joy of cooking.

SYMMETRYBREAKFAST was created by Michael Zee for his partner Mark in their Hackney flat in 2013. Since then, SymmetryBreakfast has become an online phenomenon that incorporates world cuisines, contemporary design, and a story of love over the meal of breakfast. Featured in the *Guardian, Washington Post,* and *Telegraph,* amongst other media, and endorsed by Jamie Oliver, it is one of the favorite accounts of Kevin Systrom, Instagram CEO and co–founder.

Michael studied Photography at the Arts Institute at Bournemouth and later went on to teach Art and Design in secondary schools in London's East End. He then completed his masters in Museums and Galleries in Education and worked in public programming at the Victoria and Albert Museum, London.

Michael's passion for cooking comes from his parents and his mixed English, Scottish, and Chinese heritage. In childhood, weekends and school holidays were spent working in his father's Chinese and English chippies in Liverpool and teaching himself to bake to satisfy his mother's sweet tooth. Now, Mark's hectic job as a menswear fashion designer means late nights and weekends in the office. Early on in their relationship, breakfast became a sacred moment in the day and Michael started on his mission to make each meal as celebratory as possible.

Over 1,000 breakfasts later, Michael still wakes up early to make breakfast for Mark, looking carefully around the world and at home for inspiration, taking a simple idea and making it beautiful.

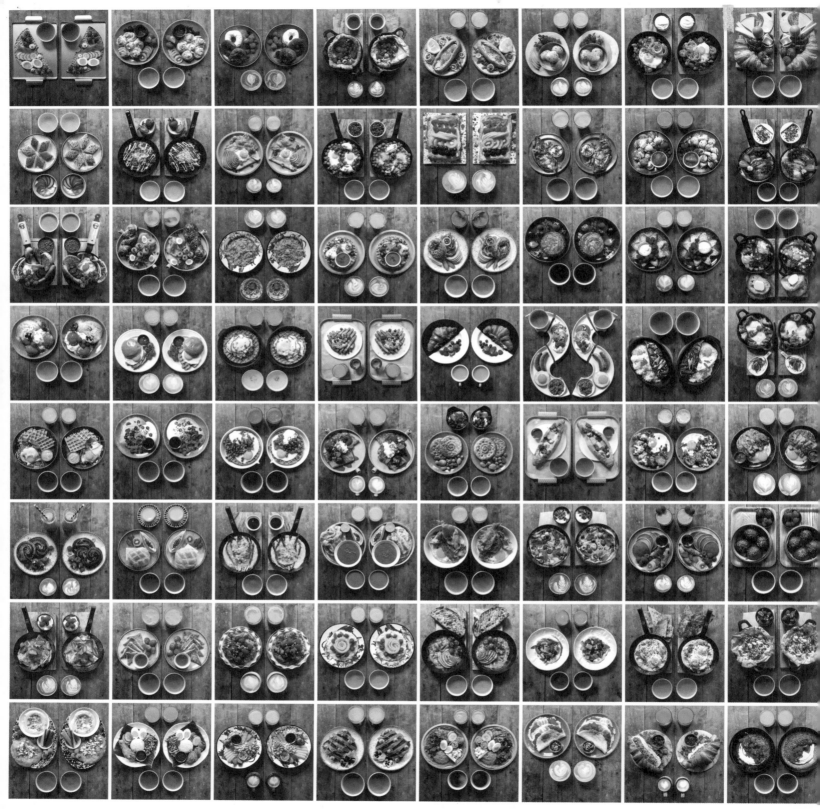